Joyce's Comic Portrait

THE FLORIDA JAMES JOYCE SERIES

Florida A&M University, Tallahassee
Florida Atlantic University, Boca Raton
Florida Gulf Coast University, Ft. Myers
Florida International University, Miami
Florida State University, Tallahassee
University of Central Florida, Orlando
University of Florida, Gainesville
University of North Florida, Jacksonville
University of South Florida, Tampa
University of West Florida, Pensacola

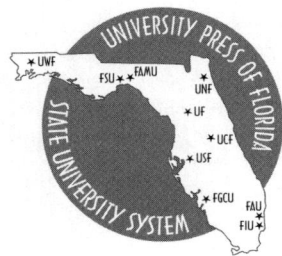

THE FLORIDA JAMES JOYCE SERIES
Edited by Zack Bowen

The Autobiographical Novel of Co-Consciousness: Goncharov, Woolf, and Joyce, by Galya Diment (1994)
Bloom's Old Sweet Song: Essays on Joyce and Music, by Zack Bowen (1995)
Joyce's Iritis and the Irritated Text: The Dis-lexic Ulysses, by Roy Gottfried (1995)
Joyce, Milton, and the Theory of Influence, by Patrick Colm Hogan (1995)
Reauthorizing Joyce, by Vicki Mahaffey (paperback edition, 1995)
Shaw and Joyce: "The Last Word in Stolentelling," by Martha Fodaski Black (1995)
Bely, Joyce, Döblin: Peripatetics in the City Novel, by Peter I. Barta (1996)
Jocoserious Joyce: The Fate of Folly in Ulysses, by Robert H. Bell (paperback edition, 1996)
Joyce and Popular Culture, edited by R. B. Kershner (1996)
Joyce and the Jews: Culture and Texts, by Ira B. Nadel (paperback edition, 1996)
Narrative Design in Finnegans Wake: *The Wake Lock Picked,* by Harry Burrell (1996)
Gender in Joyce, edited by Jolanta W. Wawrzycka and Marlena G. Corcoran (1997)
Latin and Roman Culture in Joyce, by R. J. Schork (1997)
Reading Joyce Politically, by Trevor L. Williams (1997)
Advertising and Commodity Culture in Joyce, by Garry Leonard (1998)
Greek and Hellenic Culture in Joyce, by R. J. Schork (1998)
Joyce, Joyceans, and the Rhetoric of Citation, by Eloise Knowlton (1998)
Joyce's Music and Noise: Theme and Variation in His Writings, by Jack W. Weaver (1998)
Reading Derrida Reading Joyce, by Alan Roughley (1999)
Joyce through the Ages: A Nonlinear View, edited by Michael Patrick Gillespie (1999)
Chaos Theory and James Joyce's Everyman, by Peter Francis Mackey (1999)
Joyce's Comic Portrait, by Roy Gottfried (2000)
Joyce and Hagiography: Saints Above!, by R. J. Schork (2000)

Joyce's Comic Portrait

Roy Gottfried

University Press of Florida
GAINESVILLE · TALLAHASSEE · TAMPA · BOCA RATON
PENSACOLA · ORLANDO · MIAMI · JACKSONVILLE · FT. MYERS

Copyright 2000 by the Board of Regents of the State of Florida
Printed in the United States of America on acid-free paper
All rights reserved

05 04 03 02 01 00   6 5 4 3 2 1

LIBRARY OF CONGRESS CATALOGING-IN-PUBLICATION DATA
Gottfried, Roy K.
Joyce's comic Portrait / Roy Gottfried.
p. cm. — (The Florida James Joyce series)
Includes bibliographical references and index.
ISBN 0-8130-1782-3 (alk. paper)
1. Joyce, James, 1882–1941. Portrait of the artist as a young man.
2. Humorous stories, English—History and criticism. 3. Dublin (Ireland)—
In literature. 4. Young men in literature. I. Title. II. Series.
PR6019.O9 P6444 2000
823'912—dc21   00-028700

The University Press of Florida is the scholarly publishing agency for the
State University System of Florida, comprising Florida A&M University,
Florida Atlantic University, Florida Gulf Coast University, Florida
International University, Florida State University, University of Central
Florida, University of Florida, University of North Florida, University of
South Florida, and University of West Florida.

University Press of Florida
15 Northwest 15th Street
Gainesville, FL 32611–2079
http://www.upf.com

To Mary Comfort

Contents

Foreword by Zack Bowen   ix

Acknowledgments   xi

Introduction. "To Tumble" Rather Than "To Fall":
   The Comic Portrait   1

1. "The Comic Irishman in the Bench Behind":
   The Portrait with Two Heads   24

2. The Surd and the Absurd: The Conflated Language of Comedy   48

3. Two Comic Contexts   83

4. Obscure Arts and the Economy of Vulgar Language   117

5. The Portrait Alternately Portrayed   148

Notes   161

Selected Bibliography   175

Index   179

Foreword

Roy Gottfried's splendid book is the first full-length work to address the rarely discussed subject of Joyce's use of comedy in *A Portrait of the Artist as a Young Man*. Far from the usual opinion that *Portrait* is anything but a comic work, Gottfried to my mind proves conclusively that the comedic, so readily apparent in the rest of Joyce's fiction, is also everywhere in *Portrait*, buried often just beneath the surface and affording the book's predominant irony a comic doubling or mirror against which the character of Stephen Dedalus, its *Kunstlerroman* protagonist, may be measured. Gottfried details how Stephen, lofty and solemn in his solipsistic thoughts and language, lives in a vulgar comic world just beneath his flight from the nets he imagines enveloping him; and how those low, essentially comic metaphors of existence inevitably ground his flights of spirit with comic reality. The book forces its reader to come to the conclusion that *Portrait*, rather than being a totally ironic work, is really a work of "muted" comedy to the degree that comic elements play a far greater role in the irony itself.

Finally, Gottfried's book indicates how *Portrait*, instead of being a deviation from Joyce's continuing progress as a comic writer, is rather a subtle development of his comedic gift before its full blossom in the comic representations of *Ulysses* and *Finnegans Wake*.

Zack Bowen
Series Editor

Acknowledgments

For one to write single-mindedly about comedy often tests the humor of others, and I have been fortunate to have found in many Joyceans much good will and high spirits. My gratitude goes to Zack Bowen for his characteristic exuberance, good nature, and constant support. I also appreciate the wit and insight of Claire Culleton, and found as a tonic the fairness and openness of the anonymous reader for the University Press of Florida. The support of the Robert Penn Warren Center for the Humanities and of the University Research Council of Vanderbilt University is gratefully acknowledged. The patience and help of my colleague John Plummer in matters technical made for light moments. My three sons, Oliver, Edward, and Henry, with their general antic quality, did much to make carnival when I was too solemn. The dedication is to my wife who, as her name suggests, was great solace.

Introduction

"To Tumble" Rather Than "To Fall"
The Comic Portrait

The effective and affective movement in *Portrait* is one of falling and rising, into the square ditch then onto the shoulders of fellow students, down into sin and then up into piety, and finally, "falling but not yet fallen . . ."(162), followed by his soul "in flight" and "soaring" (169).[1] This movement certainly charts what Joyce called, in the earliest essay version of "A Portrait," "the curve of an emotion."[2] Such a pattern is accretive; each lapse and then correction lead to new awareness and give a directed impulse to the narrative. Within these trajectories the character moves on to discover himself, the self he was preconditioned to become (as Stephen would say in a later work). This linear motion of improvement is necessitated by the genre of *Bildungsroman* (and its corollaries *Erziehungsroman* and *Kuenstlerroman*):[3] development paints an obvious, overt telic purpose: "the end he had been born to serve" (169). This end, Stephen thinks, is to engage in the sinuous rhythm "to live, to err, to fall, to triumph, to recreate life out of life" (172). All this is serious and important: engagement with and struggle against life, the interaction of failure and triumph, at stake the development of a person, particularly an artist.

Seen as a novel of development, *Portrait* must be somber and enlightening: one definition of the Latin *protrahere,* from whose past participle *protractus* ("portrait") is derived, is to bring to light, illumine, reveal. To this sense of "portrait" belongs its didactic intellective effect. Its generic status as a novel of development as *Bildungsroman* or *Erziehungsroman* (novel of education) is concerned with learning, with the instruction of both the protagonist and the reader. It is also here that the prevalent ironic tone derives, as the means to demonstrate the shortcomings and misunderstandings of the protagonist while indicating to the reader the actual case of the world. This ironic tone further adds to the intellectual and serious cast of the text. A portrait (*protractus*) may also be something drawn forward or drawn to a conclusion (again showing its etymological connection with the German *erziehen* as impelled or directed, also led as in educated); this definition additionally underscores the sense of impelling direction which readers experience in Joyce's novel (and for those who find the novel prolonged or tedious, *protactus* also etymologically yields protracted). Such is a weighty work on the growth of what will become the poet's soul, a romantic theme of much introspection. The consequent internalization of the narrative (along with adolescent earnestness) adds to its absolute focus, seeming to exclude any but the deepest earnest thoughts.

Additionally, the autobiographical basis behind the work has lent it a disproportionately heavy aura of importance, that of the hagiography of St. James. Yet in actual life, there was another Joyce, less earnest, less somber than the autobiographical figure on the novel's canvas. Joyce of the *Portrait* years, as Ellmann and others note, was nowhere near the tedious prig of the novel that Kenner finds.[4] Joyce, even if driven to be an artist, was known as "Sunny Jim" and he was funny. Letters from his first years abroad when working on *Stephen Hero* suggest a young man of ready, if sometimes scabrous wit.[5] The *Portrait* may be of the young Joyce, but it only depicts one possible pose. Joyce was proud to derive his name from the French "joyeux" or the Latin "jocus";[6] one might argue that in finally choosing "Dedalus" (rather then the original "Daedalus") there is a deadening effect of the character on the innate humor of Joyce.[7] And as there was another sort of Joyce, so there may be another *Portrait,* too. Any completed portrait is a product of many sittings and each portrait itself is achieved through the contrasting interplay of light and dark. Criticism of *Portrait* has always been a tension between alternate views, a successful development against a failed one, a serious text against an ironic one. More recent readings have suggested that *Portrait* is a text at odds against its context, its culture, or its genre.[8] There may be, however, another "sitting" to the portraiture, an alternative to the tension of success or failure, sincerity or irony; it is one that takes those alternatives as its own opposite. There may be within the somber, serious, ironic artistic *Portrait* another, lighter one, not so much concerned as comic; it would be dilatory, not driven; diffuse, not directed; amusing, not instructive. To the accretive motion of rhythmic rise and fall it may offer another motion. Rising and falling are the dynamic of religion and myth, noble and uplifting; they are the motion of redemption. There is another movement in *Portrait* of turning in circles without aim or advance, of moving without end or goal, of jesting rather than striving, of pratfall rather than tragic fall. To the progressing and elevated rhythm of rise and fall, whether successful or failed, *Portrait* may also depict an alternate motion of tumbling.

At the beginning of chapter 3, a mood is set right in the middle of the novel, when Stephen, already wise in the ways of the world, contemplates his sexual sins during a class in mathematics. The opening sentence reads, "The swift December dusk had come tumbling clownishly after its dull day and, as he stared through the dull square of the window of the schoolroom, he felt his belly crave for its food" (102). The text resists (because Stephen resists) saying "dusk fell" as too plain a style for his impressions, and the seriousness of his thoughts is contrasted with the subsequent frivolity in the classroom around him. As usual, Stephen is so absorbed in himself as to be beyond the clatter and chatter of the classroom, where at a time slightly later his fellow students will be eager to "scut" because the absence of the rector means "that's game ball" for the class (105). (The distance between Stephen and his classmates is easily measured by the large gap between his poetic diction and their common, vulgar one; Stephen also imagines the vulgar language of whores, although he would never himself use such language.) The elevated language of Stephen, thinking about his sins or the mathematics problem in his scribbler, stands outside the colloquial sounds around him, and Stephen is usually a creature of intellect. Even his failures are a palatable pleasure for him: "detaching himself" from what is in the world, he is given to "testing its mortifying flavour" (*P* 67). It is this desire for "morose delectation" (as he names it in *Ulysses* 3.385) that usually governs his appetite and while it has a savor, it is in the service of the intellect, not the body. What interests him at this moment are physical appetites, first for the flour-fattened stew and then for the brothels (and surely the reader might already see a faint glimpse of something humorous in Stephen's heroic sinfulness—the dinner stew and the brothel as a "stew"). Stephen's mind is not engaged here (nor is he making the pun); rather his belly counsels him and the belly as a source of appetite is in contrast to the mind and head. Because those immediate appetites of Stephen are for food and sex, corporal and common concerns, the belly is a site of a world wholly different from what is found in the *Portrait* world of classrooms, chapels, and books; it is the world of the real, of gross behaviors, of the lowering effect that brings down elevated thoughts.[9] The presence of the vulgar word "belly" here indicates a change from what are the usual concerns of the novel, and along with it there is another turn here, a change in direction from high to low: the verb "tumbling" is a lesser poetic choice than "falling." The shift from elevated to common diction introduces the countermeasure of the text, a countermeasure that is part of the contrast of mind and belly. Instead of the world of the intellect, the prime focus of the narrative, the world of the belly is one of things comical, festive, and carnivalesque. Moreover, "to tumble" is indeed to play the fool, the antic figure of circus and festive activity, rather than to fall as a tragic hero or a Luciferean sinner. Tumbling is not linear or progressive, but circular, even repetitive; rather than advance, it undercuts, rather than elevate, undoes: it has no aim but fun. The contrast of the two is strong, even in so brief an example, the belly rather than the *nous,* tumbling rather than falling; their contrast embeds a sense of an alternative, an otherness, to the text of *Portrait.*

While *Finnegans Wake* is of course predicated on rises and falls, it is precisely their repetition that gives the compulsive quality of comedy. Even in *Ulysses* Stephen still retains a sense of the clownish nature of "tumbling" when in "Circe" he sees in a hallucination the figure of Punch Costello who *"tumbles in somersaults"* (15. 2152); his nickname indicates precisely the carnivalesque nature of the activity. ("Circe," we shall discuss in conclusion, is the full comic flowering of elements in *Portrait.*)

The idea of clownish tumbling as an alternative rhythm and tone to the text of *Portrait* is firmly established later, and by Stephen himself. Stephen is in the physics theatre at UCD (another classroom as the one from Belvedere, above; its subject, physics, like math, is one of the real world). There he recognizes the presence of the comic that exists behind him in contrast to his seriousness. To the physics lecturer's discussion of ellipsoidal balls, a modest touch of humor from the conventional source in Gilbert and Sullivan, Moynihan's ribald response goes downhill farther toward the less acceptable: "What price ellipsoidal balls! Chase me, ladies, I'm in the cavalry" is one of the few overt examples of low comic effect and vulgar diction in the novel. Stephen notes the effect on his own thinking: "His fellowstudent's rude humour ran like a gust through the cloister of Stephen's mind, shaking into gay life limp priestly vestments that hung upon the walls, setting them to sway and caper in a sabbath of misrule" (192). The somber ideas that clothe his mind in ritual thoughts are made glad and "brightened"; humor is in contrast to his usual tone (rather than somber, it seems rather "sunny" here). It is, however, only a momentary respite, a sabbath.[10] This tone is to be hidden away, the cloister that Stephen imagines is shut up, closeted as it were, from the rest of his life, in a very private place along with his clothing; humor for Stephen must be locked away behind him and rarely allowed any outlet.

Stephen goes on to envision all his teachers (elsewhere described as "sober honest men"), the men who wear those vestments, in "the forms of the community," acting antically: "They came ambling and stumbling, tumbling and capering, kilting their gowns for leap frog . . . , shaken with deep fast laughter, smacking one another behind and laughing at their rude malice, . . . whispering two and two behind their hands" (192).

The scene Stephen imagines is in every way antithetical not only to the rules of the priestly order but also to the rules of the telic order of the text. The priests' usual task is extremely serious—to instruct and to lead to salvation; the text has a similarly earnest purpose—also to instruct and to lead protagonist and reader to the higher end of art. Stephen's imagining purposes a shift, a sabbath respite from the focus not only of Stephen's isolated development but also from the rigor and discipline of the novel's telic drive.[11] The scene glimpses misrule rather than rule. In this scene, the "clownish tumbling" as countermovement briefly introduced in the mathematics class is fully expanded at the university level to offer an alternate depiction of the novel; this imagined scene characterizes and portrays all of the comic elements of *Portrait*. "Tumbling" again entails a motion of no serious purpose; "ambling" is without direction; "capering" is whimsical movement. All these are in contrast to the earnest drive of the text: they all are the activities of carnival.

Rather than intellectual, this imagined scene is physical; it is something other than the world of serious thoughts and ironic correction. The leaping and capering movement, the deep laughter's "shaking," the "smacking" of one another are burlesque, the features of the slapstick: here is pratfall rather than tragic fall. The priests' "kilting their gowns" is cannily descriptive of what they would do if they were improbably to play leapfrog (when he wishes, Stephen can have an eye for detail). The kilted gowns also connect (by way of substantiating Stephen's image) to two other places important to the text's development; such connections of Stephen's image with other events in the text give the scene, while imagined, a quality of substance: the skirts of the capuchins, discussed by the director when he talks to Stephen about the priestly calling (155); and the "kilted" skirt (171) of the girl on the beach who evokes Stephen's esthetic response. And where there is this sort of misrule, there is the possibility of comic confusion: the idea of the "gown" or skirt introduces here (as it does in the interview with the director) a disjunctive note of gender conflation (the priests more like women than men). That confusion is worse confounded by the "kilt," a masculine article of dress that adds a mixture of ethnic elements to those of gender. These connections ground Stephen's reverie within other parts of the novel.

However brief and anomalous, the presence of this scene is certainly an opening into the comic possibilities of the novel. Its completeness as a vignette, its very separateness as a set piece, suggests that it evokes an already established image. Stephen's depiction of sacerdotal license is a long-standing feature of pre-Lenten excess and pious challenge; such humorous behavior of the saintly is a major component of comedy in a culture that is theocratic, particularly associated with the Middle Ages (as Stephen correctly historicizes in this passage with the image of the "cloister") but equally true of the theocratic culture of Ireland.[12] The seriousness of clerics in such a pious culture is occasionally to be tempered with playfulness; in like manner the seriousness of the *Portrait* text is to be lightened. This reverie of Stephen is itself a respite from his serious thinking and from his habit of morose reflection.

Stephen's depiction of the priests is not only a recognition of the comic potential in his life and the work about it: it is precisely a consideration of the issues of comedy. Certain words in his reverie are distinctly ones that have been used to define and describe elements of comedy. The obvious playfulness and boisterous rebelliousness of the priests is revelry, and that word is embedded in the origin of comedy as κῶμος, revelry. The priests are constituted as "the forms of the community," the clerical division of orders, but also of the communal life, one that resembles the village (κωμη) from which comedy is also derived. "Misrule" is clearly such another word to describe comedy because it denotes the festive and carnivalesque that defines comedy; it evokes the world of Rabelais's Brother John. One other crucial word is "tumbling" itself, as it is one that suggests the very physical energy of the jester or fool, one who takes the pratfall that makes for laughter or one who trips up a serious other by the heels.[13]

The presence of humor as an alternate portrait is made emblematic in Stephen's imagined scene by the doubling of those priests who whisper in comic collusion: the figure of two indicates a pairing, a mixing of complementary opposites such as light and dark, high and low, serious and comic. The priests are described by physical opposites: "florid" face with "grey hair"; "little priest," "squat . . . form of the professor of economics," "the tall form of the young professor"; "the grave troubled prefect" with "the plump" professor with the "rogue's eyes" (192). The imagined scene by itself presents the possibility of misrule and antic behavior as an alternative to usual somberness; and the doubling within it, along with the comic confusion, points to the way in which the presence of comedy is to be found in the text. It is present by pairs, as alternatives to raising and falling by tumbling, in pairing diction of high and low and by confused and conflating entities and concept (such as gender). Moreover, as this scene is imagined, so that it has a presence in the text but also stands just outside the events of the plot, comedy is also furtive, slightly to the side. Stephen has placed this scene away in a closed space, the cloister. As the priests whisper "behind" their hands or mock each other "behind," so too with the placement of the comic—behind, just off the trajectory of the novel of development. Behind or beside the purposeful is the place of comic amusement. Yet to be off to the side is still to be present; just as the "sabbath" is a regular if limited occurrence, so humor is a regular if occasional part of the text. Humor will appear in the text only a portion of the time, but it will reliably peer out from behind the order.

As tumbling is in contrast to rising and falling, so comic misrule is the alternative to rule: even if temporary and imagined, all is in humorous otherness in Stephen's response to the "rude humor" beyond him in Moynihan's comment. Stephen suggests the presence of the opposite pole of humor; the seriousness of the instructors or of the novel is given a respite: the sabbath of misrule is the day of rest from the Sunday of redemption or the weekday earnestness of the novel. A comic view is not predominant in the text, only one in a series of plural readings, but it has the virtue of running counter to (or behind) the usual critical assumptions of seriousness and irony. The reader may wish a relief from the earnestness of *Portrait*. Driven, as the reader is, by the "end" to which the novel seems to move inexorably, rising and falling in serious emotion, he or she might well seek a respite from the direction of much of the text, or from a reading that requires either a serious or an ironic pose. The reader might welcome a reading of the novel that is in opposition to the expected order of inevitable development and triumph over rules and authority; the reader too might wish to tumble rather than to fall. The reader might long to see disorder, confusion, misrule in the life of the novel that is always around and in Stephen: language less lofty, more common, ideas less serious than humorous, movement more antic than elevated.

Such respite and humor does not seem, however, readily apparent in the book, even at measured intervals. The most pertinent reason why there is so little humor evident in the foreground of the text is due to Stephen himself.[14] Foremost (and more obviously) because the text focuses extensively on his inner life, his psychological state is the main concern; second, he is so serious about himself that he cannot by himself notice what is around him or take a respite from the concerns of his own life. There is an active world around him, one of capering motion and playful ambling, from which he turns away inward. He puts such a world behind him. To return to the Belvedere mathematics class of chapter 3, which begins with the dusk "tumbling clownishly," and in which Stephen seems to stay aloof from the noises of his peers: alternately working on his equation and recalling incidents of instruction in the class, Stephen is absorbed in a narcissistic memory, aptly introduced by "his mind" that "wound itself in and out of the curious questions proposed to it" (106). It is a goal-oriented activity, "following up to the end the rigid lines" of doctrine. The labyrinthine inwardness of Stephen's self-concern is to be expected, as are the arcane theological questions proposed to his mind: "If a layman in giving baptism pour the water before saying the words is the child baptized?" The Eucharist occupies a prominent place in these questions, as it always does for Stephen, precisely because the Eucharist does what Stephen cannot yet do, bring the spiritual into the everyday. He continues, "If the wine change into vinegar and the host crumble into corruption after they have been consecrated is Jesus Christ still present under their species as God and as man?" This last thought is interrupted by a cry from a fellow student: "—Here he is!" This is not, however, the incarnate presence of God and man, but rather only the return of the rector to the class. The boys, having had a brief respite in his absence (where they could "scut," his absence being the "game ball" end to the instructional hour), must now return to their catechism; Stephen takes no break from his. Stephen, always by contrast, is reluctantly turned away by another voice beyond him from his abstract and serious musing toward the life around him, if only briefly. This rapid change from his inner thoughts and the falling off from his higher ideas certainly has a comic effect.[15] The violent juxtaposition of Stephen's last question "Is Jesus Christ still present" with the schoolboy's cry of "Here he is!" is the sort of disjunction that causes an ironic reading of *Portrait*, where Stephen's earnestness is shown to be excessive; the interior monologue is cut off, so that what Stephen thinks is diminished and disabused. Stephen of course does not see the irony, the reader does. Yet the effect, while reflecting ironically on Stephen, must be humorous to the reader. The irony is present only when Stephen is looked at exclusively as the focus of the text; to the reader who can look just beyond Stephen, the alternation of Stephen's thoughts with the classmate's cry is comical as a tumbling of misrule. If the reader looks to the entire portrayal, looks at light as well as the shadow of seriousness—that is, keeping in view the background beyond Stephen's interiority—the scene is humorous; it is not judgmental irony but comic capriciousness. There is a certain chaotic quality to that world around Stephen. The reader will find these moments of comedy in the places around and beside Stephen, the places other than his spot of piety and self-absorbed seriousness; it is to the side of Stephen, in the places just around and beyond him, in the real world just over his shoulder beyond him.

This comedy appears tangentially, which is one reason it often has been missed (the other reason is due to the drive of the *Bildungsroman*, which does not suggest the presence of the comic). Yet this humor, while indirect, resembles the comedy elsewhere encountered outright in Joyce, a comedy that challenges and jokes with the fabric of the text. It is only the single focus of readers on the directed course of Stephen's development that causes these small but comic features to go unnoticed and unappreciated in the portrayal. They are moments of comic freeplay, antic gestures, that exist not to the end of *Bildung* but to the levity of a text.

Chapter 5 chronicles the breaking away of Stephen from all orders that have held him back; it is the part of the book in which the expectations of the genre come to fruition. Its importance seems to weigh down the action. He has left the Church for the university and, in the opening pages of the chapter, is about to leave home (rather late) to go to class. His father yells down at him in a comedy of language and gender confusion: "Is your lazy bitch of a brother gone out yet?"; his mother regrets the change in him: "you'll live to rue the day you set your foot in that place [the university]" (175). This first comment suggests the throwing over of all orders that is essential to the novel; the last, the maternal solicitude, indicates the inevitable change in the protagonist, separating him from his family and society. To these comments, Stephen makes a gesture of some theatricality: " — Good morning, everybody, said Stephen, . . . kissing the tips of his fingers in adieu." That gesture is a suitably worldly and dandified one of French manners. That the (also French) word "adieu" rhymes visually and aurally with the "rue" of his mother's comment gives an additional gloss and comic pointedness to this exchange. Yet in French "rue" is also a street and, when the narrative turns its attention to Stephen's exit into the "lane" behind the Dedaluses' shabby home, the diction is tripped up into a comedy of pure diction "rue(street)lane"; it is a manic sort of polyvocality that characterizes all others of Joyce's texts. This series of words in the narrative is exceptionally valuable, as it implicates both Stephen's actions and the narration into a comic imbalance that does not directly affect any part of the text but clearly maintains a comic presence just behind the action of the novel's generic direction, much as the lane is behind the serious domestic difficulties. That is to say, this play of words does not ironize anything in particular but is pure comic play on the page that we expect in other of Joyce's work. The entire text of purposeful change and development has an antic disposition behind it, diversionary but present.

When he rejects the possibility of entering the priesthood, which he thinks will entertain him with questions such as those he posed to himself about the Host, Stephen has claimed that the "vegetable life" of his father's house, as illustrated above, will win the day in his soul, that life of "disorder, the misrule and confusion" (162). That is the world of the real, of the belly, of the decay of rotted cabbages and hamshaped icons he sees across the ash pit of his back garden. Stephen knows and acknowledges that the real world is something other than the cloistered world of idea and image he so assiduously courts; he passes the actual cloister behind his house in that comically polyvocal lane, above, only to hear the mad nun call from behind its walls. Yet so little of the world of Dublin that Stephen encounters appears to him in any way as humorous. Much as Stephen claims to seek the real world, yet so rarely seems to find it, rather his own preconceived images, so too, Stephen claims that the real world of misrule will win his soul, yet he resolutely seems to turn his back to it. The details of life in Dublin, the street furniture of *Dubliners,* is not present in *Portrait's* house of fiction, that labyrinthine and indoor soul of Stephen. One can catalogue the few details of the world in which Stephen lives: the shrine of the virgin "fowlwise" on the pole he sees as he thinks of the vegetable world of his father's house; "the grey block of Trinity" (180) he passes on the way to University College; the stonecutter Baird which makes Stephen think of Ibsen rather than see any detail of the stonework itself (nor does he think of the spirits commemorated by the stones). The newsagent's placard (177) tells him what day it is, but he takes no cognitive notice of the headlines he stops to read. By contrast, the earlier text of *Stephen Hero,* more open and more detailed, will not only note that Stephen and Cranly read the placard, it will also list what the headlines are: "EVENING TELEGRAPH [Meeting] Nationalist Meeting in Ballinrobe. Important Speeches. Main Drainage Scheme . . . Mad Cow at Cabra, . . ." (*SH* 221). The conjunction of "Important Speeches" with "Main Drainage Scheme" reads like a touch of Flaubert, as it replicates the quick shift from high to low that makes the comic impulse. There is the vegetable world of misrule, which Joyce relishes in all of his works, even there in an early text discarded; and the Stephen of *Portrait* will not see it, rather shut it away in the private closet of his mind. The humor is locked away and obscured, but the reader might and should glimpse it.

Portrait has few such overt moments as does *Stephen Hero* (a point to be discussed in chapter 4); the best may be the old Irishman talking about the queer creatures at the latter end of the world whom Stephen can only treat with disdain and fear for his comedy as much as for his Irishness.[16] The move from *Stephen Hero* to *Portrait* is a move that Joyce makes not only to be more economic, more terse, and more focused; it is also a move of a sort of repression, since Joyce removes many of the figures of women,[17] and the death of the sister Isabel—in short—removes emotions of all sorts. And there is a move to put behind the text of *Portrait*, behind both temporally and locally in space, the sort of comedy that Joyce practiced in all of his other writings. *Hero* contains the life of misrule and the vegetable world (where, for example, Stephen asks Emma for one night together and then farewell), the sort of vibrant reality and absurdity that characterize *Dubliners, Ulysses,* and the *Wake,* and that are turned back in *Portrait*.

The contrast Stephen makes in the physics theatre of monastic seriousness with antic activity is a genuine one that shows he is beginning to be aware of what exists alternatively around him; only much later will he reinforce the contrast when in "Proteus" he distinguishes "monk words" with "rogue words," and presciently recognizes a heteroglossic tension in his own discourse. At other points in *Portrait*, Stephen persists in seeing himself exclusively as a monk, a way of separating and distinguishing himself from others, a further turning of his back on the world in cloistered retirement. Stephen certainly maintains his monkishness with Emma, even "that night at the carnival ball" (219). In the very place of antic merriment, a place of license and amusement, he insists that he is "born to be a monk." In his narrative of himself in *Portrait* he goes on to exacerbate this separation: "his mind, in the vesture of a doubting monk [those somber vestments again], stood often in shadow under the windows of that age, to hear the grave and mocking music of the lutenists or the frank laughter of the waistcoateers" (176). While this is a piece of adolescent self-dramatization, to Stephen the stance is almost inveterate. He is displaced, in the "shadow" of the music and laughter, presented as the negative image of his actual presence in the novel, where he is foregrounded with the humor and melody lurking behind the frame. He claims that his "monkish learning" makes him "but a shy guest at the feast of the world's culture" (180). This bathetic self-projection not only separates Stephen, locking him away in his own private closet, it also intellectualizes him as a scholastic and restricts him to a monovocal language. In a rare moment of self-awareness in "Proteus," Stephen notes his tendency to "morose delectation" (3.385), delight in the sad and serious; fittingly he takes the term from the scholasticism of Aquinas. The omniscient narrator of *Stephen Hero* has claimed that the Stephen in it has an "indurating shield" (*SH* 34) that *Portrait* represents by the cloistered and immured nature of Stephen's thinking. The reader, so closely following Stephen in *Portrait*, is similarly given to monastic interpretation, hearing only serious words, and inclining to read the scholastic instruction of irony.

In the reader's experience of the language of the text, *Portrait* is devoid of a discourse of common language and carnival. Stephen never speaks the language of the streets and the schoolyard; the slang that enters the novel comes rarely and always from others such as Moynihan. It is this outsideness, this place just beyond Stephen, that produces a counterpoint to the novel and it is where the comedy is located. The same physics lecture (where Moynihan's ribald comment creates momentarily for Stephen an image of comedy) ends with Moynihan yelling out, "closing time, gents," a phrase so familiar in Dublin as to be ubiquitous. Stephen never descends to the coarseness of Moynihan, even if he appreciates it. Vulgar speech in the traditional sense of common and unelevated is always around Stephen, forming an alternative to his highly embroidered poetic assays. Yet Stephen does not hear or reproduce it. (There is, by contrast, more direct and suggestive speech commonness in *Stephen Hero*.) Stephen is too serious to hear or transmit the common speech that is part of the "vegetable life" of misrule; he is too self-absorbed to have a carnival holiday of comedy, a sabbath from seriousness. Yet it is in that common speech that the comedy of the real world resides. Stephen has turned his back on that world of misrule and vegetable life, just as Joyce has put the real world around Stephen (or that of *Stephen Hero*) behind the text of *Portrait*; it is in that anterior space, however, that the antic is to be found.

The humorous detail of the real and the comedy of common speech have place in Joyce's texts before *Portrait*. The stories of *Dubliners* had their own purposeful intent, like the telic direction of the *Bildungsroman*, that of presenting the paralysis of which Joyce famously writes; yet they also contain a tone of humor in the language that runs alongside the naturalist presentation in Joyce's "nicely polished looking-glass" (*Letters* I, 64).

Take the following sentences from "Grace," that story from the world of commerce, on the trajectory of McCoy: "His line of life had not been the shortest distance between two points and for short periods he had been driven to live by his wits. He had been a clerk in the Midland Railway, a canvasser for advertisements for *The Irish Times* . . . , a town traveller . . ."

(*D* 159). The repetition of "shortest distance" with "short periods" collapses Euclidian notions of geometry's lines and points into confusion (and thus connects to the gnomon of the first story, "The Sisters"). The life as not "the shortest distance between two points" tries by a common cliché to change the diction by poetic euphemism away from McCoy's feckless and habitual divarications, but surely the "distances" and "points" make a comic connection to "traveller" and to the "Midland Railway" (not to speak of the railway with "driven"). The humor in this language is just beside the story's plot and purpose, parallel to them like Euclidian lines, implicit but present. (The ways in which Joyce comes to develop this style of verbal humor just behind the focus of the text, and the context of that development, will be discussed further in chapter 3.)

Parts of *Portrait* have long been seen as overtly humorous: Stephen's excessive piety in chapter 4, for example, or the exchange of students at University College in chapter 5. These scenes are connected either to the distancing ironizing of Stephen's inwardness or to the humor found in the situations of external events. In such scenes, the reader sees what is overtly funny, with language being transparent. These moments are therefore already marked out as separate, discrete intermissions within the more purposeful direction of the novel. The first such scene, of Stephen's excess, contains of course the hyperbolic quality of Stephen's solipsism, the narration of which makes funny things happen externally. Such intensity, moreover, seems to require from the reader an ironic response that calculates Stephen's intended course of developmental advance. Even so independent a critic and so iconoclastic a reader as Kenner senses the restrictions of irony when he says that "our impulse on being confronted" with Stephen at such moments "is to laugh: and laugh at this moment we dare not."[18] The drive and purpose of the novel seems to have checked laughter and turn it at best to irony.

The second sort of comic scene recognized in critical appraisals is those realistic actions, something from the world outside of Stephen, presented directly in the text: these are often extended dialogues where other (and lesser) characters speak and act, their behaviors and words creating a comic effect represented within the text. Yet such a scene is not comic because of its production by the text, rather merely by its presentation. Both sorts of scenes are separate from the fabric text, the interior ones corrected by the direction of the novel, the external ones humorously enacting real life; and thus the humor found in existing criticism seems to overlook the way in which there may be humor integral to the text itself, a comedy involved with the very words of the novel, much as the polyvocal "rue/lane" or the "distance" of the "Midland Railway." Discrete moments have been noted, but no sense of a comic alternate portrait in the medium of the words where the language—even serious—is itself in play.[19]

So it is that few critics (or readers) would consider *Portrait* as frequently or even integrally comic. The august *Concise Cambridge History of English Literature* says of *Portrait* that "no one has ever called it a comic work."[20] Despite the transparent humor of *Ulysses* and *Finnegans Wake*, and even the wry wit of *Dubliners* (not to mention that attic salt and salaciousness of Joyce's letters in his youth and the early years of writing), *Portrait* seems to be a separate work, written for a different purpose by what seems like an artist with a different temperament.[21] To go for the first time from *Portrait* to *Ulysses* is to experience a change, a kind of tumbling from the heights of self-absorbed seriousness to light, airy humor. While on the parapet of the Martello tower Stephen is still somber, dressed in Hamlet- and priest-like black; by obvious contrast, Mulligan wears an open morning gown. The "gown" resembles that of the solemn priests of Stephen's years of schooling in *Portrait* (with the "tonsure" adding to the sacerdotal quality), but with the contrast that Mulligan's gown, being "open," brings him in line with the capering, leapfrogging priests in Stephen's image from the physics theatre. *Ulysses* enacts what *Portrait* can only imagine, that a priest can be a joker, or a joker a priest. Like the playful reverend fathers in Stephen's imagined scene, Mulligan is said to have "skipped," pointing a finger in "friendly jest" and making "mockery": he calls himself "tripping and sunny." Tripping is a sort of light-footedness, or even tumbling, motions that do not seem to describe a work that has the morose Stephen in it, but it is not only Mulligan who is sunny, bright, and jokingly light: in the other "portrait" of his youth Joyce was known as "Sunny Jim."[22] *Portrait* apparently has none of this sunniness, as does the opening of *Ulysses* and did parts of Joyce's life. In the evening in the classroom when Stephen thinks of "clownish tumbling," the day and the sky are described as "dull" (used similarly eighteen times throughout the novel). A reader or critic might be surprised to find that versions of the verb *laugh* ("laughing," "laughed") and the noun *laughter* appear in the novel more than eighty times. Certainly the mood seems to be obscured, subdued, and closeted away.

The laughter in *Portrait* seems not to be a raucous kind but rather silent; it has an unvoiced quality, a muting. The absurdities of the language, we will find in chapter 2, are connected to a certain silence. What voice is most evident in *Portrait* is that of irony, which is used to display the limits of Stephen's understanding; such irony is especially possible because of the interiorization of the narrative that creates a judgmental tension implicit in the indirect style.[23] Irony has a didactic purpose, raising points for the development of the telic direction of the narrative; irony is a corrective touch to the enlightenment of the reader and the protagonist who is being led to the desirable end of the development into an artist. (Joyce's end was to be an artist, albeit a comic one, not a moral one.) Irony involves the wish to be both direct and correct, where comedy, by contrast, exists only for the respite from order and for the pleasure.

To say that *Portrait* is comic is to seem to claim the preposterous, to state something in and of itself funny. To say that it is ironic is, of course, to say the commonplace. Irony involves the reader in a complicity of superiority, whereby a knowing stance distances him from the text; as the etymology of *irony* indicates, the reader expects the text to dissemble. To be aware of the dissembling leads to truth; thus the text fulfills its intellective purpose of education. Moreover, irony is to be expected as it is the privilege of the modernist position, detached, intellectualized. Irony requires a distance from the real world, a distance by intellection from the messy material of actual life.[24] Comedy embraces the real, revels in its resistance to ideational order. To be funny would be much less, as the point of something humorous is foremost pleasure, not exclusive knowledge (even if some knowledge might be a side effect of humor). In the driven *Portrait* knowledge always is a premium, pleasure infrequent and often associated with wastefulness and sin. Comedy exists as a respite from order, exists for the amusement and pleasure such respite affords. The comic element unsubstantiates representation and the signifying focus of irony, and substitutes a *jouissance*;[25] Joyce presciently calls this "joy."

Even in his earliest esthetic writing Joyce develops this sense of the self-sufficiency of comedy. Still shouldering distinctions from Aristotle regarding kinetic and static art and the cathartic effect, Joyce writes in the Paris Notebook that improper art excites in the reader a feeling of desire that "is the feeling which urges us to go to something," that is, it causes us to go beyond what is presented to us. Comic art is rather the "feeling of joy." Surely an ironic reading (which may have some comic elements) is "improper" because it is one that is not satisfied with the work as it is, but instead impels the reader to a judgment beyond: this desire for something else takes the reader "from rest that [he] may possess something," presumably a knowledge or a reading that takes us farther than what is presented to us, something that is "not sufficient in itself inasmuch as it . . . seek[s] something beyond itself" (*CW* 144). The stasis of the comic moment is in obvious contrast as well to the purposeful movement of the novel of development. Comedy "does not . . . seek anything beyond itself" and rather gives us the "feeling of joy." It is sufficient end in itself.

Grandly, the young Joyce claims that "it may be seen that tragedy is the imperfect manner and comedy the perfect manner in art" (*CW* 144). This averred triumphing of comedy over tragedy is Joyce's release from the drama he valued as a university student but could never come to write; it is his turning from Ibsen to Meredith and to fiction; it clearly indicates the work he comes to value and to do. And it also indicates that comedy in *Portrait* has no directed end but exists in itself within a novel of much direction and aim.

So for all of the novel's seriousness and development, it has a comic countertone. It may be offside and silent, but it is present. As evidence of this displacement, this putting of comedy into the closeted parts of the novel, *comic* appears only three times in *Portrait, comedy* never.[26] One use is related to Simon Dedalus's memory of his jovial fellows, one of whom "could sing a good comic song" (91); Stephen is enured to his father's advice, yet the sense of fellowship and community his father tries to convey is essential for comedy. The second use of "comic," which is discussed in the next chapter, comes from Stephen's disdain for his fellow student as a "comic Irishman"; the phrase helps situate the comic elements in the novel. The third use is in a question Stephen asks himself about an object as "either comic or tragic," following in the footsteps of Joyce's own essays in the Notebooks; it is discussed below.

Because it is as counterpart, an alternate portraiture, comedy can be found precisely in the places that contain the high purpose and even the intellectualized irony very essential to the directed plot of the novel. One such part, Stephen's esthetic discussion with Lynch, is of course an important component of his growth and of the articulation of his ideas about the vocation of art. The ideas are important to the status of the text; and the theory, seen as a whole, is ironic not least of all because Stephen's theorizing outstrips his practice, he having written only the villanelle and a few verses for Emma. (And Stephen will continue to do so little for far longer, beyond the text into *Ulysses*.) For Stephen thoughts must precede experience; as with all of the events and actions in *Portrait,* ideas come to him before action. Everything for Stephen must be *a priori;* as he must behold an image in his soul before encountering it in the real world, so he must think about art before he practices it. Any abstract ideas Stephen promulgates are subject to the correction of reality, and irony may judge his pretensions. Thus it is that irony is so much of the apparent tone of the esthetic theory, but there is another note.

In chapter 5, Stephen mentions to Lynch that he has written down questions "which are more amusing than yours" (214). Their amusing quality notwithstanding, "In finding answers to them," Stephen says, he "found the theory of the esthetic which I am trying to explain." This is a serious intention, one that drives him and the reader. Yet the *Grundrisse* of his theory, its origin, lies in something amusing; from the ridiculous arises the serious. Stephen has earlier noted to Lynch that "this side of esthetic philosophy" is carried by Aquinas "all along the line," a very purposeful aim. This Aquinas, however, may not be the strict philosophizing moralist. Lynch remarks that Stephen quotes Aquinas "time after time like a jolly round friar" (209); in this image of the cleric as a figure of humor and pleasure, Aquinas resembles Stephen's capering priests. Lynch goes on to suggest that Stephen is joking himself by using Aquinas in such an antic way: "Are you laughing in your sleeve?" (209).[27] So here, too, the origins of Stephen's earnest esthetic are tempered with something festive and comic. The phrase "laughing in your sleeve" suggests the uncontrollable laughter that is hidden in the context of solemnity; it is a furtive and muffled laugh but yet present. While "to laugh up the sleeve" is a cliché, it is an image invigorated in *Portrait* by Stephen when he contemplates the antic behavior of his Jesuit masters: they too act out their humor furtively, whispering "behind their hands" making merry if discretely. The sabbath of misrule may obtain even in the esthetic discussion.

The set of questions Stephen poses are purposeful but off-handedly to the side, like the priests' whispering behind the hand or Aquinas laughing in the sleeve; they are amusing and more, even absurd: "*Is a chair finely made tragic or comic? Is the portrait of Mona Lisa good if I desire to see it? Is the bust of Sir Philip Crampton lyrical, epical or dramatic? Can excrement or a child or a louse be a work of art? If not, why not?*" (214). The questions have the stilted form of the schoolboy essay, but they range from actual objects of art (the bust of Crampton or the Mona Lisa) to objects in the real world, a chair or excrement. (One assumes that Stephen would theorize that excrement is not a work of art, although Joyce made it the subject of art when Bloom goes to the jakes in "Calypso"; Stephen's esthetic would not likely have extended to embrace today's art world.) Why the Mona Lisa would be adjudged good if it were the object of desire is perhaps a question only an adolescent would ask: in Stephen's constant search for the contradictory figure of a woman, the iconic portrait is a pateresque vamp and vampire. Yet the other questions amuse beyond their evident, surface ludicrousness, and they do so because their absurdity is integrated with other parts of the novel. The bust of Sir Philip Crampton cannot be lyrical, dramatic, or epic, as sculpture evades the verbal genres (as Stephen would know from Lessing). Yet the point of Stephen's posing the question surely opens the way to comedy: that bust was considered by the denizens of Dublin to be a monstrosity,[28] something whose appearance was on the order of a pineapple. To ask whether such an object was lyrical was to court comedy and to continue in it: from the proposition that such a piece resembling "vegetable matter" might be a work of art, it is an easy, if humorous, step from Stephen to ask whether the nearly wholly vegetable matter of excrement could be. And the comedy continues the next question within this list: moving etymologically from excrement to *excreta,* such as fingernails (the image of the artist God), lice (held by medieval thinkers to be produced by the body), and on the most literal excretion, a child. When a reader remembers that Stephen has earlier talked to Lynch about how he needs to find a new terminology (and a "new personal experience"[!]) for the phenomenon of "artistic conception, artistic generation and artist reproduction" (209), he sees the extension of a comic playfulness in the questions Stephen sets for himself. The masturbatory comedy of Mulligan in "Scylla" is not that far away from Stephen here.

These questions, then, are not only absurdly amusing on their surface (Stephen setting himself wild intellectual problems in his serious theoretical quest), nor only funny in Lynch's reactions to them.[29] They have the sort of comic impulse found in lists of names and places so obviously comical in *Ulysses* and *Finnegans Wake*. The features are the same—internally consistent connection, not readily apparent but manically related (an exfoliated bust: vegetable matter as art: excreta of all sorts: children as "excrementia"); extended playful echoes and reflections from other parts of the text (the child with artistic generation, or the lice with a memory of Stephen's mother). The comedy is not merely an isolated moment of respite of amusement in a serious narrative; it extends, as in all of Joyce's other works, to all parts of the text, so that the humor is integral. The reader may see these connections when Stephen cannot, as they are slightly to the side of the text, and to see them is not to ironize Stephen but to laugh.

Consider the question, "Is a chair finely made tragic or comic?" as another example of this sort of extended playfulness. This one, too, seems to yoke rather incongruously the artistic and the useful and, although tragic and comic qualities are absurd for an object, the phrase "finely made" raises the philosophical questions of the good and the *quidditas* of the object. The *quidditas* of a chair is to seat someone well: its function is to support the human form. Stephen must have been implicitly teasing Lynch, who quite obviously and coarsely jokes to him; Stephen's humor is less obvious because it is less sophomoric than Lynch's. Lynch has already shown a less than esthetic interest in the posterior of the Venus. Stephen had begun his discussion of esthetics with the definition of art as "the human disposition of sensible or intelligible matter for an esthetic end" (207). Surely he must here be playfully extending and reversing that idea, presenting a comic alternative: an esthetic chair is for the disposition of the sensible (or intelligent!) matter of the human end, what a Dubliner later calls "the parliamentary side of your arse" (*U* 12.1792). Perhaps then even Lynch's interest in the backside of Venus is not erotic but esthetic. Humor appears in just this sort of turning of the serious; jokes always take the important, and by twisting it give an alternative view.

Not only are the questions Stephen has written down amusing, so too is the writing of chapter 5.[30] Stephen is being playful here, even if he is serious about an esthetic; he engages in a comic turn. It is a sly and subtle comic turn, a sort of laughing in the sleeve, slightly to the side of the important. The seriousness is there because the esthetic is important not only to Stephen but also to Joyce, to the reader, and to the plot of the novel; yet just askew there is the silliness of the questions themselves and their extended playfulness amid the interconnections within the directed text. This absurd quality, borne by language, is humorous; it is not the deceptive language of irony, but rather the playful language of comic possibility. There is no dissembling in the questions Stephen poses; that is, there is no way in which the language is used to convey a meaning opposite to that expressed by the words used. The questions are on their face incongruous, and on reflection the intellectual activity they seem to foster creates humorous connections. These connections lie just outside the main and serious purpose of the articulation of esthetic theory, but they are comically present. What irony there is in this section of *Portrait* comes in the larger focus of Stephen's artistic development that is yet to occur, unless the reader were to take these questions more seriously than does Stephen himself. Stephen is earnest and thoughtful, not far wrong or incorrect, nor so obtuse as to deserve the corrective of irony. There resides even in the important sections on esthetics in chapter 5 a laughing in the sleeve, a humor not readily noted or noisily evident, but present. It offers the alternate possibilities of a comic novel.

It is therefore not necessary to distinguish between irony and humor in order to make the claim that there is a comic *Portrait*. Irony and humor, while different in form and effect, can occur in the same text; in fact, in

Portrait they must do so, to make the alternative pairing that is confirmed in Stephen's vision of serious priests temporarily cavorting. The point to be stressed is that there is comedy in *Portrait,* far more of it than has been hitherto recognized; that the comedy more nearly resembles the humor in all of Joyce's other works (when the persistent irony of *Portrait* finds small counterpart); and that *Portrait* is made up of light and shadow, high and low, serious and funny.

This combination is integral to the text: the focused requirements of the *Bildungsroman* genre and the dispersive nature of the antic, order and disruption, purpose and play. Their embedded opposition seems particularly Joycean, but this opposition is also fundamental to comedy as well. Comedy, traditionally viewed, has been seen as both conservative and disruptive. Moreover, contemporary critical theory on comedy (of which there has been less than for other issues) takes another position but still one oppositional, contrasting the conventional view with a postmodernist perspective.

Traditional views of comedy note its conservative character: it holds basic, eternal values dear, thus focusing on society and community; it shuns excess and its concomitant hypocrisy, hence its satiric and ironic tone; and it asserts the permanence of the human condition, thus assuring its universality. Analysis of comedy is replete with quotations that stress this conservative nature, of which a few might suffice to substantiate both the definitions and the prevailing values. "All comedy celebrates humankind's capacity to endure. . . . [T]he comic spirit expresses elation over our condition," and comic works "depend on generally accepted standards of values."[31] "Comedy . . . consists in the indirect affirmation of the ideal logical order by means of the derogation of the limited orders of actuality."[32] This last quotation notes the ways in which comedy challenges accepted orders of society and life, being in that way critical and disruptively pointed, but does so only to affirm the transcendent order of higher things. As corrosive and corrective, comedy has been itself an integral combination of orders.

Current critical theory takes a different view of comedy, but in so doing simply changes the poles of its opposition by insisting not on the assent to an overarching order but rather on the immediate value of experience. Humor can be seen as universal no longer than any other power structure with transcendent claims. Feminist theories of comedy discuss how comedy by women shatters the idea of comedy as universal; it is "subversive and gleefully threatening to the dominant order" which, conventionally seen, it chided only to better embrace.[33] As contemporary theory has changed the notion of art from product to process, so it has shifted the effect of comedy from values to possibilities, from result to cause. The material of the text is the matter of comedy. No longer an affirmation of community values or of psychological verities that substantiate a higher value, comedy becomes the expression of a subversive verbal movement. Barthes has seen the function of comedy as creating a text of pleasure for the reader through which ideology may enter, not as asserting a gospel of reconciliation to higher powers; Kristeva removes the focus of laughter from therapeutic psychological compensation to a "textual laughter"— that is, away from traditional, Aristotelian and Freudian notions of catharsis and substitution to verbal play.[34] These views of comedy invert the terms of comedy's oppositional nature to insist on its subversive element rather than its conservative reconciliatory purpose. Yet such theories only insist that the figure of comedy's character be inverted, with what was secondary now primary and what primary now subservient. Comedy is a countermovement of the text, with a woof-like thread against a dominant warp.

Such a view of comedy seems fitting for a *Portrait* whose humor is integral but just displaced, alternately present but slightly oblique; not in the foreground but in the background as contrast to the seriousness of the directed plot; just beyond or behind the serious issues, closeted away from the persistent drive of the novel. The humor that is present in *Portrait* is always just "in the sleeve," just to the side of the serious. When at Belvedere the director invites him to join the priesthood, Stephen adds his own imagination of sacerdotal posing: he envisions himself vested as a subdeacon, standing "aloof from the altar," placing himself in a position behind the solemn action of the Mass. That role of subdeacon is, of course, a seemingly modest and subservient one; yet to stand behind the serious ceremony of Eucharistic consecration is to stand just outside the other place, outside the main and important action, in the place where the comic light falls in the liminal places of humor. Stephen goes into detail about this figure of himself standing to the side: "vested with the tunicle . . . , his shoulders covered with a humeral veil, holding the paten within its folds" (158). In this vision, Stephen vividly and earnestly considers the calling, although he comes shortly to reject it; yet in that earnest depiction lies the language of comic absurdity. The humeral veil is a shoulder veil, so that it could cover nothing else but the shoulder.[35] The Stephen who, later in "Proteus" when imagining the Mass celebrated in various places at the same time will praise Occam for eliminating the unnecessary, rather obviously repeats himself here. Someone who will value words (either their rhythmic "rise and fall" or their "associations" [166]) certainly is nodding here. Even so "poor a Latinist as he" (179) confesses himself to be (and this passage has several words from Church Latin such as "tunicle" and "paten") would be aware of the repetition. That he is not suggests that he is less self-conscious in his diction than is usual. And in that lack of self-control, in this tumbling misstep, lies the antic spirit of comedy always present just behind Stephen. Humeral is derived from the Latin for shoulder, *humerus;* that is a word which sounds like "humorous," with the difference between *us* and *ous* being for all practical purposes unheard in speech to remind us of all the language around him that Stephen never hears; indeed the funny bone owes its folk and false etymology, its unscholarly and inaccurate entity, to the connection of the humerus with its sensitive nerves that tingle when struck. There is something funny in Stephen's seriousness, something that might (just) tickle the funny bone of the reader, and it is present as the alternate beside the serious solemnity. It is a humor somewhat hidden, not immediately evident; it is introduced obliquely, by indirection, through language, placed just behind the text, up the sleeve or over Stephen's shoulder, so to speak.

From Stephen's own image of cavorting priests, tumbling and clowning, we can see the character of humor in *Portrait* as an alternate to serious, telic development. It is a respite from the seriousness of the novel's education and intellection; it is a sabbath from the reader's tension of genuine or ironic reading. Stephen's image of himself as slightly to the side of the solemnity of the Mass is an emblem of the presence of comedy: that humeral veil over his shoulders, in its common redundancy and comic etymology, is a funny place, over the shoulder, just behind the serious Stephen. The humeral veil connects (as do all of Joyce's comic touches in other works) with other parts of *Portrait:* with the "sleeve" in which Lynch claims Stephen laughs as he uses a "jolly friar Aquinas" who resembles the cavorting Jesuit instructors. And that sleeve connects with the hands behind which those Jesuits laughingly whisper. There is further humor in those priests' confused and complicated behavior and dress, and a pairing up by two of such comic conversation in whispered language. Over the shoulder, just to the side, indirectly laughing in muffled sounds, cloistered away but still present, doubled in pairs, the comic portrait can be glimpsed as making a contrast. Humor is just to the side of the text, in other texts behind and around *Portrait.* (These will be the points of the subsequent chapters: doubling of language in 2, other contexts in 3, an earlier version of *Portrait* in 4.)

That humeral veil drapes over the shoulder and is put over the head, head and shoulders both being the very essential features of any portrait. In a portrait you should look at the head and behind it as well.[36] The next chapter will discuss the presence of the comic as just behind Stephen and the text, just over the shoulder of the narrative canvas that always puts him in the center of the narrative's portrayal.

1

"The Comic Irishman in the Bench Behind"
The Portrait with Two Heads

For Stephen, a model schoolboy, scenes in a pedagogical setting are capital moments in *Portrait;* for the reader they are equally essential moments of instruction and enlightenment. Classrooms are not only obviously an important part of a student's life, they are also places in which the novel's quality entity as a *Bildungsroman* obtains. Education is an essential element of *Bildung;* moreover, instruction compliments the intellectual component of the novel, adding to the sense of weighty issues being entertained. The classroom is a place of authority, which must be both obeyed and defied for the growth of the protagonist. In *Portrait* that authority limns at a distance the control of colonization and, because Stephen is taught by religious men who add dogma to the order of other powers of the classroom, they are certainly guardians of the power of the Word and, by extension, of the world. A classroom is—or should be—a place where those various authorities impose order and rule, directing while teaching about the world. Stephen must accept and adapt to this order; his response to the instruction he receives—and then transforms or rejects—operates as an analogy to the activity of the reader, who reads the text and must transform or reject what happens to Stephen, and it is here that irony plays its part in the reader's response to the novel's instruction. The classroom has a purpose to advance the student, much as the generic plot of the novel of development has a purpose to advance to its predisposed end. Stephen finds a sense of superiority and otherness in class, befitting his sense of special calling, and so he demonstrates these qualities. In the order of the class, however, there is disorder, and Stephen often misses what happens in the class around him. The reader, because he focuses on Stephen, similarly misses much of what goes on elsewhere in the classroom. And so often what happens in these instructional moments that Stephen fails to note is a sense of chaos and misrule. It is there that the comic spirit surfaces, in acts of humorous capering. Much as the novel's serious drive is interspersed with moments of tumbling, the classroom's pedagogical thrust is alternated with antic behavior. It was in such classrooms as the mathematics class at Belvedere that the notion of the alternate comic tumbling was found; in the physics class at UCD that the image of the capering clerics occurs. The reader, like Stephen a model schoolboy, takes seriously or takes offense at what happens in the instruction; the comic element occurs just beyond notice, as an alternative to the direction of the class.

In addition to the mathematics class and the physics lecture, four other classroom scenes bring into light the workings of *Portrait* as something comic, as alternately over the shoulder. Stephen ofttimes falls short in these classes, and sometimes he is merely present, standing by while something occurs. Much like his staying to the side during the rough and tumble rugby in the first term at Clongowes, Stephen is a bystander here to moods, activities, concepts that go on just behind him, and these things, indeed, are active and amusing, much like sport or a game. He partakes as little of this fun as he did of sports. These scenes are discussed here not in their order in the plot, because the elements of the comic that peer through each scene follow their own alternate process of comic misrule. Jumping around the chronology of the plot defies the authority of the genre and allows the comedy to emerge from the rules. The chronology of these scenes makes them appear accretive, as Stephen grows into his sense of his own powers; to displace that order is to see the ways in which Stephen's tumbling and error are themselves independent, equal moments of humor, comedy allowing no hierarchy. The first scene discussed is one of the last, and it is only fantasy—the English class Stephen imagines on his way to Newman House, having already missed the class proper; the second is that actual physics class where something more appears beyond the scene of uncloistered revelry occasioned by the ribald comment. After these, a transgressive move jumps back to the very first class, the one at Clongowes in which he is pandied, and then to an English class at Belvedere in which Stephen is threatened with punishment when accused of heresy. These two classes in which Stephen is in error then yield to the meeting with the dean of studies, before the actual physics class, in which, although Stephen more than holds his own in intellectual discussion, a comic sense pervades the encounter. The last classroom considered is a return to that class of mathematics in the winter term at Belvedere, where the idea of comic tumbling is first recognized, to see that the class yet contains something else besides. While these scenes defy the logic of plot and chronology, they obey comedy's antic sway.

So the classroom is a particular, important area for both the serious development of the novel and the skewed presence of the comic. By his university years, Stephen has begun to slacken in his studiousness; his own home is misruled by a clock that is wildly inaccurate, and he even fails to know what weekday it is and so only realizes on his way that he will miss his English class. He imagines being there, envisioning the other students with heads "meekly bent," dutifully taking notes while his "own head was unbent" (178), as if resisting the ideas of the lecture. He sets himself apart yet again as different, another kind, as he has been in all his school days, even in a classroom he only imagines. The head is a major feature of this imagined scene, surely because the head is the main object of the classroom's instructional intent (and heads are so prominent in the tiered auditoria to both student and instructor alike). So the focus on heads seems appropriate (and necessary) to the novel's serious intellective purpose. That prominence is why the classroom provides such a capital setting in the book. The presences of heads, Stephen's up and others' meekly bent, also localizes the figure of the body to stress its most revealing feature, the one that is the absolute center of a portrait.

After imagining the English class he actually missed and then entering the physics theatre and meeting the dean, Stephen attends the physics lecture. Like mathematics, its subject is rule and authority; it is also a subject of the actual world. This last class presented in the novel is no culmination of Stephen's education. Rather than a matriculated finish to his learning, one that would drive the telos of his development, this class is riddled with confusion and unruliness. The tedious lecture is spiced with marginal commentary by Moynihan. In particular, the one vulgar aside he makes about ellipsoidal balls produces in Stephen the image that recognizes the comic tumbling around the somber ideas of his life. In the order of science lurks the ribald biology of youthful raillery, just as within the somberness of the priests and the earnest youthfulness of the narrative lurks a comic impulse. Moreover, even as Stephen's imagined scene of the cavorting priests gives antic misrule and tumbling to the somber, principled drive of the plot, so this scene in the physics class also gives comedy something else, its particular position and place. We will not be surprised to find that it lies just over the shoulder, like the humeral veil, displaced from the apparent center. Throughout the lecture Moynihan's voice from the back is in contrast to the subject matter presented at the front of the auditorium, as serious matters are always foregrounded in the novel: as the front of the room is for serious material, so the back of the classroom is the place for vulgar speech. At the outset of the class, when the roll is taken and there is no answer to the call of Cranly's name, "Try Leopardstown! said a voice from the bench *behind*"; and the instructional hour ends as "Moynihan's voice called from *behind* in echo to a distant bell:— Closing time, gents!" (191, 194, emphasis added). Behind the authority of instruction and questions is the jocular exclamatory countervoice, the back of the classroom being the place for the unruly students. Moynihan is the very figure of the antic that Stephen evokes when he hears his ribald comment about "ellipsoidal balls": his "snoutish face" (191) is the face not only of scabrousness but of satire, marking its etymological derivative from *satyr*.

There are other voices around Stephen and their presence makes up the real world that eludes him or that he avoids. In the middle of the lecture, during the teacher's demonstration of electrical current, one other student asks a question: "A sharp Ulster voice" asked whether students would be responsible for questions of applied science. This to Stephen is the voice of the other again, which always intrudes upon his thoughts. He sees it as another head, Protestant, northern, alien. The intrusion of other voices always forces a shift away from the intense foregrounding of Stephen's own serious thoughts; they present alternative tones to the monovocal quality of the narrative. He only recognizes in such other voices the authority of their dutiful obligatory imperatives and seeks to free himself from the conformity they demand: "the constant voices . . . urging him to be a gentleman . . . to be a good catholic . . . to be strong and manly . . . to be true to his country" (83–84). Together, they all create "the din . . . hollowsounding." His escape from them is into "the pursuit of phantoms," certainly not a freedom achieved in the real world. Yet there are other voices that Stephen fails to hear, and these are ones from the real world around him that do not urge duty but misrule, not purpose but playfulness.

In many instances, such as this one from the different student, the "other voice" is heard within the tumult and disorder of the classroom that Stephen, self-absorbed and highly intellectual, ignores. We have remarked on Stephen's self-absorbed catechetical questions about the Real Presence of the Divine in the Eucharist that continue despite the comic intrusion of his classmate's noting the return of the rector with "Here he is!" Again at Belvedere, and similarly, when Stephen is greatly moved by the rhetoric of the presentation of hell at the retreat, he imagines "his brain was simmering and bubbling within" the skull, flames bursting from that skull "shrieking like voices:—Hell! Hell! Hell!" (125). What is actually going on around him is that his fellow students, completely unmoved, are remarking and joking about the sermon to others not at the retreat: "Voices spoke near him:—On hell.—I suppose he rubbed it into you well.—That's what you fellows want: and plenty of it to make you work." With a sense of the comic that appears obliquely, a reader should sense that the raucous voices of Stephen's fellows make such likely sophomoric jokes as "it was a hell of a sermon" of "it was hell to sit through it" that causes the repetition of the word "hell, hell." Such voices around Stephen, unnoticed by him, mark the chaotic nature of the classroom and the comic life of the real world. Those voices always contrast humorously with Stephen and his (here) genuine, conscience-stricken self-absorption. Importantly, those voices do not ironize his response, but offer an alternative in another tone, a comic presentation that takes place just over his shoulder.

Back in the physics theatre, the sharp Ulster voice of this practical Scot asking questions about the material annoys Moynihan, who "murmurs from behind" Stephen, " —Isn't MacAlister a devil for his pound of flesh?" (193), as he conflates Scottish parsimoniousness with Shakespeare's Jewish usuriousness. Stephen, sitting on his bench, is stuck between MacAlister before and Moynihan behind, posed between earnestness and comedy, positioned in the same space as his own autobiographical novel, doubled in between earnest development and comic otherness. A bench is also equally two things, partaking of the doubleness of diction that often produces comic paronymy: a bench is the *banc* of law, or authority and rule, yet it is also at the same time the *banc* climbed upon by the huckster, the joker, the mountebank of misrule and tumbling. Two voices, two benches suggest another focus and location to the portrait, riffled otherwise with a tension between the serious and the ironic.

This sort of doubleness is clearly continued by Stephen's heavily configured thought about MacAlister's head: "Stephen looked down coldly on the oblong skull beneath him" (193). Stephen is so firmly tied to his self, so narcissistically connected to his own portrait, that he often gazes at his own reflection. He "gazed at his face for a long time in the mirror of [his mother's] dressingtable" (71) trying to write a poem for E. C.; or he wonders what his face looks like to others, whether "there was something in his face which made him look like a schemer and he wished he had a little mirror to see" (53). It is by solipsistic extension that he so often notices the heads of his classmates, primarily as an egoistic reflection of his own search for a portrayed identity (and partially because his eyesight would limit him to noticing only what was directly before his face). Each head, of course, is a portrait that connects to the central representation of the novel, but each one is of someone other, and thus is a counterimage to the one of Stephen that occupies so much space in the novel. Many of these heads offer lesser alternatives to Stephen's exalted image within the text, and we will not be surprised to see that these offer comic alternatives to the serious sitting of *Portrait*. Stephen, bidding his mind think a "willful unkindness" about that head of MacAlister, considers that "the student's father would have done better had he sent his son to Belfast to study and have saved something on the train fare by so doing" (193), displaying solicitude for money and fatherhood Stephen has never before shown. Yet it is a thought with less malice in it than Stephen has elsewhere shown himself capable. What follows is an odd exchange in Stephen's mind: "The oblong skull beneath did not turn to meet this shaft of thought and yet the shaft came back to its bowstring: for he saw in a moment the student's wheypale face" (193). The passage has a certain quality as a set piece, a polished period of prose: "shaft," "bowstring," "wheypale." (This last is a description Joyce cherished enough to use with variation in "Proteus" when Stephen looks at the face of Sargent.[1] "Wheypale" must in Stephen's mind be associated with mother's milk and the firstborn, as he thinks in regard to Sargent; if MacAlister is a firstborn, Stephen has found in him another semblance.) It is Stephen's intent to think here, to speak weightily to himself, and the willful verbalizing is always in danger of being overembroidered because it is conscious and deliberate.

Yet the words "shaft of thought" and "bowstring" are odd figures for Stephen, resembling the adventure stories read by the boys in "An Encounter"; their strangeness suggests the strained effort by Stephen to be literary. Too often, when he consciously reaches as he does here for artistic efforts, the results exceed his grasp and become empurpled with excessive rhetorical blooms that make an inviting target for the action of comic tumbling, tripping them down from an undeserved lofty perch. Some of these figures owe their debt to Stephen's allusive mind, one that already has had suggestions of Shakespeare in Moynihan's clichéd "pound of flesh." Surely Stephen's disavowal of intent immediately following his insult to MacAlister resembles Hamlet's odd apology to Laertes about his lack of aforethought: "that I have shot mine arrow o'er the house/And hurt my brother" (V, ii, 253–254). In that speech Hamlet claims to be another Hamlet ("If Hamlet from himself be ta'en away"), and Stephen with MacAlister's skull is portraying himself as another. Stephen has found two heads for himself, as if there are two Stephens figured in any image he makes or in any other person he sees; in this alternative and doubling lies the possibility of comic effect.

This sense of otherness, of something just behind, is continued with the head of MacAlister phrenologically observed as "oblong," a shape that is like an ellipsoid. When Stephen sees that MacAlister does not respond to his sharp thoughts (the shaft of his thought came back to the bowstring), he wishes to disavow his unsuccessful witticism: "That thought is not mine, he said to himself quickly. It came from the comic Irishman in the bench behind" (193). It is not clear whether Stephen's denial of "that thought" refers to his practical one (about the train fare) or to his metaphoric one (of the bowstring); if the former, he seeks to undo his unkindness; if the latter, his awkward metaphorizing. This is the Stephen unsure of his identity and unwilling to assert it as is Hamlet; it will be the same when he goes to Paris (as he remembers in "Proteus") and keeps police tickets to prove an alibi: "*Lui, c'est moi*"(U 3.183). His comment here is another alibi, literally, to be somewhere else, neither in the one thought nor in the other. Disavowal is a doubling, a making of another, an alternative. In the need to deny either an unkind thought or an inelegant word choice, Stephen seeks the erasure of himself by positing a double, a similar but alternate entity. It is an entity neither practical nor poetic, one more humorous than earnest. It is more likely that he refers not to any thought of his, practical or metaphoric, but rather he disavows the comic thought of Moynihan. Stephen puts the blame for levity somewhere else, on someone else; that is why he is so rarely funny.

Stephen may mean to say something quite literal and correct when he says that "thought was not mine . . . , it came from the comic Irishman in the row behind": that the thought he disavows was the comment "Isn't MacAlister a devil . . ." and that it was Moynihan who made it, the Moynihan of the ellipsoidal balls who sets the tumbling sabbath of misrule in Stephen's mind. He is indeed seated in the bench behind, from whence comes the thought, and he is comic.

Yet the very notion of the comic Irishman behind in Stephen's disavowal would well describe the comic counter-narrative of the novel. There is comedy always just behind the text that focuses with directed intensity on Stephen; the text quite clearly localizes it: humor is always just over the shoulder of Stephen, that shoulder of the humeral veil. The very same comedy is always indirect, not only just "behind" (where Moynihan is always located in all these exchanges), but also just to the side, laughing "in the sleeve" as Lynch had noted of Stephen's comic use of Aquinas. That comedy is always the other side to the novel of development, in "another head" portrayed in the text, a head other than his filled with serious thoughts; *Portrait* may produce a doubled but alternate view, an opposition to serious direction.

The comic Irishman is neither the artist nor the serious boy (nor is he Joyce, exactly); he is someone other just in the margins of the text.[2] It is he who tumbles over and over in undirected antics, rather than rising to higher levels; he is misrule rather than rule, carnival rather than career. He is always displaced just behind. Ellmann, speaking of the more open humor of Stephen in the last passages of the novel, notes that comedy had before been "almost undisclosed" in the earlier chapters; he fortuitously notes that obscured and cloistered nature of the comic *Portrait*.[3] This disposition of comedy, a closeting away from the seriousness of the plot, is necessary on several grounds, although being necessary does not mean that the novel cannot be comic.

The reasons for this displacement, for the comedy appearing in the bench behind, are many—historical, psychological, artistic, and critical. There is first the subordinate condition of the colonial, for whom, as critics note, comedy is the response to imperial power. The comic Irishman is always the alternative figure standing in humorous comic dissipation and powerlessness against the authority of the imperium, much as the hapless students must use chaotic ribaldry to resist the power of parochial educational authority.

Portrait, in fact, has several hegemonic forces against which evasion and subterfuge are necessary. The political system of imperialism is not the only force that demands of its colonial subjects a surface conformity and appropriate behavior that result in a subversive humorous counterrebellion; religion is one of perhaps greater effect in Ireland and certainly within *Portrait*. The Church is the force of censure and censoring, a particular threat to the artist.[4] While politics seeks to suppress native feeling, the Church seeks to censor pagan impulses. For the late nineteenth century, of course, these were one and the same: native feeling was uncivilized, primitive, and pagan. So *Portrait,* because it centers on a protagonist caught in the system of a Church and living in a country controlled by the system of an imperium, is a novel in which the repressive forces are foremost in the events and must be challenged by the individual for a necessary outcome. (One might argue that *Bildungsroman* is the prime locus for the expression of a self liberated from all hegemonies.) Yet the very heavy presence of those two repressive systems of church and state (to which might be added others, such as culture) suggests that *Portrait* is in greatest need for humor that finds its way out from underneath oppression's weight and out from behind the powerful enfranchised systems. The pagan forces against which the Church marshals its power are those very ones associated with the body—sexuality and license—the body that is the source of comedy.

Yet there is another powerful order and authority that surrounds the text rather than appearing in it; it is an order that is artistic. The novel's very genre must also be resisted in the same ways as political order; authority, dogma, and tradition are generic as well as hegemonic and must be resisted by carnivalesque tumbling; that may be Joyce's first overthrow in revolution. To resist reading the directed plot and seriousness of *Portrait* as a novel of development is to resist the order and direction that are the main implements of power, both literary and imperialist. To read the novel as comic is to resist all orders.[5]

Freud has argued that the techniques of comedy—caricature, parody, and travesty—"are directed against . . . objects which lay claim to authority and respect, which are in some sense 'sublime.'"[6] While it is evidently true that much of Joyce's humor is directed against church and state, and even against aspects of culture and family, it should be also argued that his humor is directed against the authority of the artistic forms he chooses to employ, the esthetic sublime. Certainly the deconstructive parodic aspects of *Ulysses* work against the demands of the epic and novel form, those established norms which are for the artist an authorizing enfranchisement. *Portrait's* very genre represents the challenge of the protagonist to all forms of authority, yet within the plot of *Bildungsroman* such a challenge is rarely humor-laden. The humor of *Portrait*, however indirectly, works against the very precise claims to authority of its particular genre because the form is itself the authority that gives direction and structure. The comedy of *Portrait* is at war with the very authority it generates itself; it is little wonder that the humor must be so covert.[7]

Stephen's sloughing off of Moynihan as the comic Irishman is a critical judgment as well. He disdains the typical literary caricature of the stage Irishman as an unstable influence, belligerent, chaotic, and unserious.[8] Stephen wishes to make his own elevated art of the esthetic, as witnessed by the ephemeral villanelle. He only has to hear of an old peasant from the west, who reacts to Mulrennan's question about the universe and the stars with the comment, "there must be terrible queer creatures at the latter end of the world" (251) for him to "fear him. I fear his redrimmed horny eyes." Stephen feels he must struggle with him, resisting the Antaeus-like pull of the Irish soil that Yeats embraces because Joyce sees it as sluggish matter that will keep him from soaring with elevated art. Yet the comic

Irishman behind Stephen, just over his shoulder, is his future as it was Joyce's (a point that will be discussed at some length in chapter 3); and that figure will overtake Stephen when he comes to live with Mulligan in the Martello tower at the start of the next work. The writer Stephen might become (and Joyce does) is a comic writer, one who takes his stand against all authority, Church, imperium, and literary tradition all, through the use of comedy that he adapts to his own purposes and not to those of an exclusive national identity. The comic figure resides within the frame of *Portrait,* limited by the narrative, always there just behind, just beyond; he makes another head that is imperfectly seen in the alternative portraiture.

Scenes of instruction in the classroom, with heads attentive or not, are thus fundamental to *Portrait,* itself a depiction of a head, and to its genre as novel of intellectual development, of education. Classrooms are instructive for the attentive reader, too, if the reader can just look beyond the foregrounded absorption of Stephen and hear beyond Stephen's dominant voice, and past the directed drive of the novel that centers both; the comic alternative appears in capering confusion in that space behind, as the classroom situates the comic impulse. Such notions as comic tumbling, presented in the mathematics class at Belvedere (a class that will be revisited again in this chapter), and the image of the sabbath of misrule in the physics theatre at UCD, revisited above, are places where the reader can learn. In these classes the reader has been instructed already in two essential features of the comic: its tumbling sense of capering aimlessness and its temporary respite from the serious, and now a third, the displacement of the comic as different and behind.

There are further classroom scenes showing Stephen in less than successful achievement; indeed they show his shortcomings, his confusions, the otherness of his ideas. While Stephen is central to and his thoughts predominate the narrative, both causing and caused by the interiorization of the novel, and the classroom experiences encapsulate the internal workings of his mind, the fact that he is brought up short and seen as inadequate in these moments of instruction suggests that the scenes offer something more, and something other, than the directed drive of the seriousness of development. Stephen is often implicitly contrasted in these scenes by other, duller students and with obtuse masters: this contrast, while it works to elevate Stephen, also adds a sense of otherness and difference; it suggests the world outside of Stephen. Other voices here emerge, such as the ones noted at the retreat or at the university, and these voices give articulation to things that are different from the novel; and because the novel is so serious, that difference is often humor. This otherness is not the irony that arises within the indirect style in the disparity between Stephen and the narrative.⁹ Otherness is the distance between Stephen and text, making the space behind that opens up the alternative to seriousness: in comic otherness, in the bench behind, there is a glimpse of the carnival of misrule rather than the sobriety of ironized instruction.

It is transgression and misrule we find that prompt the first two classroom scenes in the plot of novel. The initial one, in Stephen's first school, is in many ways the most complex and determined in the novel, the scene of pandying, when Stephen falls afoul of authority without any action on his part; it is an exceptional event in Stephen's otherwise and subsequent obedient school career. Yet, in addition to the issues of authority and justice that are important to the text, the scene also establishes the primacy of the classroom setting in the novel, and establishes the places within it of the serious and the funny. Fleming is a recognized idler and dullard, with a blotted copy book and a grasp of grammar so weak as to suggest that the noun *sea* has no plural; he probably deserves flogging as an idler: even before Dolan appears looking for one, Father Arnall claims that Fleming is "one of the idlest boys" (47) he ever met. Yet Fleming's intellectual failings are placed in equal standing with Stephen's physical one of not being able to see, and Stephen feels an injustice in being considered a similar idler. He feels this equality especially as the two students are placed together when they are usually set so differently in the classroom. Stephen has a highly developed sense of place; he is insistent even in the physics theatre, in a class he no longer cares about, when he notes that Moynihan is in the bench behind. He is just as scrupulous at the outset of his academic career at Clongowes. Fleming is made by Father Arnall to kneel in the middle of the class, to come out of his place in the last row of seats, a place assigned due to his poor academic performance. The text locates him: "Fleming moved heavily out of his place and knelt between the two last benches" (47). Like the joker Moynihan at university, Fleming is in the bench behind. Stephen, or course, sits in the front row, as befitting his status as head scholar and leader of Yorkists; his is first of place, that of seriousness and achievement. He is summoned by Dolan to the middle of the class, where his punishment reduces and positions him *inter pares* with his classmates. What justified resentment Stephen feels in this scene about being beaten unfairly must be colored by his disdain at getting equal placement with a fellow student far his inferior, one in fact from the last benches, that place in the classroom of foolishness and misbehavior. In his very first class, Stephen seeks to disassociate himself from the unruly elements in the back of the class, even as he continues to do so up to the last class, where he disavows the comic comments from the row behind. (As a sign of his seriousness at the retreats in chapter 3, Stephen is twice located "in the front bench of the chapel" [108] and "again in the front bench" [126].) Order is restored after the beating when Father Arnall tells the different malefactors, "You may return to your places, you two" (51). Places are hierarchical, awarded on merit in the classroom; there Stephen receives his just deserts. The benches behind, from whence issue the ribald, the comic and the chaos, are ones with which Stephen has no wish to associate. They represent the misrule that here is punished but elsewhere lives in the world around Stephen, whether he will acknowledge it or not.

The second classroom scene in the novel occurs at the end of the first term at his next institution, Belvedere, and also involves a failing of Stephen's, this one of the intellect and not of the body. He remembers, invoked by Heron's beating him to confess Byron a heretic, an incident in which he is accused by the English master of having heresy in his essay. "Mr Tate withdrew his delving hand and spread out the essay.—Here. It's about the Creator and the soul. . . . Ah! *without a possibility of ever approaching nearer.* That's heresy. Stephen murmured:—I meant *without a possibility of ever reaching.* . . . It was a submission and Mr Tate, appeased, folded up the essay and passed it across to him, saying:—O . . . Ah! *ever reaching.* That's another story" (79).

The gap in this brief moment of heresy, spiritual misrule, and submission is one that further opens up the possibility of the comic. "Approaching nearer" and "ever reaching" might well be a slip of the pen (especially by someone with weak eyesight, the cause of the other classroom confrontation); the eye might slip by omitting "approaching" and misreading "reaching" for "nearer." (The diphthong *ea* in both is always elided when the name Dedalus appears, making another sort of gap.) The distinction between "nearer" and "reaching" (like that of Tennyson's "reach" and "grasp") is something that falls just short of absolute control or completion; it is, in fact, much like the comedy of the novel that never actually reaches the forefront of the text but always approaches nearer, over the shoulder, in the last row or the bench behind. And the echo of Tennyson must surely stand comically behind the confrontation of Heron with Stephen, who must defend Byron against Heron's choice of the Laureate. The interconnections of this classroom scene with the confrontation with Heron can be given a comic gloss. Further elements of a comic language are to be found in the memory of the beating by Heron that evokes the classroom scene with Mr. Tate: as the teacher has asked Stephen to "submit" a paper, so Heron commands Stephen to "admit"; words can seem much the same and yet humorously different. The instructor is pleased with Stephen's retraction and restatement of his essay, its being a "submission" to indicate that Stephen is subservient to authority. Yet a submission, so rare a thing from the proud Stephen, is also an activity done every time a student hands in an essay, an activity Stephen is eager to do; this alternate meaning of language makes for comic possibility. When at Belvedere, the young Joyce sought to submit comical sketches to *Tit Bits*, showing not only his eagerness for submission for public fame but also a tendency to humor in contrast to the somber self-portrait at this same chronological point in the novel.[10] Admission, as confession, and submission, as placing beneath, are the movement of Stephen's life; but their interplay in the text is a comic shadow of Stephen's development and rebellion.

The delving hand of Mr. Tate as he sifts the submitted essays resembles that of Father Dolan at the pandying; the strong arm of authority ends with forceful hands. Yet that delving hand, going beneath the papers, can also be viewed as the hand behind which the priests whisper their laughter when Stephen imagines them in misrule. The subject matter of Stephen's essay is serious: the soul and its relation to God, a relationship that has its analogue in *Portrait* obviously in Stephen's relation between his soul and the world; the relation also pertains to the space between the character and the author, that source of irony. The gap between God and the soul replicates that seemingly unbridged gap in the novel between Stephen and the world outside, so that he only glimpses and faintly hears its misrule and comedy far behind him. The idea of nearing but never reaching also obtains between the reader and the text. The idea of otherness, of distance between God and the soul, or of Stephen's soul and the world, and the reader and the text, is continued by the fact that his error in the essay is itself something else; it is not intentional but a *lapsus scripsi*, that is, a tumble that opens up comically misunderstood possibilities within orderly dogma. A gap, within a word or in a text, is a likely place for comedy, where something falls short of an ideal, where something is less than intended, or other than expected. When Stephen submissively notes his error, the teacher offers in reconciliation that his essay is something else, another type of literature, "that is another story." As another story it is like the alternate *Portrait*, not serious but funny, whose missteps are places of comic discovery.

The originary failing of Stephen in the classroom at Clongowes, that of his pandying, makes up "another story" told twice in *Portrait;* in fact, this story is told once as the noble history of justice served after the beating and the second time as farce. It is what Simon Dedalus calls "that story about you" (72) he heard from Father Conmee, who gave "a great account of the whole affair." It, too, is another story: "*Manly little chap! . . . You better mind yourself, Father Dolan, . . . or young Dedalus will send you up for twice nine*" (72). This repetition is a doubling over, and it is an emblem of the way in which the comic appears in the novel: first a serious account, told from Stephen's interior point of view, and then a more antic rendition told—or frequently glimpsed alternately from outside. As the text presents the father's recounting of Conmee and his "great account," the novel has something told, retold (recounted), and valued ("account")—all the function of literature but also the substance of fanciful stories, *contes*. In the discussion of Stephen's admission to Belvedere (the place in which so many instructional moments occur in which the serious is mingled with the comic) there is something humorous. Simon begins by telling Stephen that his "long holiday" from school is over, which is to say that the sabbath of idle pleasure is now to come to an end with new application to order and discipline; comic freedom is to give way to serious purpose. When it is clear that there has been an "arrangement" about Belvedere, Simon then remembers that Stephen's brother Maurice is also to be included in it. Marginalized in the text (this his only mention) and here brought in only as Simon's afterthought, "Holy Paul, I forgot about Maurice," this brother is a completely comic figure: "they'll teach you to spell c.a.t cat. And I'll buy you a . . . handkerchief to keep your nose dry" (72). Maurice "grinned at his father and brother," apparently accustomed to being the butt of such low bodily humor; just behind Stephen in years, he is another figure of the comedy that surrounds the major character. Yet that first son and prime focus of the novel is himself in this account an unaccustomed source of humor to others: Conmee says, "Father Dolan and I had a great laugh over it. . . . We had a famous laugh together over it. Ha! Ha! Ha!" (72). By way of comic exaggeration and repetition, this punch line is repeated for a third time, the text setting it in italics so as to suggest that it has become a source of legend for a circle wider than the original two: "*Father Dolan and I and all of us we had a hearty laugh together over it.*" This account, with its vocalized laughter ("Ha! Ha! Ha!"), contrasts with the solemnity with which Stephen undergoes this experience of visiting the rector (and there is an echoic similarity and difference, as the laughter "Ha! Ha! Ha!" contrasts with the historic landscape feature of the school, the ha-ha). Stephen is first presented as purposeful and solemn, and yet this scene described by Simon offers a counterexample of accounting and recounting that is quite raucously funny. Conmee's account is one of comedy. It has a reversal, a misrule, in that Stephen will now mete out punishment to his superior. As well, the retelling has inversion: Stephen, then elevated on the shoulders of his schoolmates, is now the figure of contradiction, as both "manly" and "little." The retelling also has exaggeration, where Stephen's two hits are enlarged gargantuanly out of justice to the threat of twice nine.

As he quietly goes up the storied and historical long dark corridor to the office at Clongowes, Stephen imagines what he does is sanctioned by history "by some great person whose head was in the books" (53); again he situates the serious at the site of the intellect, the head. Yet portraiture has many sittings and other poses; the other story about Stephen is quite loud. The "hearty" laugh of Conmee is situated in an organ in contrast to the head and its intellection, an organ of the body that is the source of humor (hence the belly laugh); the contrast between the head and the *hearty* and *great* and *famous* laugh is the alternate portraiture of the novel.

These classroom scenes of pandying and heresy are Stephen's lapses, if both inadvertent and excused; they are two lapses of a sort not normally granted model schoolboys, if in the real world such missteps are common. St. Stephen, for the similar lapses perceived by his elders in authority, was dilapidated. Unlike the saint his namesake, however, Dedalus achieves a victory of sorts in discussion with the elder dean of studies. This is another pedagogical scene, which takes place in the empty physics theatre just before Stephen's next class, in which he will envision the misrule and locate the comic Irishman. The meeting with the dean is more a tutorial than a class, where Stephen interacts with a lesser member of the hierarchy, the exchange with the dean being one in which Stephen smugly maintains his superiority. Here Stephen feels he is the instructor. His points about "the esthetic question" seem to convince the Father temporarily. The culmination of the conversation is in the discussion of the word *tundish,* where Stephen seems to defeat the dean by asserting that the word is common and English. English things are to be disdained, but so too are things too Irish; all are too common for a young man who wants to be distant from the real world of the vulgar. Indeed, much of the discussion about language is about otherness and displacement. The dean is an Englishman, an outsider to the Irish Stephen, and more, he is an outsider brought into the Church by conversion, a figure of change or turning about. As such, he is another figure behind or just to the side who, fittingly with the sense of otherness and displacement in language, is a source of comic possibility.

The language in which we are speaking is his before it is mine. How different are the word *home, Christ, ale, master,* on his lips and on mine! . . . His language, so familiar and so foreign, will always be for me an acquired speech. . . . My soul frets in the shadow of his language. (189)

Stephen feels further displacement because he considers that the language spoken is the dean's before it is his; for Stephen, it is an acquired speech (although an alert reader might ask for whom is language not acquired speech? And as to Stephen's claim that the language was the dean's before it was his, surely the difference in their ages makes that an idle and self-concerned piece of pathos). The secondariness of the language, however, seems to be a pertinent condition for a comedy situated behind; and the words that Stephen chooses to suggest that he and the priest have a different purchase on language all contain enough dissimilarity to suggest comic alternatives: *home, Christ, ale, master.* The first and third are English words, as simple as "tundish"; the second is Greek, the last Latin, as is "funnel." While the list begins with the familiar and common, it moves next to the special and unique; back then to common ("ale") and then returns to the superiority that Stephen always seeks. The list has its own comic possibilities, unknown to Stephen; it might resemble a list Stephen makes for Bloom in "Circe" which he knows to be funny, but pitches the humor beyond Bloom to maintain the sort of superiority he tries to gain with the dean of studies: "Cicero, Podmore. Napoleon, Mr Goodbody. Jesus, Mr Doyle."[11] Doyle is the anointed one, the Christ and the master; Cicero is connected to Latin; so the comic connection of these two lists spans several years and texts in Joyce's mind (and Stephen's). Such connections, we have observed, confirm the presence of the comic in both *Ulysses* and *Portrait.* In Stephen's first list, "home" and "ale" are common, "Christ" and "master" are superior; the list has its chiastic conflation. "Home" is familiar, "Christ" is unique (and there is also the connection of the Gospel, "in my father's house there are many mansions"). The anointed one must be anointed, and ale could function in that way, especially as it is a fermented spirit (and again, the miracle at Cana occasions Mulligan's jokes about free drinks [U 1.590]). Language at odds here creates the sort of gap or distance out of which the comic can peer. Stephen seems unaware of the connotations of the words he uses; in that space between connotation and denotation is another spot for humor. The sense of distance and displacement is continued with Stephen's bathetic claim that "his soul frets in the shadow of his language," which he takes to suggest his art languishing in the tenebrous power of the other culture. But the space between the soul and language is a place just behind and over the shoulder, and a distance maintained from language can be a virtue, because in that space verbal comedy can be forged.

Stephen is not merely unaware that what he thinks could be humorous; he is too serious about his own displacement to see that language, when displaced, can be comic. Extending the idea of distance between Stephen and language, what is additionally comic is the way that the language of the passage refers to a world outside Stephen which he refuses to recognize and that gives a comic and deflationary tumble to the weight of his ideas and the metaphoric language in which he expresses them.[12] The actual figure of the dean is a good place to start; he is described in the homely task of removing candlebutts from his soutane. The man who will be the butt of Stephen's smug superiority and university-wit nimbleness (and Stephen remarks to himself on the way to UCD that it was the home of Buck Whalley of the Hellfire Club) was called in *Stephen Hero* Father Butt, so that the object he takes out and his function are more comically evident in that earlier text; in the *Portrait* the name has been displaced and redirected into oblique anonymity, relegated to the behind bench of an earlier version to hide the obvious comedy. (More of this issue of how the overtly comic earlier text of *Hero* frets in the shadow of the *Portrait* will be discussed in chapter 4.)

To his action of removing the remnant of candles, Stephen thinks of the dean as humbly serving "without growing towards light" and that his body and soul both had "waxed old" (185). Although the dean in fact lights the fire, Stephen can find in him "no spark" of Ignatius's enthusiasm (186). The dean's simple task is to light an actual fire in the empty physics theatre, and he manages to bring actual light and heat when Stephen, not yet achieving his esthetic, speaks of those qualities only as metaphoric substitutions for knowledge and fervor. All of Stephen's diction, even before the choice of "tundish," is attenuated and unreal: thinking about esthetic "by the light of" Aristotle and Aquinas, of using and guiding himself "by their light" and of trimming the lamp if it smells (that is, if the thoughts are unhelpful) is clearly his tongue-in-cheek way of ridiculing the figure before him. When, to Stephen's use of lamp as a metaphor for reading and lucubration, the dean asks about Epictetus and his actual lamp, Stephen linguistically extinguishes the conversation by noting "coarsely" that Epictetus was "an old gentleman . . . who said that the soul was very like a bucket of water" (187), the water extinguishing the metaphors of the light Stephen tries to shed. Characteristically, Stephen turns to make metaphor, in large part to maintain his superiority to those around him, as he had always held his higher position among his classmates. Yet the clash of reality with his metaphors makes a comic turn; the intellectual light Stephen sheds, metaphorizing and theorizing, creates humorous shades in the scene portrayed. The discussion with the dean is crucial to Stephen's burgeoning sense of an artist thinking on his own, yet it has comic elements. The scene can stand in for *Portrait* itself, as one of the meanings of the root *protrahere* is "to bring to light" and thus not only to elucidate but to alternate light and shadow, seriousness and comedy.

The use of the lamp metaphorically or actually, Stephen claims, is a contrast between literary tradition and the marketplace; yet giving the difference to these terms overweighs the argument with a value judgment. The question is directed not only to the use of words as poetic or vulgar, highly valued or cheaply employed (the subsequent subject of chapter 4), but also to the use of words as literary or as actual, as belonging to the realm of the isolated artist and not to the world of common experience. By stressing the realm of the isolated and rarified artist, the context of literary words, Stephen can too readily catch the dean with Newman's use of the word "detain," which the father hears as simply a social phrase; it is a poor joke too easily bought. Common experience Stephen always neglects and diminishes; and it is that experience that forms the antic comedy of the novel. Stephen catches the dean with a piece of arcane diction; yet he himself is always tripped into comedy by the common language of others around him.

When the conversation takes its turn from the metaphoric lamp to the actual one of Epictetus (before Stephen's bringing the whole conversation to an end by extinguishing it with the "bucket of water"), the realm of the actual intrudes. As Stephen's mind is checked "in a false focus" (187), "a smell of molten tallow came up" as the actual candle brought by the unnamed (and erased) Father Butt, who has waxed old in service, has had an actual effect in the useful arts. Reality intrudes everywhere to create a similar comic effect; humor lies in the ordinariness of the world (especially when it comes up against Stephen's isolated otherworldliness). The dean's genuine surprise at the word "tundish" causes him to mutter "I must look that word up. Upon my word I must" (188); he naturally and realistically repeats himself to a comic effect (and also mixes literal with metaphoric "word"): this, Joyce knew, is the way events happen to fall out and tumble up humorously in actual life. Alongside this humor is the more prominent foregrounded seriousness of Stephen's esthetic considerations, to which this undercurrent of humorous touches makes a pleasing contrast of shadow. Until Stephen sees that such tumbling and commonness can be art, he will not be an artist, despite his working in the light of ideas.

So the otherness that Stephen strives to maintain in the exchange in the empty classroom between himself and the lesser-ranked and -gifted dean, between himself and the use of English, and between himself and the world of actual words and things, turns out to be the otherness that always separates him from the world of confusion and material life that breeds the comic. In the same way, the reader frequently is separated from the real world around Stephen and consequently from its humor. Stephen's serious feelings about esthetics are genuine, and the scene does not ironize Stephen's feelings; however, his seriousness of purpose, his impetus to special separateness, keep him (as they do the reader) from glimpsing the possibilities of comedy in the actual actions and conversation. In a similar way, we have seen how Stephen's further theorizing about art with Lynch had comic elements that did not reflect ironically on Stephen. The fact that Stephen ridicules the dean shows that he is aware of what can be humorous, but the fact that he uses his wit only for ridicule says much about his selfishness and immaturity. His exchange takes place in an empty classroom, and, like much of Stephen's efforts in the novel, it is a vain and empty activity, producing neither heat nor light.

It is to the physics theatre, where he will find the image of carnival and the figure of the comic Irishman, Stephen has come, arriving late and missing his English hour, where he imagined the heads of students. In that reverie which takes place before he talks to the dean and hears Moynihan and MacAlister in the physics lecture, he also fancies yet "another head than his," that of his friend Cranly; still walking to Newman House, his thoughts become increasingly complicated by the sort of otherness and difference that filled the exchange with the dean or the recognition of the other, comic Irishman in the bench behind. "Another head," Cranly's, is like "another story" that Conmee laughingly tells of Stephen's triumph; it is the depiction of yet another head of a fellow student of Stephen's. This other head is a contrast and a compliment to Stephen's own, a further alternative as tumbling is to falling and as a pun is an alternative to denotative single meaning.

One reason for Stephen's question, "Why was it that when he thought of Cranly he could never raise before his mind the entire image of his body but only the image of his head and face?" (178) is due to the nature of portraiture always at the center of the novel's focus: the image portrayed on canvas, as it is also conveyed to Stephen's mind, is focused on the head. The prominence of heads in the novel so titled makes Stephen's question almost rhetorical; and he notices many other heads. As Stephen mediates Cranly by not remembering his actual face but only an image in mind, so too does the portrait present not the actual features but an image mediated by art. The artful and yet attenuated nature of Stephen's thinking about Cranly's image is further suggested by the distant allusion to a text Stephen has certainly read, "Macbeth," with its suggestion that "there is no art to find the mind's construction in the face" (I, iv, 12). Yet in that small art lies the possibility for Stephen to imagine Cranly's portrayed head as an image increasingly out of the ordinary and grotesque, finally being so extended as to collapse into the comic: "he saw it before him like the phantom of a dream, the face of a severed head or deathmask, crowned on the brows by its stiff black upright hair as by an iron crown" (178). The fantastic and the revenant are the ultimate others, outside and beyond the rational; they hover in shadow just over the shoulder of reality as does the comic. The severed head also leans to the legends of hagiography, the Baptist precursor to Stephen's own Jesus with His crown of thorns, and the iron crown in particular points not only to royalty but nationality: the Iron Crown of Hungary, that country whose political situation was a model for Irish nationalism, was kept even as late as Stephen's university years in Vienna's St. Stephen's Cathedral. Thus in many ways, inevitably, on that face of "another head than his" Stephen sees and reads his own face, doubled into possibilities, alternatives, extremes that lead to grotesquery. He, who has rejected the pastoral calling, calls Cranly's head "priestlike" (178), seeing in Cranly's demeanor his own until recently, and because Stephen acknowledges that he has confessed to Cranly, a compliment to him. Yet the similaic "priestlike" face and pallor indicates another difference, another space between one head and another, as Cranly tumbles from the power of the priesthood into the impotence of being unable to grant absolution to Stephen for his confessed sins: "a guilty priest who . . . had not power to absolve . . ." (178). Stephen's sins are falls into what he terms "tumults and unrest and longings of his soul" and all the words apply to what he calls the "life" of his father's house, the unrest of the actual, vegetable world, in which are the tumult of tumbling and the comedy of misrule.

 Cranly's head has further sources of difference and comic confusion, related to the sorts of "longing" to which Stephen confesses. Longing is an appetite, a source of desire and therefore potentially of the comic; Cranly's face is doubled in gender to serve other desires. The "priestlike" face is intended by celibacy to be neuter, but in that it is guilty of hearing Stephen's confession of sexual "longing" without being able to absolve, it is impotent, and thus its "guilt" is marked in his face by the difference of "dark womanish eyes"(178). For Stephen, viewing the unsure sexuality of the celibate and the too close proximity of a male friend, begins to turn that other head even further into something completely other, the opposite sex: one head may confusedly contain two genders. (And here again the image of the head on a platter connects not only to the Baptist, but also to the Wilde play of *Salomé*.) To imagine Cranly's head as womanish is to make him completely other; yet, insofar as Stephen reads his own face in Cranly's, his own portraiture contains a potential doubling comedy of sexual confusion.

The literal confusion of this sort of two-headedness, Stephen/Cranly or man/woman, leads to further confusions: these are to be found in language. In its possibilities of comic alteration, there is an inevitable interplay of puns here in Stephen's thinking that show potential comic misunderstanding. The elevated introspection of Stephen about Cranly, which occurs in an imagined scene, is tripped up to tumble into humor. To Cranly's "gaze of . . . dark womanish eyes," Stephen extends his reverie; he regards the feminine listlessness of Cranly as an opiate, a "deadly exhalation" of "nightshade." The exotic image appeals to Stephen's reading, the decadent aura of narcotic hebetude and sexual attraction, and thus fits well with a portrait of Cranly as esthetic priest or object of desire. (Particularly suggestive in this is the "dark cavern of speculation," seemingly Platonic, but also homoerotic.)[13] Yet into this dreamily allusive speculation intrudes the antic comedy of paronymy: "Dark womanish eyes"—or woman's eyes made dark—are those of actual temptresses (such as prostitutes in "Circe," with Zoe's eyes *"ringed with kohol"* [15.1319], or the women Little Chandler evokes) or imagined sirens such as Pateresque Mona Lisas; all cosmetically enhanced their eyes and made them more lustrous and provocatively languid by the application of "nightshade." Thus the elaborate portrayal of Cranly's head as "other," like Stephen's priestlike but also like a woman's, is doubled further into anticness by language that makes a comic turn in diction, so that the purple exoticism of the languid plant and the temptress hidden in Cranly's head is humored by language into a comic capering. Another synonym for "nightshade," because of this very cosmetic use, was "belladonna," also a beautiful woman. Thus there is a turning over and constantly tumbling from Cranly as priest to Cranly as woman, from dark womanish eyes to nightshade and finally to belladonna; that tripping and tumbling prizes the confusions of gender and language and lets misrule have its sway in the earnestness of Stephen's thoughts. The actual word "belladonna" is hidden, just beyond the margin of the text, in that place behind where the comic Irishman resides, speaking the language of ribald misrule. It is unlikely that Stephen sees the humor of his thoughts, in no small measure because he is afraid of what he feels about Cranly; yet the text can interpose from behind him a note of levity. Cranly's head, imagined by Stephen, has two identities conflated together to make a comic effect, a prophet with priestlike seriousness and a female with exotic allure. Stephen's thinking about that head opens up language so that it plays, turning (unbeknownst to him) paronymically into a comic pairing of "nightshade" and the figure of a belladonna. It is a comic turn mischievously just behind the serious language of Stephen's inner thoughts.

Heads, doubled as alternates to the seriousness of Stephen's education and the development of his life in the novel, thus appear in classrooms where those heads are to be instructed with information conveyed in language. Language is also potentially to be doubled, two-faced or twin-voiced, and behind this doubling effect lies comedy. Puns give language two heads simultaneously: one meaning is serious and direct, the other humorous and oblique; one is in the foreground, the other behind. This combination comes to a point in the very mathematics class in which dusk came "tumbling clownishly" for Stephen, the place where the first suggestion of the countermovement of the plot of the novel arose. We should return to that class, as a student must go repeatedly and regularly to a class meeting, to find there another idea that opens up the places within language, behind and oblique, where the comedy of *Portrait* is to be found.

Unlike his earlier years, Stephen commits no error in this class, yet he is not interested, either. He is sitting to the side of the teacher's instruction and comment, but his thoughts are filled with his lapse into sin, which is the ultimate misrule but with tragic, not comic, consequences. He works on an equation in his scribbler, which begins "to unfold itself slowly and to spread abroad its widening tail. It was his own soul going forth to experience, unfolding itself sin by sin . . ." (103). The equation, like error, has its own graph and balance sheet. Yet the phrasing of "going forth" and "spreading" echo the etymology of a "portrait" as "dragging forward, drawing to a conclusion." Mathematics is knowledge, irrefutable and authoritative, much like physics. Yet it is in this class that the dusk came "tumbling clownishly," a motion that Stephen later (and the reader then) should recognize as the antithesis of order, the notion of misrule. Even in the class of mathematics there is an alternative to fact and certainty.

When the instructor intrudes on Stephen's musing to correct a dull student, what he says presents the very same contrasting alternative. The instructor berates a student, much like the idler Fleming, one in contrast with the model Stephen; yet Stephen here is conveniently inattentive to the lesson, deeply introspective, and seems no less censurable than is this Ennis. The instructor asks: "—Well now, Ennis, I declare you have a head and so has my stick! Do you mean to say that you are not able to tell me what a surd is?" (104). Ennis gives no answer.

The teacher's comment is banal, suggesting colloquially that Ennis's intellect is wooden. It may as well evoke a very particular feature of Irish education in the common hedgerow schools, where students had a stick suspended around their necks with notches, each for a lapse into Gaelic.[14] This fall from the superior language, a *lapsus linguae*, replicates what has happened to Stephen in his sin (where the prostitute's tongue is clearly mentioned); the stick is a sign of both language and lapse. Yet the prominence of the head suggests that there is something more in the example. The teacher's attempt at humor must surely evoke in Stephen his own early sense of language as doubled, possessing, Janus-like, two faces; he, after all, came early to the recognition that a belt round his pocket was also used to give a fellow a belt. Suck, too, had two meanings, one clear, one metaphoric; one right in some contexts, wrong in others; one direct, one humorous. He will note in his discussion with the dean of studies that a lamp may be figurative as well as literal. Heads can have contradictory countenances, and these often stand in comic alteration and cancelling.

There is even more in the instructor's comment; unlike the certitude and authority of mathematics, language is deceptive and ambiguous, so that what he says resonates through the novel (beyond merely having chided Ennis). The teacher's joke is an admission of a futility: as the head—the seat of the intellect—is the intended target for all the pedagogical activity of a class, the authority of the classroom and the nature of *Bildung* in the novel are compromised when both sticks and men have heads. Esthetics is also seriously tumbled: the answer to Stephen's question of esthetics as to whether the bust of Sir Phillip Crampton is epical, lyrical, and dramatic, has as its answer the same comic point: the bust, too, has a head.

The surd in mathematics is an irrational number, yet a surd also defines an entity in language, an unvoiced sound. So not only are there two heads, on people and on sticks, there are two terms for surd, irrational and unvoiced. In concert with the spirit of a *Portrait* with two heads, something alternate as a comic counterpart in the bench behind, there is something just beyond the surd, something other: the absurd. And the absurd is the realm of comedy; it marks the boundary between rule and misrule, the place where language is both one thing and another. Wordplay, so dear to Joyce, always embraces the absurd: to pun is to make two heads, a doubling alternative to meaning that often undermines the foregrounded serious purport of language. And as the surd is silent, it is like the comedy of "laughing in your sleeve" (as Lynch says, 209) or of whispering silently "behind their hands" (192) by the imagined cavorting priests; and as the absurd stands beyond, so too does the comedy stand just beyond the seriousness of mathematics of Stephen's own charted growth in the novel. The humor of heads is that they are absurdly doubled, they make comedy by interjecting over the shoulder from the bench behind.

Hitherto we have seen the comic otherness of *Portrait* in scenes and situations, those elements of the plot, but there is a more oblique and indirect presence of humor in the language, a humor essential and integral to the text. It is with verbal comedy that Joyce makes his largest and most displaced effect, with multiple possibilities making for comic confusion, and the language of *Portrait* is subject to a comic doubleness of diction that undercuts and makes tumble its highest solemn moments. Language is the essential means of comedy in *Portrait* as events are always secondary to the means to think about and describe them; more attention will be paid in subsequent chapters to the issue of language in terms of the notions raised, in the class above, of surd and absurd, silent and silly. We will see the effect of popular comic journals on the style of *Portrait* as another version of the comic Irishman behind (in chapter 3). *Portrait* obscures but saves vulgar speech like Moynihan's in contrast to Stephen's prim rhetorical strivings, as it places its earlier comic version of *Stephen Hero* behind (the subject of chapter 4). Immediately, the next chapter will focus on the further meaning of the teacher's question, which is to extend the portraiture into comedy by a language which itself has two heads.

2

The Surd and the Absurd
The Conflated Language of Comedy

The prominent head of contrast and divarication has further comic weight to bear in the compromised authority and instruction of the various classrooms. In the same mathematics class that introduces for the novel the countermovement of clownish tumbling, the teacher poses a question about numerical identity and definition to Ennis, another of those marginal students who, seated at the back bench of the class, seem to be beyond the reach of education. The teacher raises the issue of seemingly similar heads on sticks and students, by declaring, "you have a head and so has my stick"; and then the instructor asks the incapable Ennis: "Do you mean to say that you are not able to tell me what a surd is?" (104). As with the joke on heads, this question, too, has a wider relevance to the comedy of *Portrait;* it involves facts about identity, not only those within the system of mathematics but those within that of language; and it too contains its own ambiguity, making a doubling alternate. The identity of a surd in mathematics is an irrational number; yet there is an alternate meaning for surd. As head of stick and student demonstrates, language is always capable of providing an alternate, and in this case "surd" has its other identity within language itself: as a sound that is not voiced (from *surdus,* deaf). Thus the question of the teacher plays with many sorts of alternate doubleness just as does the ambiguous "head": sound and silence, voice and voiceless, rational and irrational. The very question has within it an imperative—"to tell"—that proves to be, in one way, impossible. Because in language, unlike mathematics, a surd is unvoiced and unspeakable, it is impossible for Ennis to do what the teacher asks, even if he were to know: "tell me what a surd is. . . ." In a way, he cannot. The question not only impossibly asks to speak the unspoken, it also additionally confuses by being logically redundant: "do you mean to say . . . you are not able to tell." Both the question and the very way it is spoken collapse into confusion. The doubled quality of language is repeated by the redundancy of the question, and it enacts the very tumbling and undoing that are the dynamic of comic capering, in which one thing is set up to alternate in the opposition and contrast of comic possibility.

With this question and the definition it seeks, the doubled alternatives of the "surd" further extend playfully the obvious doubled nature of the teacher's derisory humorous comment itself, "I declare Ennis, you have a head and so does my stick." Beyond the obvious point of Ennis's woodenness (and the glimpse at the history behind Irish pedagogy),[1] the sentence raises the fact that all language potentially marks something else; it offers in its very nature one thing and its alternate, a doubling effect that has one meaning and then another off to the side, both vocalized and not. "Surd," a word with two definitions, joins with the doubled pun on "heads" of sticks and students, to indicate the presence just behind of humor. It evokes misrule and disorder in the place to the side of the words and lines of the text, in whose silence the comedy of *Portrait* resides. Much as in mathematics, where the entity of a number might be rational or irrational, prime or surd, language has as entities words that can be one thing and another; different meanings can be in one word, similar words can evoke different meanings. To engage in this license of language is to play with words, and the spirit of play (like the imagined somber priests cavorting) is the respite of comedy. There is something just beyond but paired with the surd, that is the irrational or the ab-surd; there is an alternate language in the seriousness of the text. When comedy goes unrecognized in *Portrait,* it functions as a surd and suggests the unrecognized humorous quality of *Portrait,* laughing up the sleeve. The serious tone is always heard, but there is a muted counterpart in absurdity.

Consider the following interplay even in this moment in the mathematics class as a means to see how alternate meaning of the words extends to the other parts of the text (as is always true of Joyce's comedy). Along with the obvious pun on heads of sticks and students, there is the name of the boy, Ennis. That is also the name of a town in the county of Clare, so the name makes an unrecognized (or unspoken, and thus unvoiced) play: Ennis a boy and Ennis a town. Such an unstated ambiguity is not too different, in fact and in geography, from the riddle made by the boy Athy to the young Stephen at Clongowes. Athy, discussing his name and Stephen's, those markers of identity, says that his is a riddle that can be asked "another way" (25), so that the nature of the doubled quality of language is evident even to a young schoolboy. The unstated pun in chapter 3 connects back to Stephen's earlier instruction (outside a classroom, to be sure) at Clongowes. The "stick" itself also looks ahead to another of Stephen's learning experiences (before a class, in the empty physics theatre) in his tutorial exchange with the dean of studies; he imagines that man's servitude is like a *baculus,* the staff to help an old man. From these scenes the text makes a playful comedy just behind Stephen's learning.

So this passage itself both defines and portrays a certain kind of wordplay. It makes two heads, two ways, in which an absurd comic function lies with the normal order of language, making a momentary misrule. These particular wordplays are silent in the text, that is to say they are not raised often to Stephen's consciousness (he is puzzled by Athy, not amused), nor are they part of the reader's initial notice. They are present enough, however, in a sideways glance, to provide in their doubling of meaning and reference an alternate place where the comedy of *Portrait* is to be seen. As humor is always to the side in this serious text, not the foregrounded part, such indirect, mute play on words is its most useful means of expression. In order to work, something like a pun must have a basic, direct meaning in its use, otherwise it is nonsense; yet it must have a secondary meaning that is an alternate, to the side of the main sentence, often absurd. A pun very often mixes a high serious meaning with a low, silly one, where the two different meanings create a disjunctive alteration. Wordplay thus is fitting for a portrait that is primarily serious but alternately funny in moments of respite and antic behavior. Its quality of doubling is an important method to illustrate a comic impulse that alternates the action and effect of the serious text.[2]

What is true of comedy overall is equally true, condensed and made sharper, by wordplay. The comic otherness is an essential stance against monolithic, and monologic, authority. In fact, such wordplay is an inevitable and necessary function of humor. If comedy is essentially a stance against all serious orders and solemn powers, then it must use language of otherness and doubling to achieve its end of subversive tumbling. Language of an inherently doubled nature stands behind any statement, turning an innocuous one pointed, a favorable one critical, a serious one silly. The comedy of otherness (as we have discussed in the previous chapter) is in *Portrait* a stance particularly against the orders of politics, religion, and art. Freud notes that puns are expressions of repressed elements;[3] those dominated by colonialism have long used discourse to make laughter and to escape from the dominating power. The authority of the classroom, an authority in Stephen's experience both political and religious, is undermined early and late by Moynihan's ribaldry or Ennis's persistent dumb response—dumb as both unknowing and unspeaking. The dominated students, twice suborned by religious masters ultimately in collusion with political ones, have only the mischief and carnival as their means of protest. And the novel needs rebellion as well: Joyce's work, written by a young man about his adolescence, must chafe against the dynamics of his culture and his upbringing. Moreover, to be true to its expression of artistic freedom, it must also rebel against the tyranny of its generic dominance, that directed form of the novel of development which must go inevitably to its predetermined end.

There are many explanations to suggest that *Portrait* is open to influences that mitigate its seemingly monolithic effect. The perspective of both character and narrator leads to a dual presentation.[4] Bakhtin has suggested the double-voiced discourse that infiltrates all monoglossia to create a dialogic.[5] Kershner has fully explored the ways in which *Portrait* is open to the influences of popular literature.[6] Yet the issue of the doubled language is one even more integral than the interchange of outside sources, literary or cultural, because with it *Portrait* creates its own internal otherness.

Because a pun is a means of conveying different meanings, it seems to fit well with the ironic tone of the narrative: the dissembling of irony, of saying one thing and meaning another, resembles the differing of the pun, saying one thing and then saying something often clownishly other. Yet it is important to distinguish: irony is intellective and instructive, while wordplay has no purpose other than the amusement in absurdity and oddity. Irony belongs to the directed, telic part of the novel's development; wordplay to that capering tumbling with no purpose other than its own frivolity.[7] The effect of doubled language is to give an alternate shading to the texture of the novel; its aim is not to instruct but to offer a momentary deflation of the serious text.

So besides its subversive element, language that turns on itself is a particularly apt means to undercut the seriousness of *Portrait;* it is the means by which solemnity is tripped up at the heels to cavort and tumble. Wordplay projects an alternate meaning, an otherness just beyond the original meaning, that makes a contrast. The doubled language of wordplay resides primarily within *Portrait* itself, not dependent on textual voices outside, yet as such this function of language within the text has not been noticed, much as the humor of *Portrait* has not been noticed; it seems to be silent in the text. Language is central to the novel, and it is so for the same reasons that other elevated contexts are: that is, it is art.

Much, of course, has been made of the language of *Portrait,* by the protagonist himself as well as by critics, about its essential role in the development of the artist and about its poetic and symbolic qualities. Its presence as the indirect style, opening a measurable distance between the character and the narrative of character, is the source of the novel's irony, an irony still tied (vide here, chapter 1) to the protagonist's painful errors that lead to triumphs. The presence of Stephen's symbolic language seems to affirm the goal of the plot, that of creating an artist. Little, however is recognized or made of the possibility of humor in a language seemingly both so instructive and artful. However, as it is a language always open to alternation and to duplicitous, doubled contrast, it is by its very nature a fusion and confusion of meanings. As the words "head" or "surd" have multiple meanings that define different entities conflated by one word (head as top of stick or student, surd as irrational number or voiceless sound), so it is clear that language often can be so doubled. Being two things frequently very different, one and its opposite, one high and one low, one noble and one antic, language is the prime locus both for the serious purpose of meaning and for the comic otherness capering behind that intent. Language, not plot or incident, is the foremost place for comic misrule.

There is little or no slapstick in *Portrait* (as Stephen envisions the cavorting priests); there is wordplay. And that wordplay is doubled, like head and surd; words are often set in pairs to replicate the ambiguity of language and the presence within *Portrait* of both the serious and the comic. Repeating itself by variation and ambiguity, it gives a counter and deflating air to what is conveyed; like the comic Irishman in the row behind, a doubled language presents an alternative, an otherness. To the authority and artistic expressiveness of language there is the possibility of fun. Lofty ideas and images conveyed by words are taken down, tripped up in comic motion of tumbling; at every point language, expressing some serious concept, tendentious thought, or developmental description (all part of the serious uplifting drive of the novel) may have its words and diction turn into antic otherness by its potential contrasting duality. In such alternation of contrast, *Portrait* can be two things at once, high and low, light and dark.

From his earliest moments, Stephen has considered language as a determiner of identity, a notion essential to his development of self, yet he has likewise been forced to recognize that language is often doubled. Language mediates between world and self, with that entity from the first page vocalized for Stephen: "He was baby tuckoo." Identity is the nomination of otherness: "the green rose": it is the mark of spoken ambiguity, the pants leg and the town in County Kildare, "a thigh/Athy." Language seems to promise clarity (by "thinking of things you could understand them," 43) but only if the aim of language is didactic and intellective, only if its aim, as it will be for Stephen, is artistic and poetic. When its aim is comedy, language can also provoke confusion, such as the meaning of "kiss" (14), or descend to the diversionary frivolity of punning. Stephen intimates early on that language is doubled, that there are two sorts of belts even as the teacher later claims that there are two sorts of heads. Language has rules, such as those in mathematics or spelling, which determine meaning, yet all rules are capricious: the "sentences to learn the spelling from" are words of silent sounds, of surds, and they are confusing. In the first term at Clongowes, Stephen intuits that language, while potentially order and clarity, is easily confusion and disorder, not only rule but misrule.

Those spelling sentences set apart in the text seem to Stephen to be "like poetry" but art for Joyce always contains various elements: "*Wolsey died in Leicester Abbey/Where the abbots buried him./Canker is a disease of plants,/Cancer one of animals*" (10). While readers of Joyce will see in the last sentence the shadow of Stephen's mother's death, in fact immediate thoughts of Stephen's own death are what trigger this morbid exercise. This passage, seemingly so innocuous and naif, whose purpose is initially to illustrate the rule of the pen, has much layered in it. It demonstrates that even something as ordered and rule-governed as spelling presents possibilities for more, with language doubling up on meaning. The name of Wolsey raises the issue of history, specifically in Wolsey's function as agent of the Reformation for Henry VIII: imperialism is encoded in the very spelling textbook. The meaninglessness of such sentences, however, also contains possible ludic play that Stephen cannot see (neither at that early age, nor later) even if he suspects language of both power and paronymy. First off, these words are paired together, so that their being set next to each other replicates the possible comedy of punning, words with two heads. Moreover, as the words can make error if misused, they are potentially funny; misrule in orthography would make for an antic quality. Incorrect spelling or usage might trip up good students, so they represent possible pratfalls in academic achievement, Stephen's forte. (They often go by the name "devil words," showing that inclination to imp-like confusion and mischief.) And in the rather gratuitous sentence, "Wolsey died in Leicester Abbey/where the abbots buried him" there seems to be a shadow of a joke—that the abbots buried him prematurely had he not died—a joke of the sort Joe Hynes makes in "Cyclops" when, to Bob Doran's disbelief that Dignam is dead, Hynes answers, "They took the liberty of burying him this morning anyhow" (*U* 12.332). Humor in Joyce is often extended over many passages of different texts. That weak joke is the comic Irishman's contribution, the humor of Simon and his cronies, that comes from the bench behind, but it is also the sort of possible comedy that is always around the edges of the text (the more so, when Stephen confuses these lines of examples in a book with the art of poetry).

Yet if Stephen intuits the duplicity of language, he seems unable explicitly to recognize or use it to his advantage rather than to his ironic correction. So serious, he neglects to look over his shoulder, to see the other head of language, which presents a comic contrasting alternate to his expressions. He most readily sees only the higher meaning or effect of the language he uses, turning his back on the lower, comic alternate. Just as he turns his back on the raucous voices of his classmates who treat the retreat sermon as "hellish" rather than as truly hell, he does not see the comic possibilities of the language he uses. This is so for all the same reasons in *Portrait* that Stephen errs and misprizes: because he is far removed from the actual. He sees the ideal, the image, the metaphor before he sees the actual, the real, the thing compared. He misses the real world around him of childish laughter and physical play; he fails to see, in his artistic strivings, the actual world of objects and places that as an artist he must come to embrace and transform. And in those objects and places lies the banal and the commonplace that often make for humor. So in the same way (and indeed because of it) he cannot be aware of the language of the lesser, the commonplace, he cannot hear the low murmur of the comic: to him, it is a surd. And if he fails to recognize it, the task for the reader becomes more difficult to do so; the hiddenness, the behindness of the humor makes the reader miss it. Reader recognition is too often in the service of irony of directed instruction rather than in the pleasure of comic capering.

The narrative does hear the silent alternate language of comedy. The notion of the surd introduced in the very center of the novel (in chapter 3) furthers this sense of the doubling of language and of the comic entity lurking behind the text, in the otherness that contrasts the seriousness with humor. Mathematics, like a narrative, is grounded in factuality, the narrative sharing with the order of numbers a sort of first-order reality; both are the rational exercise of authority, of structure and system. Yet as mathematics has lurking within it its own release of irrationality, so too does the narrative. The surd's doubleness contains both mathematical irrational number and linguistic unvoiced sound, yet it also contains by contrast another entity, its alternate, the absurd. Pertinently, what is absurd is out of place, just beyond order and rule, like the humor found in "the comic Irishman in the row behind"; it is the comedy that just lies beyond the direction of the text. The absurd of the narrative is found in this particular sort of wordplay and word pairing: conflated diction, doubled language, deflationary opposites. Quite frequently—more than is recognized—a factual entity, a word choice in the narrative has an other entity, unreal and comic, just beyond or behind. As every sound might also have a silent surd, so every serious word might have a silly opposite. In the comic conjunction of the surd and the absurd, in the doubled diction of the novel, lies another way to glimpse (another way to hear) the humor of *Portrait*. The text becomes textured with doubled language, not only serious but silly. Direct punning is rare in the novel, usually restricted to lesser figures such as Athy and Moynihan, or to the mathematics instructor. More frequent is a wordplay more supple and more subversive at the same time: a pairing of words in the narrative, words that seem similar in appearance and in sound, yet which bring disparate things together comically.

Here is a pairing of words that exactly portrays the doubled nature of language in *Portrait* in which the lofty is conflated with the low, to make a comic effect in the narrative direction, to turn it capering instead of moving upward. In an important moment to the plot, Stephen falls away from childhood innocence into sin. The lapse belongs to the direction of development that drives the novel and, as such, is a central moment: he falls into the arms and bed of a prostitute at the conclusion of chapter 2, marking an end to one stage of his life. The consequences of his fall give him a divided consciousness that is seen at the start of the next chapter, when, in that mathematics class, he desultorily writes his equation but thinks rather of his appetites. That divided sense is enough to make him aware (as we have seen) that the day came "tumbling clownishly," but it is not enough to enable him to understand that language, too, has the divided, fallen nature. The scene in the brothel has its odd touches such as the room adorned with the puerile and comic presence of the doll with its "legs spread apart." At the moment of desire, the prostitute is said to embrace Stephen "gaily and gravely" (101)—a pairing of adverbs that in small portrays all the doubled effect of language. First of all, because the words are near contraries and yet modify the same action, the direction of the novel is compromised. Second, the pairing is similar enough in sight that the words resemble each other (and have enough similarity in sound to be confused); they have the similarity that heightens otherness. Their semantic differences, however, are crucial in that they are opposites. "Gaily" is lightened and without concern (when Moynihan jokes about ellipsoidal balls, Stephen thinks the comment "gay"); "gravely" is with weight and seriousness, *gravitas*. Echoed in the manifold possibilities of language is a contrast between the deadly, the wages of sin, and the pleasure that leads to it, the lively. This doubled conflation of opposites, over and above making the rhetorical balance, draws the balance of the novel, an equipoise not always recognized: here is both seriousness and humor, with the humor slightly out of place, absurd. As the impetus of the novel's serious development of falling and rising can be said to be done "gravely," in seriousness, so the antic alteration of humorous conflation is done "gaily." Gravely is the manner of directed, telic purpose, yet it projects a partner in absurdity, gaily, the manner of comic tumbling.

In fact all elevated language of striving and reaching is the likely focus for the comic deflation of the doubled effect of language; inflated pretensions call for deflationary tumbling. In this deflationary process, the doubled language of *Portrait* offers a conflation; that is, two sorts of interpretations, an alternative reading, wherein the serious, the somber, and the elevated are given a comic commentary right within the narrative. This conflation is not in the service of irony, because irony is a correction of one statement by another, a supplementing of meaning; this conflation is an equal if silent counterpart with the serious to provide a comic contrast.

So the context of these word pairs is predictable; their doubled presence can be found behind serious statements. Just as authoritative classes of instruction were primary places for the presence of misrule and tumbling, so authorized religion will be a likely context for wordplay as an alternate and respite from dogma and seriousness. Similarly, Stephen's artful strivings to reach the artistic end predetermined for him will also attract an alternate wordplay that takes his posturings into the absurd.

The comic appears even in such serious moments, and does so through the doubling that is found in repetition and in the commonplaces of everyday speech. The Christmas dinner scene is fraught with polemics, ill temper, and harsh language. Its effect is one that lingers with Stephen and with the reader. Yet even within the harsh interchange of anger there is a comic overtone. Uncle Charles, who eponymously gives rise to Kenner's critical terminology of a principle of language,[8] tries to mollify the assembled: "Can we not have our opinions whatever they are without this bad temper and this bad language? It is too bad surely" (34). It is not only regrettable, "too bad"; but as well there are two "bads" in his own conciliatory pronouncement. Similarly, because of the comic possibility in Irish discourse of politics and religion, Simon at the same dinner angrily exclaims, "We are a ... priestridden race and always were and always will be till the end of the chapter" (37) scant paragraphs before the ellipsis that ends the section. Unheard, such comic doubling gives a very brief relief from the great tension of this famous scene.

In this way, the obscure and sometimes unvoiced otherness of comedy of a language potentially doubled at any point in the text takes the reader from the earnest directions of the plot and away from Stephen's relentless self-absorption and internalization. A distance is achieved from the text through this alternating language. It is a distance in which irony may seek an advantage, but it is a distance that causes a surcease of intensity and instruction, wherein the reader gets a sort of respite, the sabbath of misrule in comedy that Stephen envisioned. The text becomes occasionally and unobtrusively knotted with small confusions of language. These are never intrusive, not so foregrounded as to become the focus of the portrait; rather they are contrasts making the background of the portrayal. They are the small moments when the narration makes antic gestures of cocking a hoop that lead to absurdity (making raisins in the pudding of Stephen's solipsism). Once aware of the presence of a language of two heads, alternate and absurd, the reader begins to suspect any voice or claim, to wonder whether everything grave might also be gay. The contrast of "gravely" and "gaily" makes for both the light and shadow of the comic *Portrait.*

Every moment may have comic potential, a freeplay that runs throughout the text. Take again the climactic scene of Stephen's visit to the prostitute at the end of chapter 2; this is a crucial event for the plot of the novel of development, as it signals not only the physical maturity of the protagonist but also his falling from both innocence and his religious upbringing. It is his entry into the world. Stephen is passive as he walks through the brothel district, and the narration describes the following: "A young woman dressed in a long pink gown laid her hand on his arm to detain him" (100). The intimate and erotic gesture of the hand on the arm will recall to the reader, with a certain degree of ironic suggestion, Stephen's awareness of Cranly's arm, and the possibilities Stephen fears of homosexual contact. So much belongs to the possibilities of parallel moments. Yet the word *detain* accrues a particular usage in the novel. When attempting to impress (and defeat) the dean of studies in the impromptu esthetic discussion in the physics theatre, Stephen talks seriously of the different use of words in common speech and literary speech. (We will discuss this issue and the scene in greater depth in chapter 4; here the point is the particular word that sets off a counterbalance of comedy): "I remember a sentence of Newman's in which he says of the Blessed Virgin that she was detained in the full company of the saints. The use word in the marketplace is quite different. *I hope I am not detaining you.* —Not in the least, said the dean politely" (188). The joke at the expense of the dean aside, an overt moment of humor in the novel, here is repetition, but with a difference. In the earnest literary talk, Stephen accounts for the word *detain* in both its literary and commonplace registers, but surely the greatest difference is one for which he fails to account. Here his talk with the dean is intellectual; there the action with the prostitute is exclusively physical; and the enjambment of those two different contexts by the same word makes for a comic tumbling; the reader might be "detained" when reading. The comic contrast extends further, even into the realm of symbol: the young woman "in a long pink gown" is a venal inversion of the Virgin traditionally garbed in a blue cloak, so that there is an antic quality at play. Stephen is not privy to this humor of repetition and pairing, but the reader is, and the comic pairing of the word *detain* brings into tangience two very disparate parts of the novel, two different chapters to different purposes in the plot of development, to comic misrule and antic tumbling.

This doubled usage of language occurs in the narrative voice, although not exclusively so. Because it expresses both Stephen's inner thoughts and external observation (as little of it as there is), the narrative is already paired into dual purpose; thus a language that is itself paired by parallel diction or homophonics fits easily with a narrative of two perspectives. Stephen also engages this language of doubling, although he does so unwitting of the comic effect (as his use of *detain*).[9] He is trying to be serious, to engage issues of life at the highest plane. Stephen's most excessively "poetic" figure of inversion has frequently been remarked. Not only is it a rhetorical flourish that demonstrates Stephen's esthetic posturing, it also can be seen as an excessive verbal tic that indicates ironically how far Stephen is from his own artistic premises and promise.[10] The passages of increased chiastic *polyptoton* are clearly places where Stephen strives for literary effect; and, as such high moments, they must be ripe for comic tumbling. In fact, the very doubled quality of the *chiasmus* is an ideal place for humor to reside. The intricate balancing of words in alternation makes for the comedy of the text. The ways in which words recur is also a shadow sort of pairing that adumbrates comic conflations—that is, inversion presents words that are then used again in doubles of slight variation, which seem to glance slyly at the sort of outright pairings that the novel exploits as comic. So that in Stephen's verbal posturings there is the possibility not merely of ironic ridicule but also of the comedy of tumbling. Not only does the high esthetic line (to use a term from Sullivan's own parody of dandyism) appear in the description of the girl on the beach: "Her long fair hair was girlish: and girlish, . . . her face" (171); it seems to precede Stephen's sight of the girl and almost guarantee that moment. He begins his walk on the shore by noting in the distance "lightclad gayclad figures, wading and delving" (170). This last word, evoking the world of hard and sweaty work, is itself precious in its contrast to the "gay" and "light" suggestions of the description. (And we can see here another joke to be extended into *Ulysses*, the figures of "cocklepickers" who also receive from the Stephen of "Proteus" the artistic touch of his language, turned into "gypsies" and "strolling morts" along with the midwives of his parable in "Aeolus.") Approaching nearer, Stephen finds the figures are hardly transformed into "gayclad lightclad" ones, of children and girls. There is no real difference here, only a change in word order; the change is in Stephen, who, in the interim of the several paces from first description to second, has thought of his past as a child, his "boyhood," and of his vestments, his "cerements" that are the opposite of gay and light, being rather heavy and grave. The opposition of lightly/gravely has been firmly entrenched in the novel, from the initial encounter with the prostitute who "embraced him gaily and gravely" (101) to the director, who spoke "gravely" (154) of his calling in phrases that "had been spoken lightly with design" (155). It is not only the recurrence of these words in different contexts, but the recurrence of the pairing of words that gives a comic thread to the solemn fabric of the novel's plot. Stephen sees only the artistic effect of this pairing, where the reader may see the humor lurking behind its repetitive excess.

The narration, because it is always intimate with Stephen's thoughts in language and thoughts of language, and because it is also distanced from him, maintains the same location with regard to the doubled language. That is, it uses the language whether Stephen does so knowingly or not. What is crucial to Stephen is crucial to the narrative, but the narrative stands not only with Stephen but at a remove from him, beside him but also just over his shoulder. In all elevated contexts of faith and art, language can be made lower as well, so when the narrative portrays the crucial parts of Stephen's experience, it does so by playing with a doubled language, making contrasting cruxes that lead to comedy.

Religion is founded on a crux (and, as Joyce was fond of noting, the Church was founded on the wordplay on Peter/*petros*). As well as being the authority and order of Stephen's life, religion is something that seeks the higher plane of transcendence and thus is easily turned to low tumbling. We have noted Stephen's thought about the presence of God and man punctuated by his classmate's shouts of "Here he is" at the mere advent of the instructor. The Jesuits who taught Stephen never used "a flippant word" (156), yet they are made by him to tumble and caper in antic misrule in the revery following Moynihan's rude comment on ellipsoidal balls. The grave and death that are defeated by the seriousness of the Resurrection can easily be turned into gay frivolity. (Joyce will recognize this in the *felix culpa* that continually reanimates the cyclical comedy of the *Wake*.) Because of its absolute nature as surety in salvation, religion seems to belong to the novel's certain development to the higher end of art: indeed Stephen exchanges one for the other, art for religion. Moreover, religion has the same rising action of the novel and this is a very likely context for the comic capering of doubled discourse. Religion enacts the ultimate dynamic of rising and falling, sin and forgiveness, death and resurrection, so that its linear, truly telic motion, like the direction of the novel's *Erziehung*, might also move to the alternating motion of tumbling comedy. It is a ready, open space in its high seriousness for the contrast of antic comedy.

Religion's all-encompassing effect is tacitly recognized by Stephen in a word pair within a phrase that figures the issue: encoiled by sin, the Stephen of chapter 3 knows that "he would never be freed from it wholly, however holily he might live" (153); surely the homonymic pairing ("wholly/holily") expresses the absolute quality of religion as well as the absurdity of any attempt at such perfection. Religion is absolute, but the positioning of piety with relativity both makes a statement and overturns it. Stephen's pairing is similar in sound, thus approaching the concept of the voiced and voiceless. That is, along with "wholly, holily" there is an unstated, silent other pair, equally comic, "entirety, piety," whose silence and shadowy presence makes another comic comment from behind. For every sincere effort, there is a potentially comic one, no less true of worship than of the novel. Such a pair again draws a balance for *Portrait* and counterweights its sincerity with silliness; to the expressed contrary pairing there is also a soundless pair that extends the absurdity to offer an alternative of comic capering even to the important context of religion. Even in moments of sincere solemnity, there is an impulse in the language, conveyed through the indirect style, toward a place outside of the narrative, out of place, the absurd; it is a voice in the row behind the narrative to present a moment of misrule.

The voice of authority, speaking *obiter dicta* or *ex cathedra*, as it were, is not immune to the antic possibility that lies in all language potentially doubled; indeed, it would be omnipotent were it immune. The Catholic Church may speak with one voice, but language has its voiceless alternatives. The sermons of the retreat, those set pieces for the priests (as well as for Joyce), most frequently contain the doubled quality of lofty language that conflates into comic collapse. Father Arnall seeks an effect that will elevate his rhetoric so as to give a memorable cast to his talks, which effect will consist of balanced periods of parallel diction and chiastic pairings; such is the art of sermons.[11] When he speaks of the eternity of hell, he remarks on a saint who claimed to hear a large clock ticking in the vastness repetition of the words: "ever, never; ever, never" (132). The rhyming pair makes a sound very effective to a listener, although the effect is taken from Dante; yet it also betrays the doubling effect of language's sounds. Another such parallel appears in the sermon for the effective balance of speech, a pair that merely begins in the rhetorical balance of similar words, but increasingly makes possible comic playfulness. Father Arnall describes the damned and their punishments, remarking first on how there will be a "second pain which will afflict" (128) their souls, a pain of conscience; the memory of past pleasures will be the "first sting inflicted." While this sense of gnawing conscience probably stays with Stephen his entire life, in the mordancy he comes to call the Agenbite of Inwit, the pairing is so close in his hearing (and for the reader, to sight) and close in etymology, that the words begin to lean toward the comic: "afflict/inflict." The meaning behind both words is aggressive, to "strike," both down *(ad-fligere)* and against *(in-fligere)*. The power of guilt and the Church is always present, but this pairing begins to play with that power.

    The rhetorical flourishes of such like pairs, however, can skirt dangerously close to the doubleness of comic contrast and absurdly conflation. In beginning the retreat, Arnall comes to speak of the host of Jesuits flung far and wide in the world, proselytizing or working "in the burning tropics or immersed in professional duties" (109). He tries to suggest a varied span of the globe and of service in it; yet the mixture, if poetic, is unstable: "burning" and being "immersed" are self-cancelling opposites of fire and water. They connect by comedy to Stephen's later ending of his exchange with the dean of studies by dousing the "bucket of water" on the lamp of Epictetus. The mischief of language begins to caper with Arnall's serious intent and to tumble his purpose. (That "immersed" begins similarly to "immolated" adds further possible humorous confusion.)

    The language plays with the serious effect especially at moments of great emotional appeal. Arnall draws a pointed image to demonstrate to his hearers the violence they do to grace by sinning: "Every impure thought . . . is a keen lance transfixing that . . . heart" (134). He continues in the same way, making a homophonic pairing: "Every word of sin is a wound in His tender side." Yet such a balance of figurative diction, even well-intended and well done, and despite its rising intent, will inevitably tumble down the slippery slope. "Word/wound" is a pair that begins to sound alike, and the soundlessness of the surd will always raise the presence of the absurd just behind it. And that absurdity duly appears, in language's double-headedness, as lofty soon turns low. When Arnall next says, "Will we too, like the Jews . . . , mock that gentle" Savior? he begins to invite the conflation of the unstated contradictions inherent in language. The adjective "gentle" here, being placed close to "Jews," suggests a word of balance, similar in sound, but opposite in meaning: sitting just over the shoulder of the word "gentle" is the homophonic "Gentile." The text mimes the tension of the Pauline letter between the circumcised and the uncircumcised, so that otherness falls into comic combinations of voiced Jews and unvoiced Gentiles, and a serious rhetorical flourish about man's lapsed state capers close to comedic collapse.[12]

Arnall's sermon is effective and in great measure influences Stephen's response. As the reader recognizes in Stephen's heartfelt repentance the connection between sermon and sentiment, however, the possibilities of comic language double over the seriousness even in this solemn high point of the text. Stephen's various reactions to the sermons of the retreat are places where his intensity is matched, from behind his awareness presented in the foreground of the text, with comic alternates. In fact, the very presence of his intensity is an invitation to look over his shoulder at comic conflations.

Before the second sermon, he imagines, in his sinful state, the rain falling as continuing into another Flood: "All life would be choked off, noiselessly—birds, men, elephants, pigs, children" (117). This list, attempting to be universal, retains a carnivalesque quality in its combination as menagerie; moreover, it has, as do all of Joyce's lists, a comic drive within its suggestive combinations of the noted items. Pigs and children listed together certainly seems a sly joke at Irish life, where both abound. It may also have a literary allusion to a work read by young students such as Stephen: the combination of the two, pigs and children, seems to echo the dreamlike transformation that Alice finds when the Duchess's child turns into a sneezing pig in *Wonderland.* Birds throughout *Portrait,* in keeping with both its classical and Irish sources, are used as tokens of augury (as they will be again for Stephen in chapter 5 and again in *Ulysses,* "Scylla");

they are also used by him in his self-consciously artful transformation on the beach of the girl into a bird. A particular bird, the dove, was the agent of Noah's redemption in the very flood to which Joyce alludes. And that elephant, incongruously in the list, stands for more than the exotic and feral in a grouping otherwise domestic. It is an allusion to another text of Joyce, where humor is in the foreground. An anecdote about an elephant occurs in the precursor to *Portrait*, in *Hero*'s account of the old man of the Irish West, a scene retained but greatly edited for a diary entry in *Portrait* chapter 5. In *Hero*, the old peasant resentfully describes a traveling show that proposed within its tent just such a creature, "But sure when [a young boy] got in an' all divil elephant was in it" (*SH* 243). Joyce found the anecdote tellingly funny, so too was the very phrase used; apparently it occasioned a comment from Stanislaus as to its accuracy, which prompted Joyce to write back from Pola "Again, no old toothless Irishman would say 'Divil an elephant': he would say 'divil elephant'" (*Letters*, II, 79). (The "old toothless Irishman" is a phrase strikingly funny in its own right—as it presumes there are young toothless Irishmen—and Joyce throws it away in a letter.) So this list, appearing in a chapter crucial for the novel's plot, and moreover a chapter largely read as derivative of other, religious sources and less essentially Joycean, yet retains layering elements, and those are of a comic effect.

Stephen is directly moved by the cumulative effects of each sermon; no matter the reader's inclination to see excess in those responses, every one has a crucial presence in the plot. One such response is the scene in his bedroom after the last sermon. Before the culminating images of the hircine hell (of which, more below), there is the passage that describes Stephen, literally moved by the sermon, mounting the stairs to his bedroom. (There is a touch of the psychoanalytic in this scene, as the bedroom, above and hidden away, is always a sign of guilt.) Stephen is said to make the ascent (and the word is intentionally religious in echo) "through a region of viscid gloom" (136). This synesthetic phrase is rich with suggestiveness, its stickiness a parallel to his clotted sins, themselves caused by the "torpid snaky" penis and its "slime of lust" (140). This passage is meant to demonstrate Stephen's terror at the consequence of hearing the sermon, and it is a true emotion that propels the novel's plot (by the norms of the genre of *Bildungsroman*) of his being drawn to a religion he will have to reject. Stephen reacts to his mounting terror at crossing the threshold of his room, where faces await him murmuring "he would find considerable difficulty in endeavouring to try to induce himself to try to endeavour to ascertain . . ." (136). Stephen's confusion here is terrified nonsense:

he remarks to himself that the words had "absolutely no sense." They do, however, have a particularly verbal, syntactic, and denotative order, as they are grammatical and synonymically parallel. In those very features of order within chaos lies the sort of comic potential Joyce exploits; the scene is not only intended to be serious, but can carry over into comedy. The words themselves, seemingly nonsense, yield a comic effect. This sentence, with its synonymic repetition, foreshadows an element of Joyce's later and overt comic writing, a passage echoed by Ithaca "which example did [Bloom] adduce to induce Stephen to deduce . . ." (U 17.606); the use of "induce" is a pairing in two separate texts. From such orts of words ("endeavour/try" or "afflict/inflict") comic sketches are made.

So in some measure, Stephen's excessive responses are not wholly pure, no matter how holily he may react; his intensity has a doubled and comic effect. Nor are his fears of hell his own, but have a comic double. The connections between the sermon and Stephen's repentance are close, as they should be for any serious remorse, yet the connections are always ready to tumble, precisely because they are made almost wholly out of the holy language of the sermon. Father Arnall describes in hell the "foul demons who gloat fiendishly"(133) over the misery of their dupes; it is a sort of set piece of demonology. Yet Stephen is himself duped by Arnall's diction; if the language of religion has no entireity, piety must have some holes in it. The reader who takes Stephen's vision as unattenuated and entire, however, is a likely target for comic instruction. In his vivid private dream of a scene from hell, Stephen imagines being tormented by figures of certain "creatures," "stinking, bestial," who owe their existence to Stephen's allegorizing his own lechery and lasciviousness; yet that they are constructed as "goatish fiends"(138) has another cause more proximate than the emblematic representations of the deadly sins. "Goatish fiends" too closely plays with the description of Arnall's demons "gloating fiendishly" to escape the effect of tumbling Stephen's intense vision into comic conflation. While Stephen's remorse is genuine, its sources lie in confused comedic language. Stephen's dream has a purpose, achieving an important step in his development (and indeed in the use of language) — his renunciation of sin and embrace of religion; yet the rhythmic rise and fall of his development is undercut for the reader by such comic effects as this, where paired words, with similar sounds, make humorous comments from the bench behind the high drama.[13]

The result of this repentance, occasioned by the dream of fiends and its unwitting source in doubled language, is Stephen's eager and anxious confession at another chapel, elsewhere, away from school. The otherness of the place is not only caused by Stephen's wish to avoid confessing to those who know him but is also a gesture to the outsiderness of his own reactions. When he seeks to be different from what is around him, that space of otherness will likely contain as well the doubling effect of language tumbling toward absurdity. The urgency of Stephen's confession is serious enough, yet it has been brought about by the comic effect of using and transforming language heard in the retreat sermon. Thus, embedded in its fervid cause is a latent comic element that can be heard right at the outset of his search for chapel and a confessor. The scene is particularly unique and useful because it takes place outside of Stephen's confined life of rooms and classes and the even more constricted world of his thoughts, occurring rather out in the actual streets of Dublin, and also important because it involves Stephen in dialogue with another. Stephen is not subject to the comedy within his own thoughts, but trips into absurdity at those rare moments when he speaks to someone else (comedy always being located in that other place just beyond him). Not wishing to confess to anyone at his college (as Ellmann noted was true of Joyce),[14] Stephen is determined to visit a distant priest. Walking almost in a revery, he sees an old woman walking with a can: she is clearly an inversion of the figures in his dream, the goatish fiends of comic linguistic construction from devils who "gloat fiendishly" and who rake their tails through "canisters" of excrement. As they have spittle issuing from their lips, so what this old woman speaks is a confusion. Stephen asks "was there a chapel near" in a diction so true to actual speech as to remind the reader that Stephen does have some facility in the language of the marketplace, some diction other than that of the intellectualized monologue. Her answer is the blurring of meaning like spittle on the lips: "A chapel, sir? . . . Church St. Chapel"(141). It is an answer that causes unintentional confusion, as Stephen hears in response to his request for a chapel a word that he next questions, "Church?" The confusion is the effect of comic doubling. First, his response may indicate that he is inattentive, and not certain that he has caught the street name; if so, he has not heard all the sounds, creating a surd of her response. He might, rather, react to the word as an absurdity, as church and chapel are contradictory opposites in the sectarian differences of Irish history, and yoked together they make an antic pairing. Perhaps he thinks that the woman considers him a Protestant, his particular Irish word order of "is there a chapel near" quite common to her but alien to him, a masking of his otherness. Stephen can no more converse with this old woman with a can than to the milkwoman (with pail) who will come to the Martello Tower with her can of milk on the morning of

June 16, 1904. The real world will always defeat him, as he can never fully embrace the misrule and disorder of its vegetable life. The absurdity of a chapel on Church Street was a fact of Dublin life, and it is from such commonplaces that Joyce makes his comic sidebars: the street is named for the Church of Ireland, and the Catholic chapel of the Capuchins (whose dress will occasion a gender confusion in the subsequent interview with the director) was called St. Mary of the Angels (a rather too pat name for use in the novel especially as Stephen has imagined the Virgin as reconciling him to the innocent Emma). Additionally, real life intrudes in another way: while the word *chapel* evokes a humble site—to go along with the Capuchin order—St. Mary is in fact an elaborate structure, with a large rose window, built in the years shortly before Stephen's confession.[15] The urgency of the need to confess, the serious intent for penance, go in balance with such absurd pairings as church and chapel, or humble name and elaborate edifice, so that there is a conflation of driven purpose with a comic look over the shoulder; there are two "readings" (or hearings) of silent humor here. Joyce's comedy is to work through such disparities of the commonplace, enshrining them into his higher art; this is the central, foregrounded method of *Ulysses,* but it can be seen just to the side of the seriousness of *Portrait.*

If the seriousness of Stephen's infernal vision and earnest confession—those high moments of religious feeling—are conflated by comic doubled otherness, so too his assertive rejection of the proffered priesthood—that step toward artistic freedom—is likewise alternated with capering comic doubleness. Both religion and release from it are the sort of high emotions that call for a deflationary thrust. The scene of the interview with the director in chapter 4 is absolutely crucial, of course, to the direction of the novel, as after it Stephen can play his role as one who will not serve, rejecting the role of priest to embrace that of the potential artist; yet it is also crucial because the scene that presents the substitution of art for religion contains traces of the comic doubling of language that undercuts both the priest's seriousness and Stephen's noble resolutions.

The tension of the ideational spiritual world of the image with the real world he claims to wish to encounter arises most concentratedly and pointedly for Stephen in his interview with the director about the call to the priesthood. If he is unaware of how the actual impinges on and causes his idealized images, Stephen is aware that the calling of the religious life will separate him from the world. Indeed, his fascination with the sacerdotal is due precisely to the priesthood's semblance of reality and yet its distance from it. Stephen decides that he will not embrace the symbolic and the spiritual of the religious order, so his interview with the director is crucial for maintaining a difference, a contrast between callings in life. The tension in it resembles the contrasting tensions in the novel itself between soul and reality, things done gravely or gaily. The contrast will certainly evoke comedy in the alteration. So the interview has several conflated impulses to the priesthood and to the world, to the light and to the dark. The scene will depict Stephen's serious decisions and the comic contrasts that lie just behind that seriousness. The result of Stephen's piety—caused through the reality and the effects of the sermons, the retreat, and the confession—is to earn him an interview with the director, who makes a persuasive description of the powers of the priesthood. It is in this very scene in which Stephen responds to the call that he imagines performing the distant acts of celebration and speaks unwittingly of the redundancy of the humeral veil, the doubling that points over his shoulder to the comic Irishman always behind, in the distance of the absurdity of the comic. The distance between act and reality is also the distance between Stephen's monologue and the discourse of doubling, the open place for the absurd. The interview, with its heightened importance is also riddled with the language that jests in comic contradiction. (The reader should listen in the comments for the antic sound of the absurd.)

That interview, very alluring if not finally convincing, is serious, and appeals to Stephen, leading him to contemplate the attraction of the priesthood. Yet that attraction contains an inherent danger: because Stephen sees the appeal of the clerical life as one of otherness, "the vague acts . . . which pleased him by reason of their semblance of reality and of their distance from it" (158), he recognizes the gap between that life and the real. It is, moreover, in that space that the potential for comedy obtains. The scene has very evident ironic moments, such as where the director's overt appeal to Stephen's pride illustrates the hypocrisy that irony requires; yet it is also a scene in which Stephen's measured aloofness from that offer, while a prelude to his artistic freedom, has itself just behind it comic capering. The interview with the director is a scene with doubled word pairs (illustrating the constant presence of the comic just behind the text).

In this interview with the director, Stephen thinks of his life under Jesuit instructors and how it was characterized by "his habit of quiet obedience,"(156) a true feature of his youth and one of his virtues. The contrast between Jesuit solemnity (which Stephen recognizes as their never saying "a flippant word") and the misrule of life's humor will be apparent to him later in the physics theatre, yet even in his earnest thoughts in the director's office comedy creeps in. The director had begun the interview with some desultory comments about the various orders and the particularly funny Capuchin dress, the skirts. Yet Stephen's own reflection on his quiet obedience is colored antically by a word unspoken yet just behind the director's opening conversation: dress and robes are the clerical orders' *habits*, and Stephen's behavior, "his habit of quiet obedience," is related to it not only by schooling but also by the absurd quality inherent in a language of two heads. Even when he makes a correct assessment about himself, the world around him provides a play on words with his deepest reflections.

The interview begins uneasily, with an awkwardness that prefigures the comic contradiction within the earnestness, as the mention of Capuchin dress and Stephen's memory of his "habits" conflate levels of language. The director himself tries to make a joke about another order and their dress: "this thing up about their knees . . . *Les jupes,* they call them in Belgium. The vowel was so modified as to be indistinct.—What do they call them?—*Les jupes.*—O" (155). The term the priest uses is foreign, "les jupes," so that it adds not only an alien quality but the difference of gender and all the confusion that entails. The priest even pronounces the word unclearly; the vowel is said to be so soft as to be indistinct, like a surd, and the dialogue that ensues is filled with other absurdity. To the pronunciation, Stephen adds "O," an interjection surely, but another vowel sound. The reader's ear moves through different sound unheard when read: jupes (which should be understood as "joopes"; the priest's pronunciation, probably a flat "juhpes"; and Stephen's "O"). Before the director even speaks of a "calling," confused vocals are heard, the voiced and the unvoiced are conflated, making from the surds an absurdity.

While the interview begins, then, with lightness and levity, both the director's attempt to start with a companionable comment and the unintended confusion of sounds, the entire scene has a purposefulness indicated by the color and air of somber obscurity. The day "wanes," that ubiquitous mood setting; the priest's face is "shadowed," "its image or spectre only passing rapidly across" Stephen's mind. All is tenebrous, even ominous—that is the mood of the serious. Even Stephen absorbs the somber mood; he reacts judgmentally to the priest's remarks about skirts; "the phrase on the priest's lips was disingenuous for he knew that a priest should not speak lightly" (155). Stephen never consciously seeks out lightness of touch or thought; he is always ponderous and saturnine, in a text repeatedly filled with shadow and waning light. Yet the text cannot be so somber, nor long restrain its comedy, as the humorous always lurks behind the somber and dark. Within and among the many uses of *shadowy, shadow, shadowing, grave,* and *gravely* that run through this section are the opposite touches of "lightly" that refer not only to the priest's disingenuous opening gambit.[16] The comic otherness puts lightness right up against its opposite in the same sentence ("The phrase had been spoken lightly . . . [and] his face was being searched by the eyes in the shadow" [155]) to create a balance of elements, serious and funny, light and shadow, as countervalence to the weight of the interview. Stephen will find himself in opposition to the director, but the text from the outset already contains elements of a comic doubling in opposition, so that even in the serious, somber scene an alternate portrait is being depicted.

In finally rejecting the priesthood, on the threshold of the building as a symbolic stance of the liminal and the distant, Stephen sees the priest's face "in a mirthless reflection of the sunken day." Stephen recognizes as well "the shadow . . . of the college" passing "gravely" over his consciousness. Surely that consciousness has reacted to the mood of the interview as "deadly" where the priest speaks in "total shadow," with the skull on the desk, and the talk is of "gravely . . . indifferent themes" (154). It is a correct and seemingly inevitable move for Stephen to reject the somber quality of the priestly vocation to embrace the brightness of art, and the word "lightly" not only connotes the intensity of esthetic illumination but suggests the lively and flippant as opposed to the heavy hand of obedience and the seriousness of artistic purpose. Stephen acknowledges that there is another way than the priesthood, one of mirth and rising light, but he can nowhere come to employ it. While the text, in its thrust forward to *Erziehung* and to its goal of calling, seems to obscure that comic light, and Stephen fails to embrace it, yet there is always some levity, its humorous existence is indicated by the doubling of "gravely" with "lightly."

There is another pairing of words in this exchange that not only resembles the comic disparity of such couplings, but also directly points to the comic world that hovers just behind the novel, much like the humeral veil evoked within that interview. As Stephen listens to the initial and general conversation of the director, "echoes of certain expressions used in Clongowes sounded in the remote caves of his mind" (157); he is conscious of the nearly Platonic distance of his past, and conscious as well of those constant voices he has always heard but often ignored. He then thinks of earlier scenes and persons, whose "vital circumstances" he at the time failed to perceive (157); these "masked memories passed quickly before him." The memories are masked because, at the time they occurred, they had hidden their meaning from him; so that he again feels otherness and separation. Yet they are masked for another reason as well. Much like the voices Stephen only distantly hears, the voices of others which are the comic counterpart to his seriousness, the memories are masked because they represent that comic impulse of revelry, that carnivalesque antic behavior which, along with the raucous voices, present the possibilities of the κῶμος. When Stephen rejects the priesthood, he chooses to embrace the misrule and everyday, those very elements that go about masked as for the carnival. And that implied sense of choosing his lot with the world is indicated at the end of the interview (itself filled with contrasting pairs of "grave" and "light," as the serious and the lively); as he leaves the office, shaking hands with the director, he notes in his face "the mirthless reflection of the sunken day" (160) so that the priest's face comes to be adorned, we noted, with a "mirthless mask." This "mirthless mask" of the priest makes a near opposite in sight and sound with the "masked memories" of his days at Clongowes, in which the humor represented by the mask is either off-putting or put off.

The doubled presence of comic otherness hiding just behind, like the humeral veil, is so insistently at elbow, in fact, that even at the important moment of rejecting the priestly call, Stephen is tripped up by the comic effect of doubled language. The phrase with which he responds to the sepulchral ("grave") drag of the priesthood is one of high, empurpled sensitivity; and diction of that sort, so earnestly felt and expressed, is always tripped up by the heels from behind: "the impression which effaced his troubled selfcommunion was that of a mirthless mask . . . of the sunken day" (160). Here is the overreaching of Stephen's exaggerated self-absorption, particularly in the solipsistic "selfcommunion"; while this is a widely used phrase for conversation with oneself, it is particularly inapt in that the celebration of Communion has been a function of the priesthood which itself resembles real acts but is at some distance from reality. Stephen's selfcommunion, then, might be seen as only a vestige of something real, and equally ritualized and unreal. And an "impression," an esthetic word for feeling that it seems to be, is something pressed upon a surface, as in a wax tabula or a page, as even so weak a Latinist as he should know. To efface, then, is an erasure of an act of communion that has no reality, a removal of what was not there. It is a comic contradiction to have an impression erase something, and the more absurd to have it erase what was not there to begin with. Even at this moment that impels Stephen onward into the calling of the book's title, the doubled otherness and absurdity is always over the shoulder of his language, tripping him into a comic contradiction.

Another near pair that falls into a comic possibility concludes the interview. After he has heard the director, and residually suspects the appeal made to him, Stephen turns from the calling, because that "exhortation he had listened to had already fallen into a formal idle tale" (162). He rejects the opening of the priesthood as soon as it is made, turning the calling into something vapid; it is a measure of the power of direction inherent in *Bildungsroman* that the abruptness of this change is never questioned. Stephen turns what he has just heard into something done tediously before, "formal" as an empty gesture, such as those—to an unbeliever—the priest makes during the Mass. The tale he has heard before has been in his own mind, that chronicle of searching that he thought to find in serving God, and it has become something tedious and formulaic (a claim that could be leveled against the predictable plot of the unfunny *Bildungsroman* itself). The word "fallen" evokes not only the world of sin, but also that of comedy, as he goes away from Belvedere to embrace the tumbling misrule of his father's house. Yet "fallen" and "idle" so near to one another begin to approximate a comic pairing that is unstated but stands, like a surd, mutely behind these thoughts: placed together, they suggest "fallen idol," a comic view of Stephen's image of himself as priest, an image long held and now summarily dismissed just at the point it becomes actual. This fallen idol is a wry comment on all of Stephen's representations of himself, an attitude of literal iconoclasm (in which the antic possibilities of paired language tumble the higher elements of the text).

The tale he has "listened" to is echoed, unremarked by Stephen, by the "agile melody" of a concertina in "a quartet of young men" (160) who pass him as he leaves Belvedere's front hall. It is that lively melody that contrasts with the "mirthless" face of the director and "the sunken day." Gaiety is again in contrast to gravity, and sounds begin to make their mark in the text. That the young men are "striding" along, "swaying," and "stepping" makes another comic scene to double with the imagined frolic of the priests, and the fact the they move "towards Findlater's Church," an Anglican one, provides further comic contrast. Stephen seems oblivious to the comic possibilities of the world around him, presented in the language of the text.

As an intelligent person, Stephen is aware that there is a world outside him, although he judges it always as of less interest than his own self. He can even recognize that it can contain something common and comical, provided that it does not come near his concerns. Leaving the director, Stephen crosses a bridge, that very classical if conventional sign of a change. What he sees with uncharacteristic detail are certain items from the actual world beyond him: the shrine of Mary "fowlwise on a pole in the middle of a hamshaped encampment of poor cottages. . . . The faint sour stink of rotted cabbages came towards him . . ." (162). All these come to his notice probably because of his frequent hunger (and thus are things of the appetite, the belly) but they are things of the real, material world. Stephen then recognizes that this has won his soul: "the disorder, misrule and confusion" of his family life and "the stagnation of vegetable matter"; these are the elements, some of them very basic, of the real world. Indeed, this world makes Stephen laugh (twice: "a short laugh broke from his lips"; "A second laugh . . . broke from him"). From the prostitute's kiss to the receipt of the Host when the ciborium came to him, Stephen has moved to use his lips for rare laughter. He presciently realizes the presence of misrule, even before he envisions it as the tone of the image of cavorting priests in the physics theatre. What he first encounters (and is ready to recognize as such) when he renounces the priesthood is the world of comedy (such as the odd behavior of the man digging in the garden [162]).

Yet his recognition here is only temporary, itself a respite from his habitual seriousness that has taken him deeply into the arcana of religion and will now lead him, with that telic drive of the novel's plot, into the priesthood of art. Much as religion seeks beyond the temporal into the atemporal, Stephen's art will overlook what is in the world.[17] It is precisely Stephen's more customary inability to see what is around him, over his shoulder in the actual world in what he accurately calls (if obliquely avoids) the vegetable world of misrule, that creates another context for the comic contrasts of language in the novel, being once again of the conflation of the serious and the silly, the higher with the banal. Stephen's elaborate metaphorizing, his poetic reaching for art, strives to be as high and lofty as is religion, and it is just as likely to tumble clownishly. In substituting art for religion, he is just as solemn and just as open to comic undercutting. His figurative language first of all *is* language, which is inherently duplicitous: that is, it can have both heads on sticks and students. Stephen's striving for art—a striving that, like his essay on heresy always approaches nearer to art but in *Portrait* never reaches it—is characterized by one inherent imbalance: it is raised up without any grounding in the real world. Figurative language must come from somewhere, its comparison must connect with a thing to be compared; metaphors do not arise *ex nihilo* as his philosophy surely must teach him. It is because Stephen does not notice what is around him that his creations are mere poeticizing. Their loftiness is only empurpled prose, not grounded in the real world of actual life where the physical world of misrule can give a comic character.

Even his earliest strivings for meaning have been characterized by this lack of connection to the real world. When he wants "to meet in the real world the unsubstantial image which his soul so constantly beheld" (65), he defines a process of meaning, a dynamic that animates all of his actions in the plot of the novel; it is this that drives Stephen in concert with the impulse of the novel of development. Yet it is a dynamic that is backwards, having the meaning but lacking the experience, and such a reversal is likely to fail. He already possesses the figuration but not the actual thing on which to base his metaphorizing: he has the tenor of art but not the ground of the actual. He thinks of such moments as "magical" but he is not aware of the alchemy that it will take to make art from dross.[18] Such unearned striving is ripe for comic tumbling. Common, small, unimportant things evoke the artful figures of speech.

In the very moment of leaving the director and choosing art and not the priesthood, Stephen indeed encounters something that comes toward him: it is the sour stink of rotted cabbages. He fails to recognize that it is the source and subject of his art.[19] Such small everyday things are present in the text, but with the narrative focus exclusively on Stephen, they are easily missed, as they are always just beyond his sight; a reader can see the origins of Stephen's art in the commonplace and thus experience a comic contrast that can be glimpsed just behind the artfulness of the text. Many of Stephen's thoughts of high ideals and elevated purpose, those high moments, are ripe for an antic capering of language that, always doubled, makes them trip and tumble because of that element in it to which Stephen is not alert. Nearly each and every high moment in Stephen's secular triumph toward the goal of art and personal freedom has likewise a low element in the row behind in the other place where the absurdity of language makes for comic conflation: highlights are also lightened. The reaching for art, the soaring on viewless wings, is brought down by comic contradiction. Icarus's plunge is paralleled by the language of deflation, where in every serious artistic expression lies an unserious absurdity, a kernel of comic contradiction.

The serious discussion of Stephen's growth into esthetics is similarly made to caper in antic humor (as we have seen in the introduction, his theory has its comic features). Art, Stephen thinks, is like religion in that it is transcendent and spiritual; yet again he misses the real from which it arises, even though his esthetic claims that the sluggish matter of the earth is art's material. And that real, the banal and commonplace, contrasts comically with the elevated effect he creates when he responds or thinks artistically. While the high moments seem to delineate the stages of Stephen's inevitable missteps in the aim of becoming an artist, those moments, antically confused by language doubled in comic contortion, also show that the portrait has its comic smile. Through these conflations the novel is broadened and put into balance; artistic moments are not only serious but comic and show that comedy exists, even in art, in the row behind.

There is a scene that illustrates Stephen's sensitive appreciation of the art of poetry and yet shows as well the confusion in that esthetic response. He and Cranly, walking, overhear a servant girl singing while at work at the kitchen window (the clichéd "Rosie O'Grady"). This is a scene almost comically overdone in its parallel to the Romantic poem "The Solitary Reaper," where the speaker hears a girl singing as she works. This lyric incident is here given a realistic turn by the fact that, while the speaker in the Wordsworth poem does not know the song of the Highland girl (though he carries it in his heart), Stephen well knows the one here as all too familiar. The Wordsworth speaker focuses on the song; Stephen, the girl. Cranly, stopping, says *"Mulier cantat"* (244) speaking Latin perhaps to avoid being overheard, perhaps as a jab at scholasticism. Stephen's reaction is as elevated as Cranly's language: his sensitivity marks him as "touched with the dark of the evening" and yet his response is vague as well, because that enchantment is touched off, the text says, by "the soft beauty of the Latin word." Cranly has spoken two Latin words, "mulier cantat," subject and predicate; Stephen, so serious, can only see one possibility when the language always offers him two. The text goes on to attribute the enchantment to two things, "the touch of music or of a woman's hand" (244), music and woman both, yet the narrative has denoted only one word; for Stephen we know which word can only be soft beauty, *mulier*. It is not the Latinity of the word that attracts him but its gender. Once again he focuses on the figurative, "the figure of a woman," yet even when he cannot see her but only hear, he is deaf to the sounds of the two words Cranly speaks and the text offers. Esthetic appreciation should not be confined to the "art" of singing a popular air, but also to the comic possibilities of language.

Stephen's failure to hear the two words here, along with his lapse in thinking of the figure and not hearing the voice of the woman, are indicative of this very often missing something around and about him. More exactly, he is never aware of the alternate, what is behind, and in those omissions the disconnection between the real world and apparent inviolate sanctity of his mind is evident. In the space of those connections lies the comedy that always lurks just behind his more striving thoughts and moments.

Art that turns its back to the comedy just behind is so separated from the actual that it seems to be autogeneric, to lack any physical or even biological connection. Despite being in and surrounded by the real world, the artist, Stephen feels, must have autonomy; he should acknowledge few ancestors and should select his forbears as mythic rather than as biological. His art would be symbolic or mythic, not actual; it is no wonder he repeatedly turns his shoulder to the actual world. Consequently, a comment such as his disavowal of his family may ring high and lofty but have rather low and common roots. Following the failure of his home bank funded by his school prize money, Stephen feels acutely a separateness from his family: "that he was hardly of the one blood with them but stood to them rather in the mystical kinship of fosterage, fosterchild . . ." (98). The rising expectation of money and the fall into daily tawdriness is yet another rhythm in the novel's direction of development. Stephen's severing of biology seems a crucial and necessary step in that development, one that the artist must make in order to pursue his aim; to embrace his mythic identity Stephen must erase his actual one. Yet in fact, this very claim to lofty mythic origin has its own origin in the tepid and banal actuality of life that makes for the comic. At the start of this episode, before the extravagances of banks and dinner, Stephen retrieves those academic prizes which permit all the rest; they are given to him in a certain place. The text describes the scene around Stephen that he never notices: Stephen's mother was waiting "at the corner of quiet Foster Place" (96). She is a biological entity standing in an actual Dublin place, that of the real world. The entire scene of economic rise and fall, ending with a ringing disavowal of parentage for otherness, for "fosterage," begins with a reference to an actual street whose name must surely cause a tumbling in the posturing rebelliousness of Stephen's thoughts, "Foster Place." The bank prize fostered Stephen's brief extravagance; the name of the street where the bank was located comically lowers his extravagant metaphoric claim of the separateness of fosterage.[20] Stephen rarely notices street signs; once he is said to stare at "the word *Lotts*" on the wall of a lane (86); those legends and letters are the real life of Dublin that he so infrequently notices.

The comedic effect of Stephen's claim is, moreover, greatly enlarged to extend even the text of *Portrait*. The besideness of comedy opens many possibilities. It is this sort of comic license that, extended, will write *Ulysses* and it is first to be found in *Portrait;* what is comic in Joyce will always go beyond. *Ulysses* demonstrates this effect by carrying its humor far afield from the text; and so too does *Portrait*, if one looks just beyond Stephen's shoulder. The Foster Place named in chapter 3 is the locus for the incongruent and consequently for the humorous: Foster Place is the lane northwest behind the Bank of Ireland from which, Bloom laughingly notes, the sun of Home Rule rises on the masthead of the *Freeman* (4.102). Thus, and rather unexpectedly to critics who see *Portrait* solely as a treatise on esthetics or as a *Lebensbahn,* a recurrent joke extends into the later text from the earlier one.

There are other places where Stephen's involved metaphorizing about art and as art has a comic complement in the commonplace, so that the high thought or image connects with a lesser reality of the kind that Joyce scrupulously wrote. In these incidents, actual Dublin places frame and pull the crucial striving for artistic freedom at the end of chapter 4 back into contact with the actual that appears so infrequently in the novel. Stephen waits for his father to arrange admission to the university in Clontarf and then impatiently crosses the Bull out toward Howth. Clontarf, a place name, comes from the Gaelic, the field of the bull, and the Bull itself is an English nomination of the same term; as such, the two are conflations, different names for the same thing. And their comic coming together must certainly give a humorous cast to the cries of the bathing schoolfellows in their classroom Greek, *Bous* (168). This call may evoke a proud reaction in Stephen, but it is the sort of doubled language through which the comedy behind can be seen. The same touch must also be glimpsed in the place outside which Stephen anxiously waits for his father, Byron's publichouse, and then the excessive poeticizing quality of Stephen's reaction to the girl on the beach as secondhand Byronism. It is not heretical to assert this connection (as Stephen suffered at Heron's hands) but only comical.

Stephen again uses a word from the real world to substantiate his artful self-absorbed sense of dispossession. Again, he stands outside a building, beside an institution. The Maple Hotel, before which he waits for Cranly from the library, calls up to him the "sleek lives of the patricians of Ireland housed in calm" (238). The presence in the same place of the Kildare Street Club most obviously evokes this sense of privilege, yet his resentment of their pale aloofness and polished hauteur seems to come from a more immediate source: the name of the hotel, "a colourless polished wood." The hotel sign is unlikely to be made of such material, only Stephen's poeticizing is, going beyond the actual into this excessive burst of nationalist resentment.

The scene of the girl on the beach is apparently the triumph of that artistic vision which substitutes for religion, the making of transient reality into the beautiful and permanent; it is a high point, especially after the comic contrast of Stephen's vision of soaring and the falling comments of the swimming friends about drowning in the conflation of *Bous* heard on the Bull. When he sees the girl, the moment for which all of his life seems to have been a promise, indeed the moment toward which all the telic movement of the work has aimed, his reaction even then capers with comic contradiction. In his soulful cry, where he gives voice and sound (another vocalization, like his question to the old woman), there must be something absurd; the comic conflation that obtains within religious discourse must be equally present in that of art, diction always subject to being tripped by contradiction: " —Heavenly God! cried Stephen's soul, in an outburst of profane joy" (171). This is a short sentence if a fervent one; even so, it is filled with the opposition of comic confusion, with the "outburst" something that breaks beyond the usual of Stephen's reserve. Moreover, because the "outburst" is cried by his mute soul, it is unvoiced, a surd. Stephen explicitly realizes that this experience will replace his religious one, which is why he mentions both the holy and the secular. Yet what is profane cannot be heavenly, no matter how much one would wish to bridge the real and the spiritual;[21] to be profane is to take God's name in vain, which is exactly what Stephen does here. God in heaven is essentially heavenly and there is no need to describe him by any attribute; if Stephen neglects his scholastic training in theology, he then falls into the commonplace, and the phrase is only an interjection. (The phrase connects, obliquely as is Joyce's comic method, with the funny scene in which Stephen questioningly contemplates whether the Host is the presence of both God and man and the noisy schoolboy interjects, "Here he is.") "Profane," however, is the correct word, although not in the way Stephen means as worldly; what is profane is outside the holy, beyond the precincts of the temple (*pro fanus*); it is just the place for the absurd.[22] The outside, just beyond, is the place of the comedy of *Portrait,* it is another way to describe that row behind where the comic Irishman sits; it is the shoulder on which the humeral veil rests. Beyond the temple of the serious telic narrative lies the capering carnival. Stephen's sentence is comic, even if his ideas and feelings are serious; it is a light touch where Stephen seeks the profound. His joy must be profane, as it must be of this world, not heaven, and even just beyond this world; even as the comedy of the text must be just beyond the serious drive and direction of the narrative. To possess that comedy is joy, as Joyce defined it in the Paris Notebook; the joy of art and the art of Joyce.

To digress briefly from the issue of Stephen's esthetic experience and its artistic expression, there is a character among the university students who is clearly intended to represent this notion of exclusion by the comic contradiction of his very name, Temple. Despite the name as the essential solemn place, he is described as the ultimate outsider, "the gipsylike student" marked as different with an "olive face" (196). His eyes, differently dark when the other students' are light, are "dark, oval eyes." "Olive" and "oval" paired together begin to combine to a near repetition that suggests Temple's comic nature. When derided by the students, he confesses to them that he is a "ballocks" (231), a fool (but a dual number that gestures to comic doubleness). His comments are always *malapropos* and off-centered, yet his comic otherness at University College is a counterfoil to Stephen's somber otherness.[23] Temple is ineffectual; Stephen voluntarily makes himself an outcast.

The displacement of Stephen and Temple is echoed by the way in which the text of *Portrait* often conscripts proper names into the service of humor, such as when family names accrue other meanings. The name Lynch in *Stephen Hero* and *Ulysses* was considered by the actual model Cosgrave to be a libel, due to the ready extratextual association in the Irish mind of the name Lynch to a mayor of Galway infamous for hanging his own son. (In a letter to Joyce, Stanislaus suggests that Cosgrave might sue; Cosgrave also, with considerably more vanity, was rankled by his description in *Hero* [136] as "grave-looking" [*Letters*, II, 103].) If Dolan "was like the name of a woman that washed clothes" (55), the names of Heron and Cranly too have a humorous and suggestive slant as birds: Cranly a crane, and Heron explicitly recognized by Stephen as having "a bird's face as well as a bird's name" (76).[24] Heron even gets a comic pairing in the text when he says, "I was just telling my friend Wallis what a lark it would be . . ." (75). Thus, in the fashion of adolescence, Stephen's acquaintances figure his own sense of being hawklike, and they resist his understanding in much the same way that the actual birds resist his auspicating on the library steps in chapter 5, where, to tie disparate threads of nomination together, the birds are said to circle in "a temple of air" (224). The bird names also obliquely recall and comically invert in gender the bird girl on the beach, whose figure Stephen paradoxically elevates profanely into heavenly art.

The high striving for artistic expression, as in the scene with the girl in chapter 4, is often open to comic displacement; in the writing of the villanelle, Stephen will fall into comic conflation in his poeticizing. He is never as original as he claims, because his ideas always require something other, earlier to work on, something from the world that he fails to notice. Although he feels he is *sui generis,* without any biological origin, every word choice he makes is an echo of something before just as he is a product of his parents before him, and what was before that triggers the creation is something real but invariably less high than is the use to which he wishes to put it. This was the case with his defiant claim to fosterage from his parents in the scene that began with him standing with his family in Foster Place, an actual place name; this is the derivation of the "goatish fiends" in his vision of hell from Arnall's sermon on "gloating fiends." The otherness of a source makes for comic conflation and deflation. That villanelle, which certainly appears to proceed from a very immediate physical sensation, has this derivation of comic doubling. (It is also derived another way, from Yeats's poetry.) The text enacts the connection of Stephen's thoughts with the creation of the poem: as he thinks, "lured by that ardent roselike glow the choirs of the seraphim were falling" the poem is reworked to read "ardent ways,/Lure of the fallen seraphim" (217). Such connections can certainly be viewed as the poetic inspiration uniting Stephen's inner thoughts with his artistic production.[25] Yet the repetition within the variation comes close to the double language that skirts the comic. In fact, the most artistic feature of the villanelle, its repeated rhyme scheme, has its origin in something comical. Stephen feels "the rhythmic movement . . . pass through [the verses]. The roselike glow sent forth its *rays* of rhyme; ways, days, blaze, praise, raise" (218, emphasis added). The "roselike glow" is either Stephen himself or the wallpaper (and one might say as did the dying Wilde, one of them has got to go); its "rays" is a word told by the narrative, not Stephen, and it is that which produces the subsequent rhymes. They all are paired, as rhymes must, but the last one, "raise," is a homonym of "rays," two-headed like a student and a stick. Its very phallic gesture may, while uplifting, tumble further the orgasmic cause of Stephen's art. "Rays/raise" also suggests the homophone "raze," comically the opposite of "raise" to add comic collapse.

Stephen's theorizing is much like his poeticizing. We have discussed in the opening how there is comedy embedded in it, some of which we have seen Stephen makes himself, and how to find comedy there amid esthetic theory to be aware that *Portrait* can be funny. Yet Stephen also misses seeing other comic elements; for example, when he talks so fixedly about the act of seeing necessary for apprehension, he misses Cranly's calling out, "Bull's eye" in comic juxtaposition connection. The "Bull's eye" is a comic conflation with the figure of the bull which itself was combined with Clontarf and the Bull and *Bous* to actual polyvocal comedy.[26]

The noble statement that Stephen makes to Cranly about his future as an artist is an admirable credo of independence (if not wholly original, either). First off, even Stephen's grand gesture of rebelliousness that permits him his freedom is subject to comic doubled conflation; when he says he will not serve, Cranly observes, "That remark was made before" and Stephen retorts, "It is made behind now" (239). "Before" and "behind" are as good a pair as any to characterize the tension in the novel between foregrounded seriousness and displaced humor.[27] This comic start to his declaration is concluded with the equally grand and memorable "silence, exile, and cunning." Behind all of these noble ideals lies the always present possibility of comedy (that Joyce will exploit). Silence is the unheard, the realm of the surd, which in turn from the earliest parts of the text also involves the absurd. The comic possibility is continued by the notion of "exile," which is a distancing from the familiar, a being out of place, beyond, profane; like the comic Irishman in the row behind it will make the distance that provides humor. "Cunning" is a cleverness (such as Joyce displays) that embeds in the serious work the balance of humor. It is the cleverness of the sort that Joyce is capable of writing in *Portrait,* portraying Stephen as incapable of recognizing the comedy of his own vocalization. An example of just this very thing follows this ringing claim. Stephen says of these three that they are "the only arms I allow myself to use" (247); yet while making that proud statement, Cranly "seized his arm and steered him round so as to head back towards Leeson Park." The proud independent poet, calling up his arms, is led away, a follower, by his physical arm. The tripping up of his lofty pronouncement is surely a comic turn. His being "steered," not merely directed by someone else, describes the directional drive of the novel, and the adverbial "head" evokes the source of the novel's humor. "Steered" also evokes another doubled word, one for the gelded if garlanded ox of Stephen's noble name-calling; once more solemnity is tripped by the heels. Always striving to rise when he thinks he falls, Stephen tumbles just as often into pratfall.

When he does use his actual arms later, as he describes in the diary entry for the date 15 April, he tries to make a revolutionary gesture, but rather, he says, looks as if he were "throwing a handful of peas into the air" (252). Revolution was spoken of at the college in the appeal for universal peace; Stephen is reduced to a clownish gesture of lentils. The doubling of language unites this pair of "peas" and "peace." It is unlikely that he recognizes this comedy of himself in the sound of the surds that create absurdity; the reader must interpolate the two to make a comic conflation. The arm that throws the handful of peas, the arm linked together, the "arms" of the artist all are made comic, laughing up the sleeve, covered by the humeral veil of the text that puts them behind.

Stephen's inability to recognize comic possibilities in the language and its conflating doubleness is not only evident in his speech and thoughts, but also, as in this last example, in his own writing. He is still a long way from becoming an artist because he remains unaware of the comic shadow behind his enlightening diary entries.[28] Even when he uses language in the diary, a usage in which he must exercise some editing (in contrast to the unmediated discourse of his monologue), he unconsciously is duped by the comic contradiction; he never looks over his own shoulder when he writes, and so his diction is doubled into two-headed comedy.

Surely Stephen intends a calculated balance in the rhetoric of the written voice in the diary entry: "the white arms of the roads, . . . the black arms of the ships" (252); yet this artful touch derives from a real event in common life. When in dialogue with Stephen, Cranly speaks earnestly about Jesus and presents the original contrast: was he "a conscious hypocrite, . . . a whited sepulchre? Or . . . was he a blackguard?" (242). The various (and competing) voices within the text conflate here into comedy. The rhetorical art of Stephen's writing and the rebellious apostasy of Cranly's comment both tumble each other into a combination in which Stephen's art has a real source. The color of the arms comes from conversation, the connection of arms comes comically from Stephen's actual experience of Cranly and exile, and the contrast of white and black is like that of the somber and light of the text itself. These are the connections made by the alternate doubling up of comic pairs and parallels.

The diary contains such examples of comic conflation, each one demonstrating that Stephen, insistent on striving for his goal of art and freedom, is ready to tumble. In this writing Stephen has unwittingly adopted the absurdity of language, even in the very last entries in the diary: what other than a comic contradiction, even if an expression of the economic reality in Ireland, are "new secondhand clothes" (252)? The diary suggests that Stephen can never flee the absurdity of the language which is his, as a comic Irishman schooled and churched in the unraveling doubling of the surd and the absurd. When Stephen finally both calls out, "I go" and evokes the old artificer to "stand me . . . in good stead," he says nothing other than mute and self-cancelling absurdity. "Go" is contradicted by "stand," and "stead" is derived from "place," so that, despite Stephen's wish to go along the lines of the direction that is plotted by the generic drive of the novel, he is left in that place just behind where comedy resides.[29] (Moreover, with his wish to leave home and, having done so, be in good "stead" seems to bring another comic conflation to the much-vaunted ending: away from "home" in good "stead" comically creates "Homestead," the very place where "Deadalus" will first appear in print.)

Comic contradiction, the absurdity of language in the silence of the surd, are the means to see behind the text, in the row of the comic Irishman, in the profane space beyond the temple of art. Language describes thoughts and actions both in *Portrait* and language is always characterized by two-headedness, by an absurdity of possibilities of diction that is the means of comic tumbling. The doubled nature of language enriches *Portrait,* balancing its seriousness with the otherness of levity, adding lightness to its gravity, "lightly" to its "shadow," "gaily" to its "gravely." Portraits illuminate, but they also can lighten up. His is a portrait painted in words that erase themselves, in disappearing ink. Joyce knew this when he wrote *Portrait,* and he repeated the fact in *Wake* where the work of Shem is described as waning "chagreenold and doriangrayer in its dudhud" (*FW* 186.08) There, late in his own work, Joyce again demonstrates the comic conflation that characterizes all art, and especially that of the artistic autobiography: the chagrin within the *Portrait* of the young ("green" man), the yoking of opposite shades of color, gold ("dor" with the added fillip of "gilded" or embroidered) with the dull "gray" which is the somber tone of the novel (with a glance at the Estheticism of the '90s as "gay"). Wilde is tame (*Ulysses* tells us) and ended as an exile. And "dudhead, the "dud" pertinent here to the soundlessness of the surd, the "hud" referring to that so crucial head engaged throughout the portraiture. "Dudhud" is a rhymed word pair, a word that itself has two things, one of them a head.

The deflationary effect of language doubled, where high ideas are upset from behind by the otherness lurking in words, where diction is turned into contradiction and humor, discourse made discursive, is strongly evident in both religious language and that of art. There are as well other comic sounds beyond the text, in artistic sources that Joyce heard as a young man (if Stephen resolutely fails to hear them). The next chapter considers how Joyce engages these other comic texts.

3

Two Comic Contexts

If comedy exists just behind the action of *Portrait,* making a humorous contrast to the solemnity of the main, directed action; if it is contained in other voices in other heads rather than in Stephen's thoughts; if it is present in language of doubled effect; then it would be appropriate to look at other places just behind *Portrait* to find comic contexts for Joyce's work. Such contexts would provide the contrast to the somber direction of the novel and would themselves illuminate those marginal areas of the text in which its own humor resides. Contexts are to the side, along with something, so that they occupy the space of comedy. These contexts are not a matter of literary sources as such; rather than a dialogic relationship to texts, there is a relationship of a text to things behind it, not so much in dialogue but in displaced and diverted relationship. What will be discussed in this chapter are alternates that provide contrast to the content of *Portrait.* These are other comic expressions, possibilities, voices. The figure of two heads, and the doubled captioning of languages, are emblems in *Portrait* that there are always other sorts of headings along with the serious intellectual focus. These other writings are literally such other headings. Around and behind *Portrait* are comic influences and humorous literatures that influence the way Joyce conceives of and casts the alternate of his text. It is not Stephen, of course, who notices these works, no more so than he notices comic or ribald voices around him; these works represent in literature the sort of unserious voices that Stephen deafly ignores. For Joyce, however, these are voices of which he was aware and to which he was attuned. They act like surds, mute within the serious side of the text, but they have a presence just behind the writing, like the comic figure in the bench behind, that influences and suggests the comic *Portrait.*

Because the comedy of *Portrait* is always displaced, these texts are to be found not as models or allusions but as counterparts, not as sources but as suggestions. They are comic contrasts, as shadows, cast by the main focus of the genre. Just as there are comic characters such as Temple who are foils to Stephen, so there are comic texts that are counterparts to *Portrait*: comic others and comic authors. And what is true of the comic others behind Stephen is true of these contexts as well. Just as the voices of Moynihan and schoolmates are found in lesser degree and focus than the thoughts of Stephen, so these texts are distanced from and not clearly evident in the narrative. *Portrait* has competing voices that urge Stephen; these texts are likewise voice dissimilar to that predominant one of the *Portrait*'s narrative that raise the comedy of polyvocality and the humor of variety (virtues so well documented by Kershner, if with less focus on comedy). As Kershner has read *Portrait* as open to various influences, which give variety to the monotone of the narrative, so there are also texts to the side in popular voices of misrule and humor that give alternating context to the high purpose of the novel. As the language of those other characters such as Moynihan is vulgar and common, so too are these other texts, neither intellectual nor spiritual, rather profane and worldly. These other texts, like the voices of unruly classmates, come from lesser lights in popular culture and mass media, which have their shadowy presence in the novel without any apparent explicit appearance. They are, as it were, from the bench behind, giving voice to comic otherness. As we have come to see in other chapters, it is precisely what is not immediately present but displaced in the text of *Portrait* which has a comic purpose and effect.

In this look behind *Portrait* for humor, biography and fiction will coalesce (as they do frequently in any examination of the novel), but to a different purpose, to a sense of indirection and suggestion. What Joyce saw and read in his own life is of course enscribed as part of Stephen, but, given the developmental drive of the book's genre, attention largely has been paid to the serious reading of both. Just as Joyce was not the somber Stephen, so his reading is not exclusively done in Marsh's Library; as there is alteration in the serious text, so there is alteration in the serious sources. As the text is not unrelievedly somber, but has moments of comic alteration, so the readings are not exclusively serious. Even though Joyce presents himself as a serious reader like his protagonist, he certainly read many more ephemeral things; among them certainly were comic pieces and these must have had some bearing on the covering and uncovering of his comic portrait.

Joyce, one could say, was catholic in his reading: and surely that projection of himself in fiction and in letters as studiously scholastic may have well served not only the purpose of elevating himself in others' eyes but also of obscuring the tracks of his comic sources. (Such a move would be in keeping with the diversionary, up-the-sleeve quality of *Portrait*.) We know that he read *Tit Bits* when at Belvedere (and even thought of writing a piece for it) and the comic paper *Dublin Opinion* when in Europe.[1] An argument about what else Joyce may have read must proceed by speculation, not by assertion; we do not know exactly which popular comic works Joyce read. We can, however, see the contexts of the works around him as he studies, thinks, and begins to write. These texts affect Joyce indirectly, and because they are indirect, they make for comedy. This sort of reading makes a clear contrast to that attributed to Stephen, who, in *Portrait,* never appears to read popular literature at all after *The Count of Monte Christo* (chapter 2). The speculative record here offered of Joyce's reading forms an interesting set of markers for his engagement with comic works of others, as the first example we will examine is from the Belvedere years, and the other from his beginnings as a writer in Europe in 1905–1906. These conveniently are the dates in which Joyce both presents himself in *Portrait* and writes it. The first source is the comedy prevalent in the Ireland of Joyce's youth that he would react against—as he did with any and all literature of that time in his life—and yet come to transform and use. The second was comic work he found in his more mature years on the Continent, from which he would acknowledge and profit. Both of these comic contexts provide Joyce with contrast and possibilities to lighten and alternate his solemn fictional portrait; these are the written voices in the benches behind the serious text.

Although the contexts for Joyce's reading (and Stephen's) seem circumscribed by school, we know from a story like "An Encounter" that widely different material, such as the penny dreadful "Pluck," was read outside the class, even hidden within the texts in class. Such sideways glances away from the authority of school opens up possibilities of other literary encounters. Joyce enters Belvedere in the spring of 1893 and the central episodes in chapter 3, not only of the retreat but also of the greatly involved mathematics class in which Stephen thinks of the day clownishly tumbling and the teacher speaks in comic doubleness, date approximately from the winter of 1896[2] or, less likely, 1898.[3] We know that it was in 1894, at the start of his time at Belvedere, that Joyce both read *Tit Bits* and even wrote a story to submit to it.[4] He was likely to have read other popular publications as well, one of which may have been the *Dublin Illustrograph,*[5] a monthly quarto filled, as was often the case, with articles of general interest, items of social news, photographs, and humorous stories and sketches. It was aimed at an audience of the middle class, with its aspirations and pretensions, and consequently featured articles on the social world and the established institutions that they favored. Several factors, coincidental and provocative, argue for the likelihood of Joyce's seeing this publication. In the May 1894 issue, there was an article and photographs about Clongowes, that school for the enfranchised and the aspiring, which might have piqued Joyce's interest. Should he have felt, however, some chagrin at his having to leave that institution, he might have been solaced by seeing later in the summer (July) an article and several photographs of his new school, Belvedere College. There are photos of the various class levels; Joyce may well be in the first row on the far left of the Lower Class.[6] It is also possible that Joyce knew the article was to appear in the *Illustrograph* and that he turned his attention to it for that reason. The coincidence of life and print always appealed to Joyce because he could exploit such coincidences. In June 1894, for example, the *Illustrograph* published a piece on the bazaar "Araby," with a report and several photographs, among them the "Cafe Chantant" and a full-page beauty of Araby with languorous look and braceleted arm. (This picture seems to shadow forth the figure of Mangan's sister in the "Araby" story of 1906.) These items point to the interests of a certain class of society and also of a young boy of twelve such as the one depicted in the story of the same name as the fair, and Joyce was himself twelve in the summer of 1894.[7]

The possibility of a source for the *Dubliners* story notwithstanding, the coincidence is strong enough to suggest that Joyce read the *Illustrograph;* certainly the presence of the article about his school (and the likelihood of his picture in it) is enough to claim that he read the issues of July 1894. And amidst the article about his own school life, a life that he would turn into artful autobiography, there was a brief piece about things literary—a critical discussion entitled "New Irish Humorists."[8] Because Joyce begins thinking of himself as an artist in 1894, planning to submit a funny story to the popular *Tit Bits,* this article may have caught his eye, especially as it reports a meeting of "Irish *litterateurs*" at the "Irish Literary Society" in London, among them "A(lfred) P. Graves," the author of "Father Flynn" (which Joyce cites in *Ulysses*) and Mr. W. B. Yeats. This article seems to speak to Joyce and his sense of self as much as did the one about Belvedere in the same issue.

The article describes the condition of comic writing in Ireland in ways that anticipate the evasions and displacements folded into the *Portrait* text as Joyce was to come to write it (as in, say, the chapter 3 in which Stephen is a student at Belvedere). It reports that the speakers at the meeting were unanimous in nothing that, "considering the drollery and fun in the popular nature and heart, the amount of the laughter-moving element that has found expression in our literature is comparatively small." The wording might have struck even the twelve-year-old Joyce as cumbersome ("laughter-moving element," for example); this attitude and diction is to be repeated in "Cyclops" ("nobody who has a corner in his heart for real Irish fun without vulgarity"; U 12.545–546). The appeal to the common folk of popular nature and heart was beneath Joyce's adolescent opinion. Yet the proportion seems to describe the chemistry and even the composition of *Portrait*, a "comparatively small" expression of humor. The discussion makes a point even closer to the effect of comedy in *Portrait*. The writer (a "W.P.R." unnamed) remarks that what few Irish humorists there are "have had to find audiences in the bye-ways" (as "the great world that has shaken its sides at the quips of duller fellows has not accorded the fair meed of recognition"). Those "bye-ways" are clearly the paths of indirection and diversion, of the asideness that characterizes Joyce's comic way within his novel of development. The author goes on to acknowledge that imposition of the stereotype: that "article which is not racy to our soul at all, but a foreign imitation, a stage-Irishman growth." The Stephen of university years partakes of this same sense of otherness when he attributes the conventional ribaldry of Moynihan to the comic Irishman, the set figure with which he will have no truck; yet his placement of that figure in the "bench behind" acknowledges the points raised here. The article seems to correspond to the sense of what Joyce will do.

The article, however, moves to two concluding issues with which Joyce will take strenuous objection. The first is that "A goodly share of the heartiest humour of Ireland is to be found in peasant songs and local rhymes . . . that have never travelled to the highways . . . , the classics of rural literature." This claim of the superiority of the peasantry, even in the matter of humor (perhaps most in the matter of humor), is certainly a claim that Joyce resists. Such resistance to the peasants is a strong one, caused no doubt by Joyce's wish to see himself and Ireland in urban terms. (He notes in trying to convince Richards to publish *Dubliners* that his city, not yet the subject of art, is one of the largest in Europe.)[9] He also wished to see comedy as something less stagelike, more nuanced and social (this he gets from reading Meredith while at University College). This resistance to the burlesque of the peasantry is conveyed in the autobiographical works, in Stephen's squeamishness at the smell of the peasants' wet corduroy and of the cowyard in *Portrait*, or in Stephen Hero's disdain for Mullingar. The denial of the noble peasantry is most firmly described in a scene common to both texts—a rare moment of collusion from a text superseded by dominant other (and the process of this supersession, this putting *Hero* behind *Portrait,* is the focus of the next chapter). The common scene demonstrates how much Joyce resists the stereotype of the peasant as the sole purveyor of the honest, the authentic, and even the humorous. That old peasant, pipe in mouth much like any figure of the honest son of the soil, refuses to acknowledge a world larger than his experience (in *Portrait,* the universe and stars; in *Hero,* the animals of prehistory); for Joyce such a refusal speaks not of the limits only of *a posteriori* knowledge but of strictest provincialism. The narrowness of the peasant's view is made clear by the spatial terms used in his grudging acknowledgment: "Ah, there must be terrible queer creatures at the latter end of the world" (251). (*Hero* has this same sentence in dialect; Joyce's choosing to put in it more standard English in the final version suggests his wish to avoid direct kinds of conventional comedy.) For the peasant such knowledge is far ahead in time and space and thus unattainable; for Joyce these dimensions are within the reach of art. This is a scene of comic effect on the reader, but the comedy is at the expense of the peasant, not caused by him. The effect on the artist is different in each text: *Hero* has Stephen going on to delight in the backwardness of the peasantry and their racial inferiority (what he notes as their "Mongolian types"); in *Portrait* there is more of an agon, where Stephen imagines "gripping" the old man by the throat. The earlier text is more willing to demonstrate its humor, the latter is more likely to want to dominate it (more on this head in the next chapter). Humor is not to be found in the rural West: for Joyce that site must be abandoned, and turned behind.

The conclusion of the article "Irish Humorists" also goes rather too far in the way of false hope: "Our young humorists are coming well to the front." The phrase "our young" when used for any artist was anathema to Joyce: he would parody this sentiment in "Scylla and Charybdis," when "Mr Russell [another journalist] is gathering together a sheaf of our younger poets' verses" (*U* 9.290). And in his practice, particularly in a work about a young man and an artist, humor succeeds best when it does not come to the front but rather stays just behind.

While this article appeared when Joyce began his years at Belvedere in 1894, some of its points clearly remain with him in his university years, largely because the concept of the "stage Irishman" was in the forefront of concerns about Ireland's image in art. It is in the physics theatre at UCD that Stephen articulates his own notion of the "comic Irishman," acknowledging the stereotype that the articles praises and adding his own particular treatment of it by displacing it behind. It is at this time at university that Joyce (and Stephen) begin to consider such issues of genre and criticism; and it is a time in which another article appears that may also have influenced his sense of the comic. The period 1898–1899 was a crucial time for Joyce, as he worked on his paper "Drama and Life," whose subject of Ibsen brought him into conflict with the president and whose reception by the student body was a mixture of awe and disdain that gave Joyce a low estimate of his contemporary students which he kept for years. The scene of the confrontation with authority in the back garden of Newman House is described in full in *Stephen Hero,* but the entire issue of the paper and its reception—so important in Joyce's life—is omitted from *Portrait:* this striking omission is an example of another kind of displacement in that later text, one that removes political and social issues from the plot of the character's development as an artist. The paper "Drama and Life" marks the time in which Joyce begins an active esthetic engagement, developing a critical facility to assess all that he reads and attempting to establish his own criteria for art: this is the growth of the critic's soul. After that point (the paper delivered in 1900), there will be the Paris and Pola Notebooks (on part of which, more below) and the constant reading and judging of works when on the Continent, when he writes to Stanislaus his often quite trenchant opinions of a variety of Continental and canonical writers. The university years are ones of far-reaching intellectual inquiry; in actual life, with the large perspective on literature in the essay "Drama and Life"; or in art, with the detailed distinctions found in the peripatetic discussions of esthetic with Lynch. It is at university that Joyce reads Meredith on comedy. Yet even when engaged in serious matters of life and literature, Joyce was undoubtedly continuing his sporadic reading of popular works; for Joyce there would be no dissonance in combining intellectual inquiry with interest in popular, even vulgar, art. In December 1898, for example, while at work on the paper about higher issues of drama and life, he again might have picked up the *Illustrograph*. In fact, it is consistent for Joyce to be serious in his essays and direct in addressing intellectual ideas while simultaneously reading and obscuring the humorous material he read and encountered. The following is speculation but, despite its provisionality, speculation is a look, and looking behind the obvious will yield comic figures and other heads.

He may well have found an brief article that did little to prove the optimistic claim in "Irish Humorists" in the *Illustrograph* of four years earlier that humor was coming to the fore. What did arrive was of a lesser sort. The piece, titled "One Way of Carving a Turkey,"[10] was not intended as instruction (although there were such pieces in the *Illustrograph*), although Joyce may have found it instructive. He would have seen a piece that was intended to be comic, its limitations and sophistries an illustration of what comedy meant to a large audience, a current example of Irish humor. He also would have seen in this piece what he could work on as the matter of art, putting it behind him in order to write his own comic scene:

> He never carved a turkey in his life, and on Christmas Day, with an old maid on one side of him watching him closely, and on the other side a fair girl for whom he had a tenderness, he feels embarrassed when he begins. First he pushes the knife down towards one of the thigh-joints. He can't find the joint, and he plunges the knife around in search of it until he makes mincemeat out of the whole quarter of the fowl. Then he sharpens his knife and tackles it again. At last, while making a terrible dig, he hits the joint suddenly, and the leg flies into the maiden lady's lap, while her dress-front is covered with a shower of stuffing. Then he goes for the other leg; and when the young lady tells him he looks warm, the weather seems to him suddenly to have become four hundred degrees warmer. This leg he finally pulls loose with his fingers. He lays it on the edge of the plate; and while he is hacking at the wing, he gradually pushes the leg over on the tablecloth, and when he picks it up it slips from his hand into the gravy dish, and splashes the gravy around for six square yards.
>
> Just as he has made up his mind that the turkey has no joints to his wings, the host asks him:
>
> "I wonder who will be the Prime Minister next election?"
>
> The girl next to him laughs, and he says he will explain his views upon the subject after dinner. Then he sops his brow with his handkerchief, and presses the turkey so hard with the fork that it slides off the dish and upsets a goblet of water on the girl next to him.
>
> Nearly frantic, he goes again at the wing, gets them off in a mutilated condition, and digs into the breast. Before he can cut any off, the host asks him why he doesn't help out the turkey. Bewildered, he puts both legs on a plate and hands them to the maiden lady, and then helps the young girl to a plateful of stuffing, and, while taking her plate in return, knocks over the gravy dish. Then he sits down with the calmness of despair, while the servant takes the turkey to the other end of the table.

This piece is marked first off by its obviousness; the straining for effect suggests its desperate attempt at humor. Exaggeration strives for the comic (the gravy splashed "around for six square yards," "four hundred degrees hotter") but fails because the phrases of hyperbole are so uninspired and inartistic. The gestures are broad and large; they are not the sort that would come to the young Joyce, being, in fact, the performative theatrics of the stage-Irishman figure that he deplored. While subtlety would not be desirable in a work for the mass media, the exaggerated physical aspect of this humor (the spilled drink and gravy boat, the slipping turkey) undercuts its presence as a written text. As burlesque, appealing to the visual, this is comedy of a lower sort. In fact, this piece misses a sense of self-awareness of its own limitations that would mark a work for an more engaged and demanding audience because the directness of the comedy is the surest sign of its poor effect and low aim. First, there is no appeal to the intellect (and thus could not be read as ironic): it has neither a social context nor a political sense, nor any sense of its unreflective use of language or of its implausibility. Second, in the exaggeration and obviousness of the piece lies a danger, similar to the one faced by sentimentalism—a danger of implausibility, of an unselfconsciousness of its own bathos (another feature of popular literature). In all, its directness measures not only its feeble approach to humor but also the obviousness of its appeal to the reader, the immediacy paradoxically diminishing its effect. Moreover, there is in it a sense of incompleteness, despite (or perhaps because of) its being overdone and strained. This sense of incompleteness is not due to any unfinished action (the action in fact is so limited as to be finished). Rather, despite its exaggeration and strain, this incompleteness is due rather to the impression that the piece is not whole, that something more is possible and necessary.

Thus the article leaves the reader looking for something else, something beyond its shortcomings: in that sense, it causes a desire in the reader to move beyond it. That desire to go further is an indication that the piece is not a sufficient whole and measures its inferiority as a work of literature. Such an effect would very likely have been noticed by the Joyce of university years as he began to form his critical opinions. When Joyce comes in 1903 to write about comedy in the Paris Notebook, filling out the critical ideas begun at University College, he notes that "improper art aims at exciting in the way of comedy the feeling of desire"; desire he defines as "the feeling which urges us to go to something" (CW 144). By his own criteria articulated only slightly later, Joyce would have found this piece unacceptable not because it was the lower comedy of burlesque (that is, not a judgment on popular culture), but unacceptable by a stronger standard of art, "improper" because of a lack of quality. A work of comic art "which does not urge us to seek anything beyond itself excites in us the feeling of joy": this is a better effect from any sort of work, high or low. "Desire urges us from rest that we may possess something but joy holds us in rest so long as we possess something" (CW 144). With its shortcomings, "One Way of Carving a Turkey" makes the reader seek for something beyond; that is, it evokes a desire in the reader for something else. The comic desire in this piece, as Joyce would come to call it, not only points Joyce to the shortcomings of contemporary humor, it may lead him to do something more himself: to rewrite it. The distance of this piece from its possibility of comic completion is the opportunity for Joyce to develop his own comic practice, that of moving beyond so as to put this behind his own work.

Here we can see the impetus of Joyce's artistic methods that he will eventually come to practice, the point at which he begins in his maturity to embrace parody and pastiche. It may very well be that Joyce saw in the obvious silliness on the *Illustrograph* piece the potential for the particularly Irish means of comedy, which (according to Vivian Mercier), "is always carefully shaping its raw material: sharpening it for satire, . . . always giving it direction of one kind or another."[11] Any pastiche or parody must acknowledge not only a source but that source's incompleteness and inadequacy, which it then must move beyond for development. This is another way to understand what Joyce called the comic impulse. Moreover, a text that creates parody is one that sets something behind it, the very locative dynamic of Joyce's comedy. Pieces of literature like these, mass culture and popular, are the ones Joyce remembered in later years. Much as he may very well have remembered the braceleted girl (the "Beauty") in the *Illustrograph* feature on Araby from 1894 when writing "Araby" in 1905, so too he must have remembered this piece of poor comedy. In any case, what this offered Joyce was a model not for emulation but for improvement. The age offered him such literary moments that he would use; the incompleteness of poor comedy is clearly the opportunity for a better art by a more accomplished, mature writer, one would write about his own life, putting both its own events and such pieces of inferior work behind him to move beyond to better things.

Joyce reshaped the comic possibilities of this article in two scenes of ceremonial carving in *Dubliners* and *Portrait*, in 1907 and 1912: the similarities of these scenes to the *Illustrograph* article of 1898 are a strong indication that Joyce may have indeed actually seen this piece. He elaborates on it because it is a scene of some cultural moment, a ceremony in which values are embedded, and in this way already gives to his piece the intellectual appeal the inferior lacks. He takes the mundane scene and the poor writing and invests them with meaning and layered humor; he adds to the *Illustrograph* piece many larger issues and deeper effects. Yet withall the seriousness of the later scenes he writes has behind it a comic shadow; there is the comic other that is just up the sleeve. What is interesting to note is that, behind the seriousness and the tense poignancy of such deeply felt works as "The Dead" and *Portrait* lies this frivolous, comic scene of limited appeal. Joyce had no wish to have this piece from the *Illustrograph* be a source or an allusion in his work; it is important and enough that it be just behind. The fundamental issue is as much what Joyce makes of the scene in his work as the fact that the scene is remembered by him, and the critical point is that both of his serious works have their literary origin less in his life than in an inferior, comic text (that Joyce may have seen and if seen certainly remembered). In retaining and rewriting, he makes something anterior to his own work, something that becomes the behindness of his own humor. The seriousness of "The Dead" and *Portrait* has a comic genealogy behind and yet present in another context over the shoulder.

By enlarging the content of the scene, Joyce gives more latitude to the targets of humor; thus he can remove the direct obviousness of the article to give contrast and subtlety. To the precarious frailty of masculine privilege he asserts a domination. He might have been struck by the cultural and social anomaly of the turkey as the main feature of the meal: it was the very product and fruit of the imperial endeavor, a bird brought to Britain by colonial acquisition.[12] These contexts, historical and social and gendered, are those in which Joyce comically questions the values of his age, by exposing them in his art; consequently he deepens his work with the completeness missing from the model he may have seen in the *Illustrograph*. So what appears as serious in the broadened context of Joyce's texts is in fact backed up with comic frivolity.

The clearest parallel with the dinner scene in "The Dead" (*D* 196–198) lies in the tension of the *Illustrograph* piece between the man and his audience of a young woman, so that the context of gender is enlarged and moved to the forefront, even if the turkey is replaced by the more traditional goose. The later story turns precisely on the fact that Gabriel is more mature than the young man but no less secure in his place. Gabriel is an accomplished carver of geese (his claim to be ready to carve "a flock of geese if necessary" [*D* 196] is his own attempted stroke of banal comic exaggeration). He is the better carver in the same proportion as this scene is the better written, so that the writer of "The Dead" is more advanced than the one of "Turkey"; by contrast to the hapless man, Gabriel "plunges his fork firmly," "boldly," "at ease" (*D* 197); the knife is as mighty as the pen. Yet despite this skill, he is pompously self-conscious, still concerned with the opinion of Miss Ivors (with whom on the dance floor he has plucked another bird, the crow). Like the young man, he too becomes warm from his task: he "found carving hot work"(*D* 197). Gabriel's own judgment on the language seems to be in line with his author's on the sort of comedy in the monthly: Gabriel offers "what vulgar people call stuffing"(*D* 198). The comment seems to be an encoded judgment on the earlier piece, for by calling dressing "stuffing," the *Illustrograph* thus shadows forth its own vulgarity and the common taste of its readers. The dinner scene from "The Dead" is a deeper handling of the comedy latent in the earlier periodical. Vulgarity has its use as the contrast to the serious tenor of the longer story "The Dead."

Joyce's reworking opens up to exploit the comic, even vulgar, possibilities in the actual turkey, which seems to have particular further suggestions constellate about it. Largely because of the similarity of its neck to the human penis, turkey is a slang term.[13] In *Portrait,* for example, there is the action of the butcher who "prodded [the chosen bird] often at the breastbone" (*P* 29) as an attestation of its attractiveness, thus combining masturbation with the erotics of the word "breast." There is another riddle for the young Stephen vexed by doubleness, both verbal and physical: "Why did Mr Barrett at Clongowes call his pandybat a turkey?" (*P* 30). In the scene in *Portrait,* a child of six, in the latency period, would not know; later, when at seventeen, reading the *Illustrograph* (and certainly at twenty-eight when writing the *Portrait*), he would: both are something you beat with. Thus the turkey in *Portrait* becomes another word that has two heads. The sexual suggestiveness of both these phrases about turkey is another item of comic literature, that impulse to physical celebration that lies at the very base of all humor.

A further proof of the incompleteness of the "Turkey" sketch, moving it beyond the text outward toward desire, is the naive and simplistic use of language in the original, a use that has unintended consequences in the diction. Joyce will exploit this sense of language away from its unreflective use in the place behind his own serious text of "The Dead." To the unaware (and unfunny) language of the piece in the *Illustrograph* Joyce saw to add a knowing component, a treatment of language that would appeal to another head, and by so doing, be comic. If what Joyce might have seen in the *Illustrograph* of 1898 at the important age of seventeen was not the outright eroticism he might have found foremost in the earlier issues of 1894, when as a puerile boy of twelve he gazed at that braceleted arm of the beauty of "Araby"; he might yet, in his more sophisticated age, have seen the erotic suggestiveness of the scene and its language. He would put this as a backdrop to that climactic moment in which Gabriel's sexual desire is thwarted.

Joyce was no doubt early aware that "turkey" was vulgar, low slang. He certainly exploits the word in "Circe," where "turkey" surfaces in two sexually explicit scenes: one of Virag with his *"turkey wattles"* (15.2434) suggesting potency; the other Boylan's response to Lenehan's direct query as to whether he was sexually active by claiming to be "plucking a turkey" (15. 3746).[14] Joyce might readily have seen the (unintended) sexual slapstick in the unknowing language of *Illustrograph*. The young man "pushes the knife down towards one of the thigh-joints." When he cannot find the socket, "he plunges the knife around . . ." (appropriately "until he makes mincemeat"—a disjunctive metaphor Joyce surely would notice). As a result of this ineptitude at so manly a task, "the leg flies into the maiden lady's lap," a fair thing to lie between maids' legs, as Hamlet notes (III, iii,117), and also a proleptic glance at the song in "Circe" about "the leg of the duck." The lady's dress front is covered with a golden shower of what the vulgar call stuffing. (Even the concept of a stuffed fowl begins to seem erotic.) Not so much slapstick as climactic are the repeated spilling of liquids: he "splashes the gravy" and "upsets a goblet of water on the girl next to him." Here is unrecognized but literal *jouissance*. There is even a postcoital sadness: the young man "sits down with the calmness of despair." These intimations of sex, only distant innuendoes in the "Turkey" piece, are caused by its reticence to address sexual issues directly; as innuendoes they are merely indirect asides in a text of slapstick. For Joyce, however, this indirection serves a more useful end. The erotic quality unreflectively in the *Illustrograph* article stands behind the pomposity of Gabriel's hosting (the switch from turkey to goose notwithstanding), and is part of his own sexual frustration and failure at the end of the story. Thwarted in his mounting desire in the hotel room by Gretta's memories, he has comically (because so indirectly) had his sexual encounter at the dinner table. He himself becomes a "goose" (hence the fowl shift from turkey to goose), a silly fool, as well as a vulgarian and "pennyboy" (*D* 220); the language of two heads reflects him comically as he is reflected in the mirror in the Gresham Hotel. After that masculine carving comes his sexual humiliation; behind the serious denouement of "The Dead" is the low comedy of this context.

More of this same comic anteriority is to be found in the relation of the article from the popular magazine to the climactic Christmas dinner scene in chapter 1 of *Portrait*. Even as it contains greater social tension than marks the *Illustrograph* piece, the scene in *Portrait* is freighted with the crucial context of an ideological tension. *Portrait* clearly makes explicit the politics only implied in the little piece (the undeveloped political question about the prime minister), as Parnell is stuffed into the turkey, connected forever for Joyce through the actualities of the Christmas dinner in his home in 1891.[15] It is a measure of the cross purposes of *Portrait* that Joyce takes a scene of comic celebration and makes it into a tense melodrama. Christmas is to be a celebration, a festive moment about the Incarnation that forms and confirms the carnivalesque. *Portrait* has displaced the usual celebration to the service of politics and the terrors of the family romance. The traditional dinner (modeled on British lines, hence the irony of the turkey and the political argument) also has festive explosive crackers, containing favors and jokes. These may be on the Dedalus's table (Simon is flush enough to afford an expensive fowl), but they go unnoticed, their place being taken instead by explosive rhetoric and mean humor. The rolling napkin ring, like a child's hoop, is the only element left of play.

Yet despite (or perhaps even along with) the heavy atmosphere at the table, there is one comic element remaining that is introduced into the meal by Simon Dedalus himself, and that humor resembles the scene depicted in *Illustrograph*. Simon's carving is, like Gabriel's, accomplished, but his social offering is comically aggressive: the "pope's nose" (32) is the one part of the fowl not mentioned in the monthly. Located just above the cloaca, this part of the fowl is associated with excrement and birth; to associate it with the pope is high anticlericalism, much like the Reformation pictures of devils excreting popes and archbishops.[16] It is Simon's attempt to be both humorous and polemical at the same time. (This combination of comedy and argument is Joyce's particular addition to the scene). Simon is for Stephen a representation of a comic identity of the Irishman that he must reject.

A certain unrestrained quality of chaos is suggested in scenes of both article and novel by the overflowing liquids, their fluidity a comic excess of carnival. The spilled gravy in the story is similar to Simon, "who poured sauce freely" (30); the former caused by simple confusion and the latter by a more complex anger; yet an antic quality obtains in both results. The character in the short piece is solicitous of the young lady, Simon ignores both his wife and Mrs. Riordan; romantic unctuousness is replaced by sullen aggression, surely its opposite. The gravy and the other liquids in the *Illustrograph* piece are connected to the "famous spit" in Mr. Carey's story, an anecdote rich with history, misogyny, and bile. The emphasis on spills and spits of humorous excess makes for a Rabelaisian quality certainly obvious in the "Turkey" extremes but only implicitly behind the polemic of *Portrait's* chapter 1; its presence offers an alternate way of viewing the scene (much as the young Stephen views the scene through a mirror and beneath the table) as being ludicrous and excessive, strained and fraught. Simon's tears at the climactic end are only another in the unrestrained current of comic overflow and potential.

Potential it was because the *Illustrograph* issues of 1894 and 1899 are to be in the future contexts of Joyce's work. The magazine's issues bear fruit in work done in 1907 and beyond, although they form part of Joyce's reading as a youth as the time depicted within *Portrait*. These are the long shadows cast obliquely by the alternate comic contexts. At the time he was writing *Dubliners* and *Stephen Hero,* he was doing other reading and this, too, makes a context around the text. One source in particular enabled Joyce to refine his comic style; unlike the *Illustrograph* pieces, which defined for him something to react against, this other work by another author was a model to emulate. One way to measure Joyce's development as an artist is to see how he begins by defining his work against others but later finds works to accept and adapt. It is frequently the case that what he is against are established works and what he embraces are popular forms.

As regards his outside reading, Joyce always was attentive to voices of other texts, certainly, yet in that dialogic relationship Joyce saw himself less as a recipient or conversationalist than as a critic and even an antagonist. He reads authors as if in a contest with them, as if to critique an author were to best him. He wrestles with certain writers as much as Stephen envisions struggling and choking the old ignorant peasant from the West. The latter represents for Joyce the conventional sense of Irishness against which he must make his own literary identity; the former, the established writers, famous and published, against whom he must compete for acceptance as an artist, and he forms a sense of his own artistic method by measuring the styles and effects of other writers. His harshest criticism is reserved for canonical works; he was always more receptive to popular forms of culture than invested, approved ones. After 1904, he enlarged the arena of his interests, out of the classroom and beyond Ireland. His presence in Europe made Continental writers available to him and his readings were of works of his day; whatever knowledge he had of earlier literature came to him in school years; what he read in 1903–1906 were contemporary works.

The period of 1905–1906 was hectic and productive. When Joyce was newly in Pola, Trieste, and Rome, his career was beginning; he wrote most of the stories of *Dubliners* and began *Stephen Hero*. He read frequently and very widely, as he reported in nearly daily correspondence with Stanislaus; for each work read, Joyce clearly formed a critical judgment. Turgenieff, Anatole France, even Hardy came in for his acute analysis: France was "neither delicate nor rich enough for my taste" (*Letters* II, 85); Turgenieff "is useful technically but in European literature he has not so high a place" (II, 90); "what is wrong" with Hardy and other English writers is that "they always keep beating about the bush" (II, 200).

It is rare for Joyce to judge even established writers favorably; he always found something with which to disagree, with which to qualify a tempered approval. Because praise for another writer was infrequent, it is remarkable that Joyce singled out to Stanislaus a writer for praise without qualification, not a canonical writer but one from a periodical: "Do you ever read the *Daily Mail*. A fellow named Edgar Wallace writes in it sometimes a farcical column: it is very funny" (*Letters* II, 188; November 6, 1906). Joyce did not merely praise, but did so with an intensifier, "very funny." While the forthrightness of this praise is remarkable, it should be no less a surprise that the source of this praise is from a "lesser" popular medium. Again Joyce turns favorably to something unacademic or artistic for emulation. This comment is the only mention of Wallace in Joyce's correspondence. Yet Joyce is often coy about voices that resonate most with him and work the greatest influence; many other such sources, Berard or Dujardin, for example, receive similarly casual or oblique mention. Often the less said, the most influence. This rare acknowledgment is not only valuable in its diversionary casualness; moreover, it clearly provides a means to examine what Joyce found funny and to see how this sort of comedy came to be a method for him. Again, the argument proceeds by suggestion, looking at the ways Joyce may have looked over Wallace and how those works hover, over the shoulder, behind Joyce's own writing. That writing undergoes a change from the years in which he, as a student and first as an exile, began to be an artist.[17] From early work that is vague and abstract—highly academic—to work that is specific and acute; his art moves in the direction of detailed sharpness and effective form. Not only does Joyce's writing become clearer, it becomes more comic. This praise of one who can write something "funny" is one place to see what Joyce thought was humor and that may have formed a context he would put to use behind his own texts.

Joyce first mentions to Stanislaus, in that very frequent correspondence of 1905–1906, reading two or three London papers "regularly" starting in April 1905. This notice of reading of journalism is striking, in part because so much of his correspondence reads like an intellectual's reading list. It also points to a source that seems far removed from *Portrait,* a text in which Stephen takes so little regard for daily matters. Amid his reading of Continental writers, Joyce kept his gaze on the British imperial culture; this admixture parallels the one of his reading of both high literature and mass culture. Among these three papers, Joyce mentions specifically the *Daily Mail,* which had by that time a circulation in Britain of over 1 million copies and was also published in a Continental edition in Paris. Its publisher, Alfred Harmsworth, later Lord Northcliffe, was a Dublin man (and the original publisher of *Tit Bits,* which Joyce read avidly as a youth).[18] Although Joyce does not name it in this first acknowledgment of reading three London papers regularly in April 1905, he notes specifically in a letter of September 18, 1905, that he has seen an ad in the *Daily Mail* for Warden's *The House by the River* and asks Stanislaus to find a copy (*Letters* II, 107).

This engagement with the mass circulation daily extended over time and place. Joyce read the *Daily Mail* regularly when in Trieste in mid-1905 to 1906. When he first goes to Rome in mid-1906 he singles it out and tells Stanislaus that he can find it in the Caffé Grecco, or borrow it from the mystery man Wyndham (*Letters* II, 146). His telling Stanislaus about the presence of the paper in recounting his daily doings in Rome suggests that it was important to him, and that he sought to read it as often as opportunity would allow (this he did in concert with his reading of Continental writers). "Regularly" is a key term, suggesting that such frequent exposure was a new possibility for Joyce; this frequency suggests that hitherto he could not afford the papers, but was then able to see them for free in the Continental cafés. We do not think of Joyce as engaged with reading journalism at this time, as we do when he writes *Ulysses,* although he did actually write for it (in the *Piccolo*). Journalism is not considered a background for the short stories and the biographical novel, and its effect has not been adequately addressed.

Joyce not only read the *Daily Mail* with some regularity and attention in those early years but, as some measure of its effect, he remembered it much later. Its presence can be seen at the end of Joyce's work: for example, Joyce noted to Stanislaus the oddity of the Caruso case of public exposure, heavily featured for several days in the *Mail* in late 1905, incidents of which appear more than thirty years later in *Wake.* Joyce claims to abandon reading the literary supplement of the *Mail* in December 1906, in disgust with a serialized love novel, and he does not mention the paper in subsequent letters. He singles out Wallace for praise in November 1906, after more than a year of reading the *Mail;* this is the unqualified sentence—he "writes . . . sometimes a farcical column: it is very funny." Because Joyce was never so direct in his praise, this writer must have shown him something, speaking in a voice that resonated.

When Joyce says to Stanislaus that Wallace "sometimes" writes a column, he was accurate: Wallace's work appeared sporadically. For the months of November and December 1905, when we know that Joyce was reading the *Daily Mail,* Wallace had nine bylined articles in eight weeks, the *Mail* publishing six times a week. Most of these were a series of articles, six, on the czars of Russia. For 1906, the entire year, Wallace had nearly twenty articles bylined, including his newsbreaking scoop of the bomb attempt on the king of Spain. As well toward the end of that year there were his articles without byline about the *Daily Mail* crusade against the Lever soap trust by which time, however, Joyce no longer mentions Wallace. Some of his columns ran in series, some consecutively, sometimes parts were separated over several weeks. There were other articles for which he was responsible, but these were not marked with a byline. These columns were all located in interior pages (usually page 4 or 6 of an eight-page issue), none prominent and none marked by teasers or leads. Joyce would have had to search them out in any issue. Many columns were reportage, some were intentionally farcical, but all were touched with humor.[19]

After 1906, when Joyce's notice of and attention to him and the paper stops, Wallace goes on as well. He had a gradual estrangement from Lord Northcliffe and from reporting for the daily, so that Wallace began to write novels to support himself. It is this output for which he is best known: authoring some popular works of the time, notably *Sanders of the River* (1911, using his experience of Africa) and mystery novels, practically inventing the modern "thriller"—nearly two hundred titles in all. (As an interesting sidelight, Wallace moved to Hollywood in 1930 where his last work was to coauthor the film script for "King Kong.")

In his capacity as a journalist, then, Wallace demonstrated a perspicacity and sharpness coupled with a comic turn.[20] His pieces were focused, succinct, and clever. Lapidary terseness and comic tone seems also to describe Joyce's later stories (if not his early writings). Wallace had an appreciation for the engagement of the real that presented an idea, rather than for the abstract that merely named it. He employed a language really used by men, another mark of the engagement of his work with the culture around it. He had an acute eye, with a touch of understatement and irony, for the telling details that spoke to the layering of cultural and historical issues; and he had an acute ear for the spoken language that was evolving and reflecting the modern world. He was foremost a writer of "the crisp demotic prose pioneered by the *Daily Mail*."[21] In short, he could present actual life so that it conveyed behind it a comic view. All this must have struck a chord in the young Joyce who wanted to fix the historical and cultural moment of his nation, but initially could do only so in a prose as far from "demotic" as possible. In Wallace's combination of serious ideas and events treated in a comic light, Joyce must have found a method that addressed actual events, rather than distant concepts, but conveyed clearly and cleverly a sense of judgment. Certainly with Wallace he found someone who could combine detail with judgment to comic purposes, who could write in a succinct way rather than in attenuated and ponderous abstraction. He read a style that was accurate to the mind and true to the ear, and, because it was so, was funny.

Here is an example from the end of 1905, when we know Joyce was reading Wallace. He writes a series of set biographical pieces on the rulers of czarist Russia in connection with the St. Petersburg riots of the late fall, pieces informative and judgmental both, tinged with critical and barbed commentary. The premise of the series is that the czars of the past have led Russia to the current state of revolution and rebellion. Yet in writing this set of "explanations," it is the comic tone that seems to carry the explanation, rather than any historical or factual causes. A wealth of acute commentary rides on succinct phrases: "Peter [the Great] made Russia what it is to-day. From its alphabet to its cigarette habit—Peter created it. He established autocracy and made revolution possible." Peter "woke Russia . . . with the jab of a surgeon's knife—an amateur surgeon."[22] These sentences are terse and understated in clever balance (quite a contrast to the prolixity and hyperbole of the "Turkey" piece), yet their brevity carries a wealth of meaningful effect, as in the sentence that suggested that the creation of autocracy made revolution possible. There is more in the humorous suggestion that Peter's transformation was both important (the Cyrillic alphabet) and frivolous (a nicotine habit); he combines something serious with something funny, a combination Joyce would learn to exploit. In this pairing of words there is a fine poetic effect of the slightly echoic alphabet/cigarette. Such use of language would not be lost on Joyce, nor could the fact that in the humorous portrayal of events and characters lies the course of history.

That comic tenor was formed by whatever Wallace described in detail; it was the small observations that made the comedy, not the attitude, this the very thing Joyce misses in his earlier writing. Certainly in the example above we can begin to discern the sharp and effective tone of the later *Dubliners*. This is not the tone, however, of Joyce's writings before this date. Joyce may have made his clear remark to Stanislaus about Wallace's being funny because he was indirectly acknowledging that his writing just before this time was in need of a model for humor.[23] (This sort of indirection is Joyce's way of self-criticism and confession.) Even in the first stories of *Dubliners* of 1904–1905 he could write a vague prose and enervated narrative. His writing contemporary with the appearances in the *Homestead* were essays and reviews, pieces of academic juvenalia; these were, without exception, abstract and general, too often reaching for unearned pronouncements and posturing judgments. Abstraction, of course, is intended to address something crucial directly but has a vague emptiness at its center; abstraction is neither clear nor direct, nor, most of all, funny. The Stephen of *Portrait* is similarly abstractly ideational, without specificity or detail. Specificity and particularity, while narrow, common, and seemingly unelevated, allow meaning and judgment to find place in humor beside the detail. This combination was an essential lesson for Joyce to learn. For example, in reviewing a book he found admirable (*The Mettle of the Pasture* by James Lane Allen, in the *Daily Express,* September 7, 1903), Joyce describes in very pale terms a situation he finds crucial to his own artistic and (later) even his personal experience, that of a man who tries to resume a love affair after a remorseful separation. The affair Joyce describes is "renewed again years later when it has passed through the trials which the world proposes to such as would renew any association and so offer offence to time and change" (*CW* 118). The phrase "trials which the world proposes" suggests a lofty sense of retribution that approaches both the themes and the style of Hardy (whom Joyce will accuse to Stanislaus of beating about the bush); this similarity is furthered by the reference to a generic Wessex-like force of "time and change." The daring challenger of this universe is only generally indicated by the vague pronoun "such." Certainly the conflict of an individual in the events of a relationship would have interested Joyce (in "The Dead," *Exiles, Ulysses*), but he describes it here in such an un-Joycean way, that is to say abstractly, palely, without detail. And the strained seriousness forces Joyce uncharacteristically to overlook the potential for humor. When, having become more alert to the effect of every word, would Joyce ever intentionally speak in his own voice the redundancy of "renewed again"? The sentence is so abstract that it seems to deserve the criticism Stephen levels at his own Pateresque musings in "Proteus": "one feels that one is at one with one who once . . ." (*U* 3.146).

While such essays (and there were some twenty-five of them in 1903–1904) are intended primarily to convey judgment by a young man eager to make his mark in letters, their sort of nebulous diction and unearned rhetoric can be found even in a work intended as art, as the essay sketch of "Portrait" or a story such as "After the Race," published in the *Homestead* in 1904, itself a story about a young man of the age Joyce was in 1904. Interestingly, Joyce actually interviewed one of the car drivers for the race that figures in the story, so there ought to be a sense of actual events and lives behind it. Yet the interview (published in the *Irish Times* of April 1904) is an oddly bloodless and disinterested piece. What comes from it is a watered-down story of limp dispassion. Jimmy's reaction to traveling in the fast car (a moment, one would think, of excitement) is described in this languid way: "The journey laid a magic finger of the genuine pulse of life and gallantly the machinery of human nerves strove to answer the bounding courses of the swift blue animal" (D 45); this talks about life but does not enliven it. The artistic figures are only a hodgepodge: medical metaphors ("pulse," "nerves") mix oddly with the near-veterinary image of "the swift blue animal." The "magic finger" is a borrowed literary phrase, used without the stiffening tone of self-awareness of its conventionality. Whatever satire is intended for this piece is blunted by such dull language.

Yet between 1904 (the date of "Race") and 1906, an exposure to a comic context gives Joyce the means to change. In 1906 (when Joyce was reading the *Daily Mail*), Edgar Wallace writes for it an article on the very subject of motoring about which Joyce had already written in "After the Race." Where Joyce strains in his description of "the channels of poverty" of the poor and "gratefully oppressed," Wallace has his poor described actively, and therefore both acerbically and comically: he notes about the little urchins who ran across the road: "The little boys who were pioneers of the 'running across' [the road] game are no longer with us to encourage the present generation" ("The Chauffeur").[24] So light and telling a touch about callous death says much more about poverty, amazement at technology, and the crassness of money than do all the serious and somber elements in "Race," which is, after all, a story about a naif Irish boy who is himself rather run over by the faster members of the European generation. Joyce's languid prose makes him rather slow.

This case, strongly coincidental as it is, not a matter of influence, as there are two years between the two works, with Joyce's coming first. Rather the coincidence may have provided Joyce with the confirmation of an affinity between what he sought to do in the story and what he acknowledged Wallace could do, that is, be funny. (The "Race" story is revised in 1906, although evidently not greatly.) Wallace and his work offered Joyce foremost a portrait-like resemblance, an alternative to what he had hitherto done. Reading Wallace provided Joyce with an echo of the voice he sought to develop, one that sounded like what his own could be (Joyce was always fascinated by the Pentecostal gift of tongues). Much as with Stephen's wish to "meet in the real world the unsubstantial image which his soul so constantly beheld" (*P* 65), so Wallace was, in the daily world of the newspaper, a real voice Joyce had undeveloped within him, one that needed to find substantiation, articulated in the calling of humor. This process of finding manifest outside what is already latent within, seemingly inverted in causality, fits easily with Joyce's artistic practice, as well as his Aristotelian and religious conceptualizations. Wallace's work was a parallel track, one that confirmed Joyce's chosen direction, and provided a guide (Virgil to his Dante); it was a parallel much like the arrangement in the physics theatre of the benches, one before and one behind where the humor is. Reading Wallace, if not this piece then others, was an illumination, something like a plan or sketch of what he would do subsequently—illumination and plan related etymologically to *protrahere* and *protractus*, those words which stand behind *Portrait*. These pieces of Wallace from the *Mail*, whichever in fact they were (and this is not discoverable for sure), form a comic counterpart to the various portraits Joyce would write from 1906 on, for the remainder of *Dubliners*, including "The Dead," *Stephen Hero*, and *Portrait* itself.

With the context of Wallace thus standing behind his own work in 1906 and after, Joyce goes from a sentence in "Race" to one in "Grace." Before Wallace there is this: "Jimmy . . . was at heart the inheritor of solid instincts [and] knew well with what difficulty [the sum] had been got together. . . . if he had been so conscious of the labour latent in money when there had been a question merely of some freak of the higher intelligence, how much more so now when he was about to stake the greater part of his substance" (*D* 44). And after there is this: "Mr Hartford . . . had begun life as an obscure financier by lending small sums of money to workmen at usurious interest. Later on he had become the partner of a very fat short gentleman, Mr. Goldberg, in the Liffey Loan Bank. Although he had never embraced more than the Jewish ethical code his fellow-Catholics . . . spoke of him bitterly as an Irish Jew and an illiterate and saw divine disapproval of usury made manifest through the person of his idiot son. At other times they remembered his good points" (*D* 159). Both are about the same essential subject, money; one is preachy, the other sharply pointed. The earlier one from "Race" is so diffuse as to lose its intended crushing effect. The "labour latent in money" sounds like a phrase from Adam Smith, the "freak of higher intelligence" a text of psychology, the "inheritor of solid instincts" from biology: these are academic borrowings of abstract style, none of them genuine or demotic or funny. The later sentence from "Grace" is so precise as to puncture completely; it has common details of person, place, and religion to make it effectively and vividly comic ("Although he had never embraced more than the Jewish ethical code"). The first example is all large statements ("how much more so now"); the second is telling detail ("the person of his idiot son"). In short, the first is sententious, the second is funny. The first has its tendentiousness in the foreground; the other has humor as its background. This change is a small but sure indication of Joyce's developing tone and perspective, in the use of action and detail, and in a style tighter and more rhythmic. Such a change comes from exposure to conciseness, to detail, to a confidence in style rather than in exhortatory idea, so that the comedy has somewhere to reside and to hide. Wallace, it could be argued, was the *Bildung* that enabled Joyce to go forth on his own.

When Joyce goes forth to encounter the reality of writing, surer of his own comic ability, sentences in *Dubliners* take on a turn of phrase that allows for the comedy latent in common speech to emerge from a cloud of popular style. That is, rather than write in sardonic, judgmental but heavy academic abstraction, Joyce can write a prose that seems to belong to anyone, the common language of the daily paper, but he can give it an artful turn that makes it collapse into a comedy that stands always behind the words. No more the unreflective use of "magic finger"; nearly every sentence has the potential for humor, standing just behind the demotic speech. "Grace" provides just such an example in its description of Martin Cunningham: "He was a thoroughly sensible man, influential and intelligent. His blade of human knowledge, natural astuteness particularised by long association with cases in the police courts, had been tempered by brief immersions in the waters of general philosophy. He was well informed" (*D* 157). The first sentence provides the touch of the consensual, the average values held in common with readers; but the second sentence that tries to make an artful evaluation of Cunningham is laden with cliché and fragile: the "blade" "tempered in the waters" is dull, too much the language of the people. To compound the matter of common assumption, the appositive phrase "natural astuteness," which modifies Cunningham's judgment, is drawn on a false and mistaken etymology of *astute* as "keen and penetrating" like a knife rather than on "sagacious" or "clever." This is the sort of pseudolearning of demotic speech through which humor manifests itself.[25] This is a mixture of the serious and the silly, an attempt at elevation and a comic tumbling in the lowering possibilities of language. Such a mixture is by its very nature inveterate to the common press itself, that mass-audience publication poised uneasily between enlightening and educating a public and also amusing (and satirizing) them.

Joyce was aware of this quality in journalism. We have remarked on the passage in *Hero* where material from the daily paper appears in the novel, with its headlines realistically presented in the text: "EVENING TELEGRAPH [Meeting] Nationalist Meeting at Ballinrobe. Important Speeches. Main Drainage Scheme . . . Death of a Well-known Solicitor . . . Mad Cow at Cabra, Literature &." (*SH* 221). It was argued that, first off, this sort of daily detail is always displaced in *Portrait,* when such quotidian events of the real world are presented in *Hero* as Stephen is engaged, will he, nil he, with actual life. Secondly, and no less importantly, it was noted that this passage's comedy derives, in part, from Flaubert, whose admixture of Boulanger's wooing of Emma with the calls of the Agricultural Fair is a locus of comic disproportion ("—A hundred times I tried to leave, yet I followed you and stayed. . . .—For manures." Part II, chapter 8).[26] There may be other influences in this passage as well, ones that suggest a wide range of contexts for Joyce's work. The death of a "well-known solicitor" may be Joyce's initial working up of the funeral of his father's friend Matthew Kane, a funeral that becomes a central event in the early parts of *Ulysses* (long-range planning is always Joyce's method); that funeral is not only enacted in the text but appears later on in "Eumaeus" as a newspaper account in the very same *Evening Telegraph.*[27] The site of the headlines in *Hero,* chapter 26, is late in its composition (chapter 25 was completed in late summer 1905), and Kane died in 1904; the possibilities of the story of Mr. Hunter were probably forming in Joyce's mind. This is a time, as noted, of fruitful activity for Joyce.

Such fruitful biographical and artistic details aside, the presence of journalism is evident in this passage in another way, beyond the obvious recreation on the page. What animates this passage from *Hero* is not only something like Flaubert's disdain for the public (a disdain shared by Stephen in his own Yonville of Mullingar) but also the effect of journalism which plays to the very same public. (Journalism may at one and the same time—unlike Flaubert—appeal to the very public it holds in some contempt for the ease with which it can be manipulated.) The mix of conveying serious matter with a light tone characterizes the modern newspaper; it is this mixture that Joyce makes evident in the disparity in the headings such as "Mad Cow at Cabra, Literature &."; and it is one Joyce would have encountered in Wallace. This next example of something Joyce may have found in Wallace is again not an influence but a shared tone and concern, a parallel line going in a direction similar to what Joyce will follow. It displays a sensibility and a confirmation concurrent with Joyce's changing writing.

The year 1905 saw the Morocco crisis, a tense event in the imperial chess game when Germany's thrust into Africa brought a sharp response from France concerning its established sphere of influence in the Maghreb. A conference to establish limits was set for Algeciras in late February 1906 and Wallace, now a formidable correspondent, was sent by the *Daily Mail* to cover it (and Joyce, a formidable reader of the *Mail*, may have seen the coverage). One article in his series has his customary light tone, in part because he was not privy to the proceedings but could see them only at a distance, and in part because as British he was only distantly concerned with the more feeble French and German pretension to imperial influence. His description maintains this imbalance and aloofness: "If you can imagine so inconceivable a thing as a hundred people waiting outside County Hall (Spring Gardens, S.W.), speculating upon the passage of the West Tottenham Municipal Improvement Bill, and the interest that the discussion of so important a measure would cause, you can grasp to an extent the interest we feel while the Conference is discussing the Customs of Morocco."[28] This is the comedy of disproportion, of matters of state compared to those insignificantly local, of world issues and mere civic improvement, of weighty politics of potential historical moment with inconsequent simplicity of quotidian details. Yet it is the very same balance Joyce briefly indicates by the shift in his headlines from "Nationalist Meeting" to "Drainage Scheme." Wallace goes on to recognize this disproportion explicitly: "But behind all the quiet amusement engendered by irresponsible talk and the obvious farcical character of the Conference, there is an uneasy feeling ever present that perhaps there is some foundation for the fears that . . . there remains but one solution to the differences of the two nations." That glance at the possible future horror of war is prescient (as imperial aims and local entanglements will bring all Europe to war in just eight more years); yet Wallace seeks to calm and to humor: "The tragedy, however, is but a remote possibility; the humorous aspect of the Conference, on the contrary, is very real." He comes down on the side of the actual and immediate rather than the obscure and future possibility; he tips the balance for the everyday and its comedy. For Wallace the comic was found in the imbalance of the immediate daily simplicity with the weight of politics. For Joyce the same proportion may hold in the headlines "printed" in *Hero:* the drainage schemes are those small municipal gestures, but he may also see in their placement with the "Nationalist meeting" in the small place of Ballinrobe the possibility of a future tragedy of a rebellion. Unlike Wallace, Joyce leaves only implied the potential horror of death: his work is art and not journalism, even if it shares a common focus and tone.

The tension of the comic of the everyday and the tragedy of possible history haunts the *Daily Mail;* in the months Joyce was reading it, there was a serialization of a novel about a German invasion of Britain, part of Lord Northcliffe's jingoism. Joyce would never go so far as to be bellicose, but he recognizes the comedy of disproportion in Wallace and in the pages of the newspaper. *Portrait* turns inward from such uneasy combinations, but the same comic effect of high rhetoric and low actuality will appear most evidently in *Ulysses,* not only in the newspaper office in "Aeolus" but also in "Cyclops." There, high stylistic elements of literary importance (often Joyce's stand-in for the urgent issues of politics) mingle unevenly with the mundane characters and language of barflies and scroungers.[29] "But he, the young chief of the O'Bergan's, could ill brook to be outdone in generous deeds but gave therefor with gracious gesture a testoon of costliest bronze. Thereon embossed in excellent smithwork was seen the image of a queen of regal port . . . . Victoria . . . .—Here you are says Alf, chucking out the rhino." (*U* 12.290–294; 303) This mixture of high and low styles, of epical description and imperial presence, is a comedy in different registers of value and language, and owes much not only to journalism in general, but also again specifically to the Wallace that Joyce found funny.

In October 1906, Wallace has an entirely comic piece, one made up by him of whole cloth rather than a comically embroidered report of a real event, as was that about the Algeciras Conference; it was titled "The Makings Up of Herbert Stagg."[30] As the title suggests, this is a piece of literary self-reflexiveness, with an introduction claiming it to be the "second installment" (research has not turned up a first) of the memories of Herbert Stagg, "written on the backs of billheads ('in account with H. Stagg, General Dealer and Provision Merchant')," part of a proposed serial of an "amazing youth . . . and his . . . dissolute friend, Lord X." It is a pastiche of adventure stories, cowboy and Indian sagas and sea adventures, the stuff of popular literature and of daydreams of greengrocers. Most striking in it are the incongruities of its details: Stagg captains a ship and arrives in New York, there only to encounter hostile Indians on the "bounderless prairie" [*sic*]. The language is equally incongruous, a mingling of different discourses from various genres; the Indian chieftain speaks in a neo-Elizabethan style: "Why comest thou here, paleface . . . ? I have no quarrel with thee, so go hence and smoke the pipe or calumet of peace in thy own wigwam . . . ." This comedy is exactly what Joyce will come to practice. The jarring mixture of popular styles is in fact the method of "Cyclops," in such parts as the report of the hanging and the high epic echoes. That "pipe or calumet of peace" in Wallace is a nearly Joycean, deft touch of an appositive introduced carefully to instruct and elevate the reading public. Joyce's use of the same phrase in "Aeolus" (the newspaper again), "The Calumet of Peace" (*U* 7.464), might even be seen as an homage to Wallace. (Others seem to have been influenced as well; Wallace's article of the adventurous literary fantasies of a greengrocer seems to have inspired the sorts of pieces Thurber would write about Walter Mitty.) While Joyce comes later to the full expression of this humor in *Ulysses,* his exposure to Wallace clearly comes at a point in which his writing and thinking need to be directed, when his voice—academic, abstract, and dry—needs to learn this sort of ventriloquism, projecting away from the somber tendentious abstraction of his early writing as a juvenile academic baccalaureate into a vigorous comic writer. To look ahead is to see where Joyce will go when he goes forth to encounter the reality of writing in the real world, and to see where Joyce was prompted by a comic voice from behind.

So glimpsed here are shadows and other contexts around Joyce, not direct influences; Joyce's comedy develops slowly and implicitly in the years 1905–1906. Surely, however, the parallel lines of Wallace's articles and Joyce's future endeavors suggest that they cross. We see parallels of focus, tone, and even subject that suggest close affinities just over Joyce's shoulder. These affinities begin to shadow Joyce even in writing that is not his art but his communications; the effect of Wallace may even extend to Joyce's personal letters.

Wallace expresses his characteristic comic details with a pointed sketch of frivolous customs and manners of different Continental nationalities, in "The Diary of a 'Special' in a Hurry,"[31] part of which is a vignette contrasting Spanish beggars, crippled and maimed, gathering around the cathedral who can be deterred with a mere gesture of the hand, with those aggressive ones in Paris who flock about hotels and are, in fact, the employees of the establishment: "The Magnificent Mendicant who speaks five languages and directs the porter where to take your trunks, the lesser mendicants who carry the trunks, the little boy mendicant who runs the messages . . . , the shirt-fronted mendicant who bullies the waiters—these all wait to speed the parting guest, shameless beggars, with itching palms." This sketch, displaying precise details for comic effect rather than empty generalities, must certainly have rung true for Joyce, experiencing something similar when traveling to Rome in 1906. Joyce had made much the same observation of his dealings with porters and other who preyed on him on the way: "The money-changer swindled me out of 2 lire, the cabman out of half-a lira, and the railway official out of three lire" (*Letters* II, 145; 07.08.06. (This letter, incidentally, contains the epiphany of the Cockneys and the Coliseum.) While these difficulties were common to all travelers, both Wallace and Joyce detail them, and it is worth remarking that Wallace's article appeared only six weeks before Joyce's letter. What Joyce does here, unlike Wallace, is focus on himself: no amount of reading of other writers of whatever sort could turn Joyce from speaking about himself. *Portrait,* in fact, is the very book of himself. What he may have seen in Wallace, however, was a way to speak of himself with the distancing effect of humor. If Joyce can come to write about himself in personal correspondence, his texts can begin to develop this sort of detailed humor that will allow him to engage comedy.

There may be more than coincidence between Wallace's article and Joyce's letter; there is the likelihood of emulation. In one other letter there is something quite close to imitation; and with possible emulation or imitation there is certainly strong support for the sort of indirect influence of context offered in this chapter. When Joyce, newly arrived in Rome, is actively reading the *Daily Mail,* there is the following piece by Wallace, describing his travails when traveling in hilly Lisbon: "I alighted at the station, descended four flights of stairs, and found myself on a level with the street. Being curious, I reascended the stairs—four flights, with the temperature at 80 degrees—found another exit—on a level with the street. There was a spiral staircase that led to the roof. 'Where does that go to?' I asked an official. 'To the street,' he replied." (The article appeared on July 3, 1906.)[32] Joyce describes to Stanislaus the difficulty of looking for a flat on arrival in Rome: "If you had to traipse about a city, accompanied by a plaintive woman with infant (also plaintive), run up stairs, ring a bell, 'Chi c'è?' 'Camera.' 'Chi c'è?' 'Camera.' No go: . . . Down again. Rush off" (*Letters* II, 203). The parallelism of "plaintive woman with infant (also plaintive)" is an economical comic touch of which Joyce was hitherto incapable. The date of this description of the experience is July 12, a little more than a week after Wallace's. Joyce's letters to Stanislaus from this time begin themselves to be narrative. Always plaintive, certainly, they begin to present details of Joyce's dealings with life and offer fewer literary pronouncements, so that even his correspondence, as his story-writing, becomes more vivid and concrete.

So that, much as within his personal correspondence, the context of Wallace read—absorbed and even emulated—is what takes Joyce a long way from a student at UCD to a writer on the Continent, from a character within his autobiographical works to the writer of those works. After reading Wallace, Joyce begins to find the means to treat his story of himself. It is not a matter of distancing himself from his own experience but rather a matter of Joyce being able to get behind the writing of his story. Wallace standing behind Joyce, providing a context, is what takes Joyce from the first "Portrait" essay of 1904 to *Stephen Hero;* in both pieces the subject is the same, Joyce fictionalizing himself, but the first suffers from the abstraction that seems inevitably part of Joyce's early writing with its academic posturing, while the second is something that begins to have presence in the text and wry comedy behind it. We can measure the way Joyce begins to treat the material of his life with humor; once attained, that humor can be subtly hidden behind as in *Portrait*. First, however, it must be obtained. The 1904 "Portrait" essay has a level of abstraction so large as to attenuate it into ephemerality. The essay seems only to creep up on the life experiences it claims are so crucial to individuality; it is oddly impersonal and so unclear as to lack any specific individuation. A critique of fellow students at University College, in which Joyce's disdain for their caution and lack of intellectual adventure is an essential point, is greatly mitigated in its effect by the very similar conventionality and caution of his earlier style: "Wherefore, neglecting the wheezier brayings in that chorus which no leagues of distance could make musical, he began loftily diagnosis of the younglings. His judgment was exquisite, deliberate, sharp; his sentence sculptural."[33] With this passage, Joyce tries to fix the cultural moment of his time with attempted scathing commentary; however, insofar as this passage enacts a judgment on contemporaries, it stands in danger of being charged with the same faults. For one, the diction is too stock and ready set. "Younglings" is an odd note describing contemporaries. "Wheezier" is hardly an adjective with which to deride conventional thinking, itself being so conventional, and "brayings" is similarly a cliché in the absence of any extension into other verbal images. "Chorus" is all too ready a term for a concerted reaction to have any weight. "Diagnosis" is derived, distantly, from an Ibsenesque sense of medical precision. The entire passage is weighted with borrowed diction unreflectively employed. The perspective of the passage is supposed to have some distance, a distance indicated by the separation of the character by "leagues" from the sound of others (And isn't that leagues a Tennysonian touch?). Yet that distance is earned from no deliberation but merely from the vagueness of the wording. In fact, while Joyce's judgment about the students may be true, it can hardly be described in the terms used—"exquisite, deliberate, sharp"—nor can this sentence be at all called sculptural. This is simply straining to make a case by mere assertion, without detail or verbal texture to carry off the point. There is no life here conveyed clearly enough to have the too heavy ridicule be felt; there is nothing on which to hang a weighted judgment or to carry humor. Without the liveliness of presentation, the acerbic tone is only bile without art.

The hovering presence of Wallace has influenced the way Joyce depicts what he wishes to judge, specifically to the point of his own attitude to his past of academic posturing and that of his peers. Thus there is a more deft comic hit contained in the extant manuscript of *Stephen Hero,* which was produced in great measure in 1906. The issue is here identical, an attempt to deride the students at the college, but by 1906, after Wallace, Joyce has perhaps heard in the voice the means by which to carry out this comic thrust. (Consistent in both this passage and the essay is the claim that an appreciation for Ibsen was for Joyce a shibboleth of sensibility.) "The young men of the college had not the least idea who Ibsen was but from what they could gather here and there they surmised that he must be one of the atheistic writers whom the papal secretary puts on the *Index.* It was a novelty to hear anyone mention such a name in the college but as the professors gave no lead in condemnation they concluded that they had better wait" (*SH* 41).

Not only is this passage more focused than its earlier avatar in the essay, it is more direct, less cluttered in syntax, and more pointed in diction; it avoids gratuitous overreaching and instead, through effective word choice, points right to where the effect should go. It enacts a scene and speaks with recognizable voices and attitudes. And, for all these reasons, it is more comic. As in the "Portrait" essay, the students come in for a disdainful treatment, but here that treatment is literary and not mere name-calling. The passage brings a metaphor vividly to life: rather than being termed asses by their braying, as did the "Portrait" essay, the students are here shown to be sheepish; they are the flock of the godly shepherds of the college. There is a controlled wit to this brief description and that wit extends outward to students and teachers; it is convincing because it is artistic, not earnest.

This artistry is carried further in *Portrait,* but put at some remove because that text moves to greater immediacy in presentation. The humor, being mastered, can become more displaced and indirect. No longer is there a narrator coming between Stephen and the reader; rather the immediacy of Stephen's thoughts in indirect discourse displaces the presence of a narrator. The very students who come in for the narrator's harsh comments have a presence in this text; they talk so that the reader can hear, as in this active scene in *Portrait* where the fellow students, similar to the ones merely described in the earlier two versions, here rather speak and act up regarding the Peace Rescript of Czar Nicholas. In this dramatized scene, no longer controlled (as are the essay and *Hero*) by a narrator bent on making his point, we can trace the comedy behind *Portrait.* This humor is illuminated by the context of Joyce's having read Wallace, because there is certainly some of Wallace's ear for a turn of phrase and some of his eye for detail. There may be also some gesture to Wallace's treatment of the czars.

This confrontation about the petition is a scene which, at first glance, conveys another moment where Stephen stands in opposition to those around him, a scene crucial to a narrative of the development of his person and soul. He rejects the empty political rhetoric and gestures of his lesser colleagues in the university, placing himself in lonely opposition: "My signature is of no account . . . You are right to go your way. Leave me to go mine" (198). Certainly the signature of the artist is no small thing to be sullied by being placed on a petition along with many others. Stephen is willing to risk the ridicule of the zealous McCann, even to the point being called one of the "minor poets" suffering from "Intellectual crankery" (197, 199). Such is the price, of course, of the poet's independence, which must be maintained through acerbic and ready repartee. Stephen is up to that task, acute in his responses: (of the picture of the czar) "He has the face of a besotted Christ," a comment terse and filled with anger. He is mocking and cynical: "Keep your icon. If we must have a Jesus, let us have a legitimate Jesus"(198), the word "icon" clearly a jab at both the students' blind faith and their Russophilia.

Yet undergirding this serious and purposeful exchange, necessary for the development of the protagonist, is that comic alternative that always runs just behind the crucial and climactic. For one, Stephen's retort about Christ is—as well as pointed—humorous, because it contains studied ambiguities: the czar an unlikely Christ, and Christ unlikely to be besotted. Behind this comic idea lies an entire, other context of Joycean humor, that of Gogarty's joking "Ballad" where Jesus sings of His making and drinking wine (although Scripture would claim that He drank). The idea of a drunken Jesus in the last chapter of *Portrait* is a touch that will later open up to the overt joking quality in the beginning of *Ulysses,* so that here is the sort of connection from one text to another of humorous moments that readers come to expect and value about Joyce's comic consistency. In fact, not only is Mulligan the comic counterpart of the real-life Gogarty of Joyce's acquaintance, but he has his counterpart in this text as well; another avatar of them both, Mulligan and Gogarty, appears in the same chapter of *Portrait* in the figure of Goggins. Comic shadows such as these lurk behind much of this scene.

Temple's response to Stephen's comment on the legitimate Jesus is another place where comic alternatives can be seen connecting, not one text with another, but parts of this text (another feature readers associate with Joyce's comic methods). Temple, we have noted, is an outsider and is in some ways a comic alternative to the serious Stephen. When Temple asks, "Do you believe in Jesus? I believe in man" (198), he conflates the very nature of sotorology; this comic combination (of the doubled discourse of comedy) goes back to Stephen's own scholarly musings as a schoolboy in chapter 3, when he wonders whether the Host contains the presence of both God and man. He does not hear the answer his classmate vocally provides, "Here he is! Here he is," nor does he notice Temple's question. Stephen's all too earnest theology there tempered by the voices of others always unheard by him is extended here to meet with Temple's too earnest humanitarianism. One serious place in the text with humor behind it is connected to another by its comic alternative to make a continuing undercurrent of comedy.

In the debate concerning the petition, the earnest McCann refers to the crusading journalism of William Stead to buttress his support for disarmament and international harmony, invoking Stead's reformist zeal expressed in his crusading journalism. We have noted that Stead is a comic stand-in as well: behind the ringing heroic closing diary entry of "go forth" there is the request to "stand in good stead" to make a comic doubling. Behind McCann's invocation of the journalist Stead is another invocation of another journalist whose work wrought a reformation—that of Wallace and his effect on Joyce. The oblique reference to a journalist, presented in the indirect discourse, is an emblem of the indirect yet effective presence of Wallace on Joyce's work. That Stead was known for his anti–Boer War sentiment, while Wallace began his career as a reporter in that war, gives an additional gloss to this allusion.

The tone and focus Joyce found congenial and worthy of emulation in Wallace is suggested in this passage, mediated by the czar and Stead; *Portrait* has its comedy always by indirection, over the shoulder and to the side. Yet Joyce could be direct in his comedy. The immediate presence of Wallace and the clearest evidence of his effect on the Joyce of 1906 is to be seen in the foreground of *Stephen Hero*. That book, so long and loose as to cause Joyce despair, abandoned by him in favor of another, presents its comic tone directly. The student McCann who appears seriously in *Portrait* and receives the indirect effect of Stephen's comments there comes in for a direct comic hit in *Hero,* in the form of low punning name-calling by Stephen himself; it is the sort of humor one would expect from a collegian. "McCann was never spoken of as anything but 'Phil.' Stephen used to call him 'Bonny Dundee' nonsensically associating his brisk . . . manners with the sound of the line: 'Come fill up my cup, come fill up my can'" (*SH* 44). "McCann/my can" is low paronomasia, pairing two words only for humorous effect, quite like Wallace's pairing of "cigarette" with "alphabet" and similar to the doubled language that indirectly effects somber moments in *Portrait*. It would be difficult to consider the Stephen of *Portrait* making this sort of direct joke, although the Joyce of college days did.

The controlling narrative voice in *Hero* is as direct and unabashed in its humorous presentation as is Stephen there; his tone has an ironic understatement and a comic turn of phrase that quite resemble Wallace's. Of the issue of Stephen's paper "Drama and Life" that constitutes the rising conflict of the extant part of the manuscript, the narrator makes this observation of the attitude of the cautious faculty about their charge's free thinking: "His were simply theories and, as he had as yet committed no breach of the law, he was respectfully invited to read a paper before the . . . College" (*SH* 39). In this one can hear the same construction of a thought that turns unexpectedly to comic effect as Wallace's "the little boys who were the pioneers of the 'running across' game are no longer with us to encourage the present generation." This bemused commentary, spiced with startling comic turns, seems unique to Joyce in this period of 1906, present in many of the *Dubliners* and certainly foregrounded in *Hero*. Here is a narrative statement about Stephen's striving for autonomy that expresses a particular attitude to what is, after all, the essential direction of the novel of development; it seems a gloss on the novel's genre: "[T]he representatives of authority cherished the hope that his unguided nature would bring him into such lamentable conflict with actuality that they would one day have the pleasure of receiving him officially into some hospital or asylum" (*SH* 179). Nowhere in *Portrait* would the reader expect to find such a comic statement, least of all one that is so clearly a humorous comment on the novel's own generic form.

In great measure, *Hero* is a funny text, certainly funnier than the *Portrait* which supplants and obscures it. In fact, *Portrait,* with its displacing comedy over the shoulder, has done so with its earlier, comic version. With more depiction of the actual world, with vulgar and common language, *Stephen Hero* is the major comic context behind *Portrait,* and it has been preserved in an economical, if oblique way.

4

Obscure Arts and the Economy of Vulgar Language

Because Joyce's comic style was not autogeneric, but had some surrounding contexts, so too does *Portrait* itself have an origin. Nearly all works presuppose a predecessor, a version that stands behind the final published one. That earlier version is hidden away, unpublished, sometimes even destroyed. Frequently, that other earlier version is of a different spirit; the mind of the artist in it is unlike the mind in the later. Earlier drafts, often quite different, stand in some obscurity behind the published work. *Stephen Hero* is the earlier version of *Portrait*; so obscured that it was claimed that Joyce sought to burn it in the fire.[1] It is something quite different from the published work: longer and more detailed where *Portrait* is more focused and condensed. All of its features are put into obscurity by the final version of *Portrait*.

An epigraph bespeaks origin because it is the first part of a text, literally standing before and above the text proper. Though encountered first, an epigraph is not the essential body of the text, so it stands apart from a work in time and place. An appendage in the beginning, the epigraph falls, as it were, to the side or behind the main impetus of the plot as the new text is read so that its relation to the text becomes obscure. An epigraph additionally bespeaks origin in that it points as much to a previous text as to the one it stands above: an epigraph points to earlier texts, in the behind of the past, indicating anteriority by being taken often from a text of some antiquity. The epigraph to *Portrait* has such an anteriority because it comes from an ancient work, *The Metamorphoses*.

Having been taken from its original context, however, the epigraph's meaning is changeable. The epigraph to *Portrait* has its own determined interpretation within the context of Ovid, when Daedalus is said to have "turned his mind to obscure arts" (as Anderson translates it), going from elementary things to esoterica.[2] Yet once a passage is removed from its context, the determinants are lost, and the epigraph as it now appears has a certain latitude and license. The epigraph to *Portrait* might be seen as referring in only the slenderest way to Ovid, through the connection with Daedalus; it may refer rather more to *Portrait*.[3] Because an epigraph refers to earlier origins, it may as well indicate the earlier versions or drafts of the final published text in which it appears. It also seems to point to the earlier version of which the *Portrait* has two (the earliest essay and *Hero*), and it does so in ways that suggest why each earlier version was hidden and obscured.

So it is necessary to take a different look at the epigraph, because of the changeableness of its position and its indication of something earlier, to view it alternately as referring to something in the past, behind *Portrait*. "*Et ignotas animum dimittit in artes*" begins with a conjunction, so that grammatically it suggests that something comes before and connects its position before *Portrait* with something earlier. The epigraph might well then characterize *Portrait*'s change and development from *Hero*. It has been long assumed (and tacitly) that *Portrait* substantially supplants *Hero* in all respects, "less incriminating, more urbane," more immediate in presentation, fuller in imagery.[4] *Portrait* is, of course, more economical and formalist; the earlier version is detailed and leisurely, a projected sixty-four chapters (!). (It was written in 1905–1906, that time when Joyce was reading Wallace; see previous chapter.) The extant manuscript, covering the years of Stephen at University College (only chapter 5 in the final version) is longer than the whole of *Portrait*. The many pages projected for *Hero* led Joyce to state, "This is a terrible opus: I wonder how I have the patience to write it. Do you think other people will have the patience to read it?"[5] Ellmann goes so far as to note that Joyce rewrote *Stephen Hero* "completely."[6] That rewriting was economical and concise: *Hero* contains many scenes in detail only alluded to in *Portrait*; it has a diffuse and extended style, while *Portrait* is focused and symbolic.[7] *Hero* concerns events in external narrative voice, *Portrait* is internalized. "Dimittere" in poetic usage means to direct or apply as in turn to, so the epigraph from Ovid is apt in that *Portrait* is a text in which the mind of the artist is applied to arts (of style and language) more obscure than those in the earlier version: more elliptical, more internal, more symbolic, more figurative. The "dimittit" of the epigraph constitutes a gesture of renunciation, a turning one's back on: such is the step of moving away from an earlier version to a later.

Yet "anima" means not only mind but also memory, a remembrance of a text passed. Furthermore, it is also spirit or disposition, so that the temperament might be subject to the renouncing. Stephen theorizes in *Hero* about the classical temper that accepts and works within convention, and that term "temper" might well be understood as "anima." The epigraph suggests that the temperament or spirit of the artist is changed from earlier draft to final version.

In an alternate reading, because the alternate is essential to the comic spirit, rather than the mind turning, the temper (or spirit) turns away, and what it disregards are those "ignotas artes," obscure arts. This phrase is problematic as to what is intended by these obscure or unknown arts, even in Ovid but especially in Joyce. *Portrait* is a text that seems to avoid the esoterica that will characterize *Ulysses* or *Wake*; indeed the arts within it are studiously academic, traditional, and overt: Aristotle, Aquinas, Newman, and the like. Yet "ignotas" may have an alternate meaning, not as obscure as unknown, but also as strange, foreign, or alien. In the change, therefore, from *Hero* to *Portrait*, the mind or spirit of the artist is turned to arts that are alien or strange to his temperament. The complete lines from Ovid end with "naturamque novat," changes the laws of nature; Joyce's nature is one of humor, which he changes in *Portrait*. Such a reading makes the epigraph pertinent in that *Portrait* is a serious work different in tone from the rest of Joyce's works, and that Joyce by temperament was a humorous companion and a comic writer. So what might be turned away from are the arts of *Hero*, no longer evident, now hidden in obscurity. In Skeat's *Dictionary*, valued by Stephen (and see below), "obscure" is defined as "covered over"; this is an action similar to Stephen closeting away his humor. There is much humor in *Hero*, in many different manifestations: puns, wry satire, broad comedy, sexual suggestiveness, even vulgarity; in *Portrait* there is a turning away from these arts that Joyce practiced often elsewhere. As a funnier text, *Hero* is a demonstration that Joyce was a humorous writer and that he could conceive of his youth in that spirit. The epigraph is openly pertinent in this way, relevant to the issue of humor as well as to the quality of the manuscript itself, as "dimitto" can mean to turn away from, as to renounce, or dismiss. *Portrait* rather thoroughly renounces the open humor of Joyce's nature seen in *Hero*, placing it into obscurity, covering it over with the seriousness of the later text.

So the epigraph can be disassociated from Ovid and, coming before *Portrait*, might be seen to indicate what has been put behind it, the early version of *Hero*.[8] In general, the epigraph suggests otherness in anteriority; it signals the difference between one sort of art behind the present one. In particular, the epigraph indicates a turning from or renunciation of arts toward the foreign and alien. *Portrait* seems to put behind it the sprawling, detailed expansiveness and directness of the earlier version, and it seems to renounce the humor so evident in the draft for a somber spirit alien to Joyce's temper. What is other, what is behind, is the comic element of *Portrait*, and what is behind *Portrait* itself, renounced and made obscure, is *Hero*. The epigraph gestures to something that stands just behind *Portrait*, something in a space of otherness and alternation; it also signals the disposition of *Hero* behind in time. Behind *Portrait* there is *Hero* and in that space of behindness or alternative the comedy is the focus of the epigraph's diversionary glance. *Stephen Hero* stands behind *Portrait*, in obscurity, and because it is in that other place, *Hero*, like the comic Irishman in the bench behind, is a source of alternate light and humor in *Portrait's* final version.

There are two effects here to the relation of manuscript to published text—two effects that parallel the two meanings of "dimitto" in the epigraph (as it pertains to *Hero*) as "renounce" or "dismiss." First, there is the renunciation of the outright comedy in *Hero* for the serious obscurity of the novel's telic drive. Second, there is the dismissal of the direct style of common, lesser things in the earlier version for the narrow, elevated, and poetic style of the later text. Yet for all the turning away and renouncing, there is a sort of a return of the very elements renounced, as humor cannot be closeted away. The renunciation cannot prevent a return of the elements it seeks to dismiss. By putting away or obscuring the comedy, and all that it requires of the common and the base, *Portrait* maintains its serious tone; yet the presence, behind in the past, of the comic forthrightness of *Hero* colors and shades by contrast the material of *Portrait*, even the most solemn parts of it.

The features of *Hero* return from behind *Portrait*, something like a loan or debt that comes due. "Dimitto" may also mean to discharge an obligation or debt, and there is something that *Portrait* still owes to the earlier text. Certain elements are saved and preserved from the manuscript, elements of language and tone; while these are obscured in *Portrait*, turned away and covered over, they are to be glimpsed in intensely artful passages of seriousness. There they seem to undermine and threaten the serious writing with a comic collapse. The language of the elements Joyce found to be too common and too low for his elevated purpose in the rewritten *Portrait* he sought to renounce and dismiss. Yet his later writing owes a debt to its origin, to what lies behind it; the language of *Hero* forms a context for *Portrait* even more immediate and innate than the contexts of journalism Joyce read before writing, because that language is his own work as a source. Such common language lies just behind the serious purpose of *Portrait,* and its obscure presence gives the elevated striving of the text a comic, if distanced humor, because it is the language of the everyday and the ordinary that denotes the life that Stephen always avoids in *Portrait.* The connections of *Hero* with *Portrait* reinforce the kind of conflation of differing texts that was part of the comedy of word pairs, with one word glossed as an alternative to make comedy. The two texts, earlier and later, stand in a contrasting relationship of the humorous with the somber; so much so, in fact, that within *Portrait* is one playful pair of words that reflect the etymology of the epigraph. Stephen is twice accused of heresy, that sin of turning away from orthodoxy—once when he admits by force to Heron that Byron is no good, once in his essay submitted to Mr. Tate. Both "admit" and "submit" echo in doubled language the verb "dimitto." The presence of this language, just behind the serious text, we have seen cause the direction and drive of the novel to tumble into humorous capering; in much the same way, *Hero,* with its obvious humor and more general language, is another source of the comic behindness that makes *Portrait* caper and tumble even as it tries to keep its origins covered over and behind it.

Much is lost, when there is this turn from humor and the ordinary, much of a tenor whose absence marks *Portrait* in a harsher if more concentrated light. When *Portrait* is refocused and narrowed, there is a renunciation of the detail and everyday descriptions of the earlier version.[9] While this narrowing makes for a heightened increase in psychological immediacy, the later text is so interiorized (so focused on Stephen) that, as we have seen in chapter 1, the real, the actuality of life and therefore the material where comedy is to be found is displaced. One effect of the turning away from *Hero's* expansiveness to *Portrait's* concentration is the removal of entire dramatic scenes.[10] (One might call this removal a sort of censorship of the immediate.)[11] Here is where the other people around Stephen are removed, their voices silenced in the text.[12] What is lost, along with the dramatic immediacy and external reality, are the sources of humor: the everyday life of common elements that is the essential source of comedy. In the larger, if looser, scope of the first text there is room for actual events and for a comic tone, and that room is clearly in the foreground.[13] There are scenes important to the plot of *Hero* (important, that is, to its generic drive as a novel of development) that are not even obliquely mentioned in the redacted and refocused *Portrait:* the attempted seduction of Emma, the discussion with the mother about literature, and the conflict with the president of the college about giving the paper on Ibsen. These scenes are not only present in full, they are given a comic gloss as well (so that *Hero* can be said to have more plot and a broader tone). The humorous cast of common things is evident, not obscured.

Such openness and detail allow for comedy. The scene between Stephen and his mother is compressed in *Portrait,* where May Dedalus merely reprimands her tardy university-going eldest for his attitude and he allows himself to be infantilized by her by washing his face; their exchange is limited to a statement and response: "—Ah, it's a scandalous shame for you, Stephen, said his mother, and you'll live to rue the day you set your foot in that place. I know how it has changed you.—Good morning, everybody, said Stephen, . . . kissing the tips of his fingers in adieu" (*P* 175). We have seen in this exchange how the narrative conflates the language of "rue/adieu/lane," with this humor obliquely to the side. By contrast, this scene in *Hero* is direct and expansive; it takes place over several days in narrative time and it involves a discussion between the two, with the child teaching the parent about literature, both the roles and the subject unlikely. It begins with a particular combination of the domestic context with intellectual matters, of Mrs. Dedalus ironing while Stephen reads his important essay on literature and life; and it seems characteristic of *Hero* to have ironing as its focus rather than irony. In moments of homeliness, there can be something generous and comic. The narrator's description of Mrs. Dedalus's attitude has just this combination of perception and humor (the combination Joyce may have read in Edgar Wallace, as we saw in the previous chapter). When she wonders whether when Stephen thinks so much about "Beauty" he may in fact be rather considering something licentious, the narrator concludes with this comment on her fears: "as the essayist's recent habits were not very re-assuring she decided to combine a discreet motherly solicitude with an interest, which without being open to the accusation of factitiousness was at first intended as a compliment" (*SH* 84). The mother's wisdom is of a piece with the narrator's—both are generous and genial. Mrs. Dedalus takes an interest in Ibsen, yet that interest is open to the limit of her understanding, ignorance of art being an opening where comedy can enter. Her general question about Ibsen is restricted to, "Is he alive at present?," a circumlocutous phrasing made to sound more educated and less unsure than if she were to ask: "Is he still living?" The Stephen of another novel might respond to this query as the Stephen of *Ulysses* does when in discussion with intellectuals in the National Library in "Scylla" to the effect that, like Monsieur Palisse, Ibsen is alive right up until the moment of his death. The Stephen of *Hero* has tried to convince his mother that art is not an escape from life but is central to it, so he must take what life gives back to him. This is an attitude honored in *Hero* but breached in *Portrait;* and is precisely measured by the fact that this exchange of mother and son makes up the life that *Portrait* turns from by omitting. Stephen refrains from any sardonic reaction to his mother's unintentionally comic question and equally restrains from sarcasm again when his mother, after reading Ibsen for a day or two, makes her quite commonplace judgment: "I think that Ibsen . . . has an extraordinary knowledge of human nature" (*SH* 87). While this is as conventional and common a response as might be expected, Stephen is generous to his mother, however, with a notable equipoise: his critical self resisting her banal judgment but his emotional self recognizing her enthusiasm (he was "contented with this well-worn generality as he recognised in it a genuine sentiment"). The balance between well-worn generality and genuine sentiment is a delicate one, because it takes both intellect and emotion into account; Stephen and *Hero* are both capable of it. The entire vignette has a generosity, a sense of concern, and a communality that *Portrait* lacks: Stephen and his mother talk and exchange ideas; emotions are conveyed and understood. Where *Portrait* seeks to convey strife and tension, *Hero* (even with Stephen's attempt to break free as an artist) has a communal view and a sense of generosity that encourages humor. That is why this scene can be about attitudes toward both art and emotions, genuine enough to be generous and thus allow both art and emotion to be colored with humor.

Generosity need not be a necessary prelude to humor: sometimes a sharpened edge is useful, one that allows for forthrightness. *Hero* is certainly direct where *Portrait* is oblique, effacing the earlier text's directness into tangience. Where *Portrait* is silent about Stephen's feelings for Emma, *Hero* is far more loquacious. The scene in which Stephen asks Emma directly for one night of passion together has an immediacy that foregrounds desire and appetite. The hoped-for seduction of Emma is rendered in arch dialogue with a schoolmate: " —Would you like me to seduce her? —Very much. It would be interesting. —Ah, it wouldn't be possible . . . You know, Lynch, said Stephen, we may as well acknowledge openly and freely. We must have women" (*SH* 191). This is the genuine language of young men: it is honest and forthright about desire and humorous in its banter. Stephen would never be so direct or so funny in the later text about emotions and the lower appetites that often make for humor. Such impulses are in fact what drives life and the art that seeks to convey it (a point which Stephen argues to his mother); they are the elements that are suppressed in the *Portrait* in favor of ideational focus and oblique treatment of actuality.

Regarding another crucial adolescent concern, *Portrait* omits completely the issue of Stephen's writing and reading the paper "Drama and Life" (an event crucial in Joyce's life as it was in Stephen's); it is as if external events have little pertinence to Stephen's interiorized development. Humor, however, justifies even Stephen's signal moment in the plot of *Hero*, his being chosen for the paper "Drama and Life" because of both his mind and his character; yet his triumph is not due entirely to his sterling qualities. The passage in which the authorities of the university consider both his ideas and his as-yet uncriminal behavior has been cited as an example of a comic tone derived from sources: the young scholar "had as yet committed no breach of the law" (*SH* 39). Even the aftermath of Stephen's having delivered the paper is no pure achievement but colored with humor, because the presentation leaves some of his audience puzzled: Stephen's high-mindedness is questioned into comedy by an uncertain listener who asks whether "the essayist was supposed to intend parts of his essay as efforts at practical joking" (*SH* 102). This comment is particularly apt, as Stephen's most serious effort is seen as humorous. What are only suggestions and lacunae in *Portrait* are fully rendered actions in *Hero*, and, when rendered, are put in comic lights. With these omissions, the later text obscures the central events in the life of the protagonist, the places where he actually comes up against the conventionality of those around him, and those conflicts are shown to have even a humorous side.

In the interview with the president of the college regarding the content of this paper, Stephen's own thought to introduce the president to the works of Ibsen is conveyed with a touch of petulant humor: "Stephen had the impulse to say 'Excuse me for five minutes while I send a telegram to Christiania' but he resisted his impulse" (*SH* 94). He certainly seeks to get the approval of the master of art rather than that of the college. In fact, the repetitions of the word "impulse" in the beginning and end of this short sentence may seem (on the part of the artist) to be inattention to the requirements of art for sparseness and focus. Yet the repetition is rather an indication of the very sort of lively spontaneity that Stephen has here in the earlier text and which both later character and text lack; the sentence has an overt comic air that is quite missing in anything found in *Portrait*. The narrative immediately goes on to judge Stephen's behavior rather directly as regards this liveliness: "During the interview he had occasion more than once to put severe shackles on this importunate devil within him whose appetite was on edge for the farcical" (*SH* 94). With this, the earlier text forthrightly acknowledges Stephen's own comic impulsiveness which *Portrait* eschews and rather associates it with the humorous source of misrule and antic behavior: "impulse" and "appetite" are the features of the carnivalesque belly. These are qualities that *Hero* names directly, but which *Portrait* only obscures just as it has effaced this earlier scene.

Yet in fact, by the very nature of obscuring, traces remain in *Portrait;* such indeed is the point of having an epigraph that indicates origin while claiming to renounce it but yet retaining an impulse that cannot be renounced. Elements of *Hero* remain in *Portrait,* even and specifically (for our purposes) elements of humor. We would not expect to find this trace material in the same place, rather transferred, but it is present, as this "importunate devil" of the comic with his "appetite" for the farcical, not to be denied, recurs. Although effaced, he appears in *Portrait* in various forms, suggesting that hidden within the text is the very sort of humor that is evident more frequently in *Hero.* The word "farcical"—with the broad comedic strokes it suggests—occurs somewhat fittingly in the school play at Whitsuntide, where Stephen is said to have "the chief part, that of a farcical pedagogue" (*P* 73). What is striking here is the idea that Stephen's comic abilities appear in the later text only in a wholly postured role; that is, the comic license of his character can only take the form of playacting in response to authority (his schoolmates note his ability to "take off" the rector "rippingly" [*P* 76]). Thus the "devil" that needs to be shackled in the collegiate Stephen is relegated to the acting of a part in *Portrait* by the boy "at the end of his second year at Belvedere."

Yet *Portrait* cannot defer Stephen's tendency to farce indefinitely; the devil that is put behind the text must make his comic appearance. What is "importunate" about the farcical is the fact that it cannot be restrained— the comedy will out in *Portrait,* despite its attempt to obscure and turn away from it.[14] In one such scene, we are told that he had eaten his dinner with a "surly appetite" as Stephen considers that he had fallen to the "state of a beast that licks his chaps after meat" (*P* 111). The devil's appetite for the farcical from the *Hero* text can be glimpsed as alternately present in *Portrait,* where the need of the stomach, both venal and a source of commonness, is reduced to the feral. It is not the belly that dominates *Portrait* but rather the mind that treats all things physical as low. It is important to remember that Stephen is described in this way in the classroom of mathematics at the beginning of chapter 3, a scene discussed fully because of the antic notions which come to the foreground there; it is the same, full scene where the day "tumbles clownishly" and where both students and sticks have heads. Even in the obscurity of a clownish dusk, where *Portrait* seeks to obscure the appetite and veil the antic, there is a glimpse of the comedic counterpart from its obscured past that gives *Portrait* its lightness.

It is quite possible that this devilish appetite lurks even behind a part of *Portrait* where Stephen makes a cerebral effort at intellectual theorizing. His consideration of the Aquinian notion of the good toward which tends the appetite ("appetitus") strongly suggests such a place where Stephen's serious intellectual moments are flavored with comic valuation. The importunate devil can be counted on to appear when the text of *Portrait* strives to be most serious and least farcical. We have noted in chapter 1 that there is a humorous quality to Stephen's theories; it requires a glance at the side, through the obscurity of the serious text, to glimpse the importunateness just behind.

In the omission in *Portrait* of these entire scenes in *Hero* (the discussion with the mother, the presentation of the paper), we see how even within crucial issues a very obvious comic temper is renounced and turned into obscurity. Moreover, not only are whole scenes suppressed, but wholesale verbal humor is too. Humor is more evident and more open in the earlier text; it belongs to all of its parts, crucial or commonplace. In the fact that the text is more open, more sprawling, there is more room in it for the sort of humor which was Joyce's natural tendency, and the tenor of his own lived youth and of the contexts he read. There is no need for humor to be found behind and over the shoulder when it can take a place in the forefront. *Portrait*, with its intensity and terseness, must push comedy behind, as an alternate, just as it has pushed certain scenes and nearly all of *Hero* behind and into obscurity.

There is laughter in *Hero*. In response to a story by Maurice about his own naivete, Stephen laughs so loudly (*SH* 59) that bystanders hear it. The physical activity of Stephen's laughing is conspicuously absent from the latter text; most laughter is at his expense, such as the reception of his responses when first asked at Clongowes whether he kissed his mother (14). Even if the word and its derivatives are mentioned some eighty times, there is little action. The noise resonates in the earlier text when in the later laughter is a sound made silent, turned into a surd. In *Hero*, the humor ranges from the basest elements upwards. Characters use language to make obvious puns, of the lowest sort of vaudeville humor, thus sustaining the comedy: when in the political debates at the university one student defends in bog Latin a zealous colleague as "Patrioticus est" another retorts that, "yes, he is a patriotic 'cus" (*SH* 108); by contrast, the humor of the political students in *Portrait's* chapter 5 is of a much more rarified order. Stephen is not above making this sort of pun himself, as we have seen in his descending to a very obvious part of anatomy to make a joke on the too-serious McCann's name and "my can"(44). In *Hero* Stephen jokes about masturbation in the same terms that Mulligan will use in *Ulysses:* "my countrymen have not yet advanced as far as the machinery of Parisian harlotry because . . . they can do it by hand . . ."(*SH* 55). Readers are accustomed to this sort of base humor of the carnivalesque as being associated with someone other than Stephen.

No part of the text is immune from laughter, as even the privilege of indirect discourse descends into humor; the narrative form in which *Portrait* expresses most prominently deep psychological states can here convey laughter: "Stephen mumbled his thanks [to an invitation to dinner] and decided that he would endure severe bodily pain rather than visit Mr Garvey" (*SH* 251). The sentence seems so fresh and funny by contrast to the near-constant solemnity usual in indirect discourse. Even when Stephen's thoughts in *Hero* are presented in interior monologue (a technique little used if at all in *Portrait*) they are rendered in a humorous tone; here is one which concerns serious issues of sin and desire and impulse (those subjects that tend so easily to comedy): "There are some people in this island who sing a hymn called 'Washed in the Blood of the Lamb' by way of easing the religious impulse. Perhaps its a question of diet but I would prefer to wash in rice-water. Yeow! what a notion! A blood-bath to cleanse the spiritual body of all its sinful sweats" (*SH* 190). While the rare interior monologue here presents Stephen more directly than in *Portrait* (even with the drama of an interjection), *Hero* also directly presents Stephen's own sense of humor, unmediated by narrative style; it is a reminder of the fact that Joyce himself was witty at twenty and later. In a sentence such as this is the alternate portrait only hinted at in the somber later text, the lighter side to the figure of the Dedalus so darkly and gravely presented.

Even the narrative beyond Stephen, an entity not so separate in the later text, has its own comic tone. Where voices of others barely intrude on his mind or in the narrative of *Portrait,* in the narrative of *Hero* the voices of others in judgment outside of Stephen are heard distinctly, often with wry and comical opinions:[15] the religious "representatives of authority cherished the hope that his unguided nature would bring him . . . into some hospital or asylum" (179). (We have remarked in the previous chapter on this as an example of what Joyce learned from his comic contexts.) This sort of tone invites a common, humorous perspective between narrative and reader, so that a sort of communal judgment engages the reader and the characters in a unity of like-thinking and lightened thinking; and the common spirit creates a closeness that invites comedy. It is a tone that resembles Edgar Wallace's journalism, a medium that creates a bond between writer and reader. The village-like proximity of narrative and reader is one of the necessary features for comedy, as the etymological origin of κωμη suggests.[16] A sentence such as the following makes a similar consensual judgment: "Everyone regarded Mr Hughes as a great enthusiast and some thought he had a great career before him as an orator" (*SH* 59). This communal sentiment is always a ready place for Joyce's comic turn, and many such phrases are to be found to the same comic effect in *Dubliners*: as in "Grace," "Everyone had respect for poor Martin Cunningham . . . His friends bowed to his opinions and considered that his face was like Shakespeare's" (*D* 157); or in "an Encounter," "Everyone was incredulous when it was reported that he had a vocation for the priesthood" (*D* 19). The village of Joyce's comedy is always Dublin. A statement in *Hero* like "remunerative respectability" (49) is similar to the sort of humorous assessment attributed in "A Mother" to O'Madden Burke's name: "His magniloquent western name was the moral umbrella upon which he balanced the fine problem of his finances. He was widely respected" (*D* 145). The comic tone of the narratives of the stories is maintained in the first autobiographical text, with similar usages of language to those in *Dubliners* (all written in 1906, after reading Wallace). These show a consistency in Joyce's style that *Portrait* will renounce and seek to obscure.

Humor made evident exists in a shared foreground which is a communal space. The world so inhabited is present in all its direct features, less artistic than actual, more forthright and obvious. Humor in *Hero* is sometimes so bold and direct as to be literally broadcast in the text, where it is as present as the reality of life immediately represented and indeed is present because that life is depicted. Where in *Portrait* the reader is only told that Stephen reads headlines in a news agent's shop (another example of the lack of immediacy in the text), *Hero* presents those headlines directly on the page as if in their actual form: "EVENING TELEGRAPH [Meeting] Nationalist Meeting at Ballinrobe. Important Speeches. Main Drainage Scheme . . . Mad Cow at Cabra, Literature &."(*SH* 221). (This passage certainly has a parallel to Wallace in tone if not in material.)[17] The only material given in its formal aspects in *Portrait* are literary and higher products as the villanelle; only lofty forms find their way into the later text (there are also the songs Stephen sings but then he was very young). Despite Stephen's assertion that vegetable life and misrule are the contexts of his art, what is in *Portrait* are the more elevated things of art and not life. In *Hero* there are the matter and details of things from which humor can be drawn; as if a measure of the direction of its text, the headlines on the placard on the page in *Hero* descend from higher faculties and activities such as debates and politics to the sluggish matter of the earth, what is to be carried off by drainage schemes. Literature finishes a distant last. (In his own life Joyce takes a stance against the ephemeral and the ideational of Plato and those like Russell who would practice such art; in "The Holy Office" he claims Aristotle and his own function of carrying off the "filthy streams" of those left in Dublin.) The drain is where those streams are, and there Joyce chose to work his art. He may have obscured that source in *Portrait,* or presented it obliquely in the square ditch and the esthetic concern for the transformation of "sluggish matter," yet it is the source of his comic art: the real, the common, in fact, the vulgar.

This last example in the gutter takes us back to the point that *Hero* is not only funnier but also broader than *Portrait;* it is more forthright, more vulgar, more evident. There is more common life in *Hero,* hence there is more of the common speech of it and more of the comedy that comes from it. The arts of the earlier text are of a more prosaic, lower order than those of the later, where (as the epigraph reminds) the mind has turned to something else. *Hero* represents more common speech than does the rarified later text. Stephen remarks of Cranly's "daringly commonplace" mind that "he could talk like a pint" (*SH* 145)—a most publican measure of language. There is real speech in *Hero,* from the real world around Stephen (just as, commented on earlier in chapter 1, Stephen has a full grasp of the details of the *Hero* world). His vocabulary is not exclusively from literature but from life; we are told that "It was not only in Skeat that he found words . . . [but] also at haphazard in the shops, on advertisements, in the mouths of the plodding public" (*SH* 30). He is surrounded by a world of common language and the words and voices of the people and he is engaged with it. Stephen knows the racing names, scans the bookstalls (as he will again in "Wandering Rocks"), reads the street ballads (as does the boy in "Araby"; worth noting is that these are read in the very common "marketplace" surrounded by the naturalist details of "barrels of pigs' cheeks" [*D* 31]). It is a world of vulgar language in the truest sense of the term, of real events and people; the reader shares in it and so does Stephen.

This particular sort of diction and the commonplaces of life it denotes connects to the word *ignotas* from the epigraph. *Ignotas* can mean not only obscure and also alien, but base or vulgar. So the direct humor of *Hero* and the common language so necessary for its expression are other items left behind in the rewriting of the later text. Common speech is rare in *Portrait,* and Stephen would have none of it. That omission is another measure of the difference between the priggish Stephen and the funny Joyce. When at Clongowes, the living Joyce was punished for using "vulgar language."[18] This effacing of common language by *Portrait* is the second and more attenuated form of the turning described by the epigraph. There is in *Hero* a language of commonplaces, of vulgarity in the etymological sense of the word, which is only obliquely in the later text. Recognition of it undercuts and upsets *Portrait's* more somber moments, serious pronouncements, and artful expressions.

In keeping with the foregrounding that characterizes the text, *Hero* expresses directly a concern for the issues of language, meaning, and tone. In *Hero* Stephen has a fuller discussion with the dean of studies (more of which below) and in a part of it later omitted in *Portrait,* he talks specifically about a language used and misused by the common people, the vulgar.

> He read [works] as one would read a thesaurus and made a garner of words. He read Skeat's *Etymological Dictionary* by the hour and his mind . . . was often hypnotized by the most common-place conversation. People seemed to him strangely ignorant of the value of words they used so glibly . . . he began to see that people had leagued themselves together in a conspiracy of ignobility and that Destiny had scornfully reduced her prices for them. (*SH* 26)

It is worth noting first that, while Stephen is engaged in an intellectual exercise (that of origin in etymology), he focuses on the use of commonplace language by the people in conversations overheard; in this text Stephen can both read and listen. He is fascinated by everyday speech; however, he remarks that, in that mesmerized state, he sees that "people" in the aggregate are unaware of what language is worth. That state of ignorance is another connection to the epigraph to *Portrait* (as was obliquely the indication of origin in etymology), because *ignorant* is evidently related to *ignotas.* What Stephen means, in effect, is that people do not know—or to use the terms of the epigraph, have turned their backs to—the power of words. He will not do so, and neither does the text he is in.

What is so powerful about words is that they have a value, some measurable transactive worth, and that such values obtain in any usage. Stephen clearly invests language with worth by introducing an economic gloss to his argument. Words have value and should be used with some recognition of that value; both common and elevated diction have a currency. (The "thesaurus," etymology has told him, is a treasure house, so this metaphoric substitution comes readily to mind.) Stephen values the commonplace in this passage; he accuses other users of being unaware of its worth. In fact, in a stroke of irony that adds humor to the relation of earlier text to later, Stephen's claim against the ignorance of usage might pertain to *Portrait:* that later text ignores and forgets common language and vulgar speech altogether. In *Portrait* Stephen himself will not invest common language, any more than he will hear common speech; he is rather a consumer of the exclusively literary and his poetic usage neglects its common origin. In *Hero,* by contrast, he acknowledges the presence of common language even as the text uses it, as befits its more open manner. Common language is obscured in *Portrait* because its generic drive requires that it be serious and overvalue the poetic, but the value of words cannot be forgotten glibly; it will surface despite *Portrait's* efforts to obscure and cover it over. Common language when stored (as in a thesaurus) and brought out from storage, garnered at a crucial time, can yield great dividends, much the same as with the bringing back out from hiding the elements of an earlier version of a final text.

Vulgar language, which does not hide its metaphors but rather openly and promiscuously presents them, can produce moments of insightful comedy. This combination of common speech and its latent comic possibilities we saw in the previous chapter is something Joyce may have seen in the demotic language of journalism and Wallace. Indeed, that openness of the commonplace creates the sort of sentence which concludes the very passage above: "people had leagued themselves together in a conspiracy of ignobility and . . . Destiny had scornfully reduced her prices for them"(*SH* 26). The wry tone of the last sentence has a directness not found in *Portrait* and, due to that tenor, has humor as well. It is a vulgar phrase in part because it is about money ("prices"), yet the incipient artist who is said to read a thesaurus "by the hour" is a wage-laborer, too. The "ignobility" Stephen attributes to the common people morphemically echoes the claim that such people are "ignorant" of the value of words, and thus harkens back to "ignotas" of obscure arts of the epigraph to *Portrait* (and it is distantly related to it by etymology). So the epigraph to *Portrait* can be seen in yet a further way, as alternately stating that earlier the novel's language is obscure because it is not valued by the culture, and it is the artist who must apply his mind or memory to its use; to find something "memorable" is to be able to direct your mind (*anima*) to *ignotas artes* as phrases and vulgarities and reinvest them with value in another context, to bring them out of the storage house. What is frequent in *Stephen Hero* is this sort of popular, common writing; yet what is most striking is that the same sort of language remains, prudently invested in *Portrait,* discharging a debt ("dimitto" again).

While the parallel scenes and thematic similarities of the two works have obviously been recognized, the particular language and diction of the earlier text has yet remained unnoticed in the later.[19] And such language of the common, the vulgar, may be the very *ignotas artes* that have been retained in memory, unseen and truly obscured, reapplied from one text to the other. They are there because they retain traces of their original value as comic, and they help invest the serious *Portrait* with its comic background. To examine the ways in which the common language of *Hero* remains in *Portrait* is to see how one feature of comedy is still owed in the later text; it is to see the alternate lightness behind *Portrait* that places so much of its features in the somber shadow of its seriousness. The traces of the earlier text in the later of a language not poetic but prosaic, not exceptional but common, make for a comic tumbling of the final text's serious and striving flights of artful rhetoric. The traces of common language from *Hero* make a parallel to the inherently doubled discourse of comedy we have seen in chapter 2; there words pair into comic conflation: here two actual texts makes a conflation that deflates the narrative of the later one.

Before we see where this reapplication of common language occurs (and therefore see how much of the behindness of *Hero* colors *Portrait*), it is necessary to examine further the exchange with the dean as it appears in the two texts. For one, this is another way to see the operations of obscuring and effacing that the later text performs on the earlier, by its removing directness with obliquity, its forthrightness by figuration. For another, the interview in *Hero* develops further and more explicitly the notion of a common language and its uses—languages and uses *Portrait* seeks to hide and put behind. For Stephen to argue for a commonplace language is logically for him to imply its opposite in elevated language. It is fitting that *Hero,* which engages both actual life and intellectual life, external events and internal states, would also explicitly develop this distinction. *Portrait,* eschewing directness, naturally elides it.

Although in both versions Stephen's exchange with the dean of studies contains the subject about lighting a fire, a useful rather than obscure art, and the overt reference to Newman, not an obscure writer, to place these scenes side by side is to engage in an act of recovery. Examining these two scenes precisely because their subject is language itself opens up issues obscured and covered over. While we have looked at some differences in these scenes (in the introduction), notably the difference in humor, the uncovering of the earlier text will show the preservation of a particularly important distinction about a language of two contexts, both high and low. The notion of these two languages—of art and high meaning and then of vulgar and commonplace denotation—is actually raised forthrightly in *Hero*. When that notion is applied to the later text, it throws into question some of the high poetic cast of the revised narrative. The serious artful style of *Portrait* may have a low, vulgar note. When origin is rescued from obscurity, some reevaluation is necessary.[20]

> Words, he said, have a certain value in the literary tradition and a certain value in the market-place—a debased value. Words are simply receptacles for human thought: in the literary tradition they receive more valuable thoughts than they receive in the market-place . . . Stephen quoted a phrase from Newman to illustrate his theory.
> —In that sentence of Newman's he said, the word is used according to the literary tradition: it has there its full value. In ordinary use, that is, in the market-place, it has a different value, altogether, a debased value. "I hope I'm not detaining you."
> —Not at all! not at all!
> —No, no . . . . (SH 27–28)

> —One difficulty, said Stephen, in esthetic discussion is to know whether words are being used according to the literary tradition or according to the tradition of the marketplace. I remember a sentence of Newman's in which he says of the Blessed Virgin that she was detained in the full company of the saints. The use of the word in the marketplace is quite different. *I hope I'm not detaining you.*
> —Not in the least, said the dean politely.
> —No, no, said Stephen, smiling, I mean . . .
> —Yes, yes: I see, said the dean quickly, I quite catch the point: *detain.* (P 188)

This scene from *Portrait* was discussed earlier to show how it has unexpected comic elements in its presentation: the particular hidden humor of language in the combination of "Home, ale, Christ," as well as the obvious connection of the actual lit fire and the lack of fiery enthusiasm of the dean of studies. There is, in fact, more hidden humor in the *Portrait* scene than in the one from *Hero*; this hiddenness is appropriate to the former's effacing of the latter's forthrightness. Even the conclusion of *Portrait* has its own humor in language, as the dean tells Stephen about the tundish, "that is a most interesting word. I must look that word up. Upon my word I must" (P 188), where his repetition of *word* only demonstrates his obtuseness to language. What is to the purpose here is an examination of the issue of two levels of language and the consequences by which the language of the earlier version transforms and perhaps causes the latent humor in the later text.

In the small compass of these passages are many of the stylistic redirections of Joyce's applying his mind to rewriting *Hero*: there are the characteristic use of compound nouns elided ("market-place" to "marketplace").[21] There is a greater immediacy obtained by the shift from external narration, "Stephen quoted a line," to direct presentation, "I remember a sentence . . . ." Interestingly, the more detailed earlier text omits the very line in question which it says is quoted, and repeats a reference to it, without ever giving the line: a strange and uncharacteristic sort of displacement, seeing as the later presents the quotation directly. The earlier has a degree of repetition which, while it might more accurately convey Stephen's actual thinking, makes for a tedious written text: "quoted a phrase from Newman" "'In that sentence of Newman's. . . .'" The joke at the expense of the poor dean is retained, where it connects in *Portrait* with the prostitute who detains Stephen. It is one small place of humor for the later text, a common effect in *Hero*. In keeping with its directly presenting the vulgar elements, the earlier text portrays a slapstick "Butt," whose name is the aim of all jokes, and this one actively makes comic gestures, by rubbing his chalky hand on his chin. *Portrait,* more nuanced, restrains its humor to the dean's misunderstanding about diction (the word "tundish") so that it culminates in the more refined verbal humor of "My word, I must look up that word." To look up a word, however, is to use the thesaurus or the dictionary, to try to gauge the value of a word.

So the revised and unnamed dean in the second text raises only obliquely and indirectly the issue of the worth of words which Stephen articulates in *Hero*. In *Portrait,* Stephen merely tries to distinguish high from low diction, a lofty move commensurate with his artistic aspirations in that text, but it is an attempt doomed to failure because his text expresses no such language (and has in fact thoroughly obscured it). Stephen speaks only of the vague registers of words, tradition or marketplace, and says merely that the uses of each are different. What he says in *Hero* is—as with everything else in this text—more direct; he is aware that words have not only different contexts, but different values, one greater, one lesser.

What is changed and obscured, then, from the first to the final version of this exchange is precisely the articulation and expression of a language that is subject to the demands of an economy. What is absent from the later version is the fuller sense of how language is undervalued by a dynamic of placing value, of a measure of assessing worth. That is why Stephen raises the notion of a marketplace, where language is the specie of an artistic economy. In *Portrait,* marketplace seems only to be merely an ideational context, not an actual place of exchange and value. Fittingly, there is a description of Stephen walking through an actual marketplace in the *Hero* text, a world of commerce and value around Stephen where language is used simultaneously for "street ballads," "racing names," "scarlet police journals," and bookstalls with "old directories and volumes of sermons and unheard-of treatises at the rate of a penny each or three for twopence," this last phrase posting a clear monetary value (*SH* 145). The marketplace is where appetites are satisfied, both for food and for common literature, and so it is a place that is tightly connected both to economy and to humor of the carnivalesque.[22] The *Hero* text is therefore more detailed about what the difference of words is worth. *Portrait* speaks only of tradition in a general esthetic discussion; *Hero* rather speaks about actual currencies and needs. *Hero* specifies the term "value": "words have a certain value" in both literature and in "common usage in the market place." *Portrait* retains in its passage the distinction of literary and common (how could it not, given its disposition to the literary over the common?), yet it has obscured and generalized the worth of *all* words by referring only to utility and by mentioning only use "according to the literary tradition or according to the tradition of the marketplace." The specific value is diminished to use, and use only in an abstracted "tradition"; *Portrait* even avoids the use of the word *common* as itself too vulgar. Utility is a function of language, deriving surely from Horace's dictum of *dulce et utile,* and for *Portrait* to stress utility is to confirm yet again its disposition to instruction, for the intellective didacticism of its genre as *Bildung.* What Horace finds *dulce* in literature, the entertaining, the pleasant, and the humorous, *Portrait* has dismissed obscurely behind it.

Interestingly, however, the *Portrait* passage demonstrates its origin in the one from *Hero* in one pertinent way. While *Portrait* does not directly state the issue of "common usage," rather obscures it, it does present such a usage in a direct way later in the exchange about the two dictions by the debate about "funnel" and "tundish." Stephen's word is in fact more common in his context than is the dean's, although Stephen in *Portrait* would hardly claim to be a user of marketplace word choice. Ironically, "tundish" is also more English a word than in the Latin-derived "funnel," so that Stephen overstates his case in thinking that the dean's English is alien to him; he speaks it at home in Drumcondra. (Not unexpectedly, he fails to see this fact.) So the issue of the economic value of words literary or common surfaces in the action of the *Portrait,* even if the detailed explanation in the earlier text has been erased and is not evident even to the Stephen who makes this distinction.

What Stephen articulates in this discussion of literary language and that of the marketplace is another set of alternatives which describe the dynamic of *Portrait,* doubled and contrasted; in fact, *Portrait* seems exclusively to be on one side of this set while the elements it puts behind are on the other. For one, *Hero* directly elaborates the presence of two things in language, assessing the merits and worth of each, while *Portrait* only mentions the fact that there are two; it engages one while *Hero* uses both. This monoptic view goes in concert with the way in which words are viewed through much of *Portrait* only in their elevated form and not with their doubled comedy. For another, because *Hero* engages the low as well as high, it is the fuller text; it correspondingly has the fuller treatment of this set of opposites. The contrast of literary value with that of the marketplace is in abstract critical terms a restatement of the issue of the focus of each text: *Portrait* with its serious purpose of literary form, *Hero* with its embrace of everyday and the public space. *Portrait* has figurative language, *Hero* the commonplace. Correspondingly the diction of the reality of things (such as Stephen's wearing an overcoat and actually hanging it up [24] or having a raincoat [195]) are the sort of *artes ignotas Portrait* rejects for the elevated subject of Stephen's soul. *Portrait,* intellective, with its interior narrative, generically directed to its aim of education, is concerned with things valued highly; *Hero* seems content to develop a tone of humorous treatment of the protagonist's fuller, less concentrated life.

There is clearly an exchange in *Hero* of different values. While it is clear that tradition and thought give some words more value, all language has value. There is an economy of words, one that recognizes all the value in language. Low language, in fact, hoarded and used carefully, brings an increase in value by good stewardship. This notion of a compounded value in an economy of words and their value is made explicit in *Hero*. As early as chapter 16 (the second of all that was saved), Stephen argues that art is not profligate; rather he believes that "the poem is made not born" (*SH* 33), and that the reworking of language has a cost: "that every moment of inspiration must be paid for in advance." (As an example further relevant to the issue of recompense, this passage contains a sentence about the necessity "for the artist to labour incessantly at his art if he wishes to express completely even the simplest conception" [*SH* 32].) The author is no spendthrift; rather he is closely aware of value. Stephen then asserts that "Isolation is the first principle of artistic economy" (*SH* 33). Isolation is not merely a physical act such as exile, it can also be achieved by means of storing and garnering by putting aside or behind. To isolate is to take out of currency, to make obscure, so that what is separated is made rare and valuable, but recoverable by a sense memory of its origin. The manuscript of *Stephen Hero* was itself taken out of this sort of circulation, only to have valued parts of it reapplied in *Portrait*. Stephen's concern for an economy of language is such a reinvestment.

In the discussion with the dean, the *Hero* text in its characteristic expansiveness makes explicit how those demands on the economy of language operate by the use of the terms "a certain value," "full," or "debased." It is remarkable, when going back to the earlier text, to hear Stephen speak clearly about economies of any kind. For *Stephen Hero* to present him as direct and calculating is to make him as much more connected to the world, so that in this way, as in so many others, he is less ethereal and more vivid than his later counterpart. The passage states accurately that all diction operates as one would expect any economy to operate: words, much like paper currency, have no intrinsic value, but are "receptacles"; they depend rather on context to set their worth. The literary tradition (that is to say a system of long standing, aware of its origins) apparently finds words "in their full value" because they retain some weight of their original (etymological) meanings. Common words, by obscuring those original meanings, lower language by making it circulate more widely, in broader contexts. A debased language will find little welcome or use in a text about the growth and constant rising of the poet's soul. It is the task of the artist to increase the value of language, by reinvesting that of the marketplace into the more exclusive, more weighty contexts of literary tradition, in genres of more valued kinds, such as *Bildungsroman*. It is this impulse to elevation of common language that is the aim of the epiphany. *Hero* defines epiphany directly (when it is made nowhere explicit in *Portrait*) as a revelation, surely, that contains elevated aims but is derived from very low sources in the common: "By an epiphany he meant a sudden spiritual manifestation, whether in the vulgarity of speech or of gesture or in a memorable phase of the mind itself" (*SH* 211). It is precisely this vulgarity the epiphany seeks to make shine forth, alternating light with shadow, high with low.

Much as with this description of epiphany as proceeding from something vulgar, *Hero* expresses a concern for what is "valuable" or "debased" in words as an economy that operates according to a pricing system that seeks to make capital. This is in fact what happens in *Portrait* when the earlier parts of *Hero* are reinvested to greater dividends, as economy is the special management of resources to make them go as far as possible. (More distantly as a definition, but closer to the context at hand, the O.E.D. lists *economy* as "the structure, assignment of proportion of parts of any product of human design"—with Milton and Dryden cited as sources of great literary value.)

If Stephen hypothesizes an economy of art, it is certainly true that an economy operates in the marketplace (where need and desire are the operative features). The marketplace, Stephen argues, may undervalue words, in his view because it (and its ignorant consumers) do not have the original worth of words. They do not according to him because their use is in the service of appetite and the stomach, their immediate needs for consumption, and the basic source of the consumption of the marketplace is that site of the low, the humorous, the carnivalesque. So in fact, when Stephen discusses the cheapening of language by the marketplace he is only again (in another context) devaluing the language of the common desire that expresses itself in license, in the common and vulgar gratification of appetite, and the need for levity and humor.

His author does not set the vulgar at so low a rate, however. Joyce probably found in Skeat (and Stephen would have, had he looked at the entry for *economy* as well as for *thesaurus*) that economy is defined as "an allotment, the proportioning of a resource" from νεμειν, the Greek for "to mete out."²³ Thus the true artistic economy (that Joyce practiced while Stephen's theory is too one-sided) is to use resourcefully, with good stewardship, to put both high and low words to use sparingly but effectively. This Joyce does in both *Hero* and *Portrait,* in different proportion in each: where there are high concerns, there must be vulgar elements; if one text elevates the former over the latter, both must be present.

The point of the apportioning, the νεμειν, is to prosper the οικος the home. The proper focus of economy (if we are to value the origin of words as Stephen claims we must) is the domestic and the homely. That, surely, is a context itself of the common, of the immediate and the less than lofty. (*Hero* has Stephen talk at length about art to his mother in the kitchen.) The home is a local place, near the market; it is a basic structure in the village (the κωμη) for which the song of comedy is intended (when it is not a surd). Moreover, one might see another substitution in the valuing of the comic in this definitive exchange about value with the dean in *Hero*. From the same Skeat, etymology would treasure within "economy" the original relation of νομος (an allotment), to *nomad,* from the pasture so allotted. That nomad is not only the restless young artist breaking away from society, he is also the figure of someone outside, profanely outside the temple, one beyond the pale—in short, another glimpse of the comic Irishman behind.

When Stephen speaks in *Hero* of an economy of art, he is of course speaking of a context of money and value that seems to have no counterpart in *Portrait,* or in much of Joyce's actual life. Yet it is clear that, when *Hero* raises an issue not in *Portrait,* that issue is invariably about what *Portrait* renounces. The economy of art embraces the valuing of the common and of the comic impulse. In the turning from *Hero* to *Portrait,* this economy operates by a sort of valuation of the direct and vulgar elements in the earlier text, retained and hoarded in obscurity but meted out in the later version in small but strategic allotments. The isolation Stephen claims is "the first principle of artistic economy" (*SH* 33) has certainly placed *Stephen Hero* in obscurity within the Joyce canon; yet that same isolation has worked a value by hoarding certain parts of the effaced text, obscuring their origin and then allotting them, meted out, in *Portrait.* As far as economies go, if Joyce was profligate with money, he was parsimonious with the currency he minted himself, the paper scrip of his own words. Scraps of paper with notes, scenes sketched, pages of manuscripts unused in final versions, all these were saved for later use when they had increased in value (hoarded in fact, as was the box left behind in Trieste, which Joyce asked to be sent to Paris). His notebooks were used like bank books, places to deposit valuables to be used at a future time. The story of Mr. Hunter unused in *Dubliners* compounded into *Ulysses;* the King Mark fragment from *Ulysses* became the seed of *Wake;* the story of Buckley and the Russian general paid later dividends. Joyce clearly valued what he wrote so much as to discard so little; therefore what he wrote even in the cumbersomely large manuscript of *Hero* finds its way, recast and often obscured, into the much changed *Portrait.* What does remain are precisely those moments of common language which the earlier text expressed so clearly and directly, and which the later obscures and suppresses only incompletely.

This economy operates by revaluing *Portrait:* it is a deflation not only of an economic sort but also an esthetic one. *Portrait* is presented with an elevated purpose; the very renouncing of *Hero* has given it a monolithic tone of high art. Yet *Hero* has valued the low, vulgar elements and Joyce hoarded and allotted them in the later text in places which are the most noble in style, the most figurative, the most artful. The common language that is so much a part of *Hero's* directness remains behind the most poetic parts of the *Portrait* narrative to give the poetic a comic alteration. Much as was the case where heightened contexts of art or religion were subject to a doubled language of comedy, the highest linguistic reaches of *Portrait* have low comic elements in them that owe their origin to *Hero* and to the economy that has valued them despite their being obscured.

To capitalize on this vulgarity is itself, then, an engagement of the comedy inherent in language and in disproportion. To retain the vulgar sense of language of *Hero* is to set the later, more focused text of *Portrait* up for more comic tumbling.[24] This time the antic misrule of comedy is directed at the very figurative language that expresses the art of the novel, that style which must be artistic because of what the genre demands. The artifice of metaphors that embroider the narrative are pulled down by their origin in the common language seen in *Hero*. Only apparently lapidary in focus, *Portrait* will be blurred by vague, inelegant phrasing. The pull of the low and the common makes the serious strivings of the language tumble, deflated by the presence of the originary comic language behind it, which, turned from and dismissed, returns by the economy of the vulgar to add a revalued alteration of comedy to the artifice of *Portrait*.

Stephen's attempts at differentiating himself from his family are crucial ones that are necessary to the direction of the novel of development and heighten its plot; these moments are even more crucial when that separation occurs because of the differences between the superior young man and his more average family. So when Stephen wins academic prizes for his excellent scholarship and seeks to elevate the condition of his family, important issues are presented, and in a language of heightened figuration and metaphoric substitution. It should be remembered that this passage, examined in chapter 2, had that other comic feature of the doubled language. Stephen's sense of separation from this family is so acute that he suggests no biological relation to them, rather only a "mystical kinship of fosterage, fosterchild and fosterbrother" (*P* 98). The means, however, by which he seeks to elevate the family, the prize money, has been awarded to him as the family waits in Foster Place. Common details such as street names undercut his most fervid considerations; the low facts of real life cause his high aspirations to tumble. Yet there is another sort of comic capering involved in this passage, where the lyric diction of the narrative is undermined by something other, by the prosaic and the common that can be uncovered by reference to the earlier text of *Hero* turned away. Stephen's attempts to change his family's condition are futile, and his disappointment sharply, if figuratively, conveyed: "He had tried to build a breakwater of order and elegance against the sordid tide of life without him. . . . From without as from within the water had flowed over his barriers: their tides began once more to jostle fiercely above the crumbled mole. . . . He had not . . . bridged the restless shame and rancour that divided him from mother and brother and sister" (*P* 98). This effective narrative expression appears to describe poetically the irresistible sea change in the Dedalus family and Stephen's vain attempt, Hamlet-like, to stem that sea of troubles. As by now one might expect, however, there lurks something antic behind the earnestness and emotion of this passage. For one, the poetic diction, as elevated as it may appear, opens up possibilities of a lowering, comic effect. The attempt at calm is described as a "breakwater" with the tides overcoming the synonymous "mole"; here the poetic usage is consistent. Yet the failure to connect to his lesser family, that necessary feature of his development, brings out another usage that looks similar to the architectural ones: "he had not . . . bridged." Consequently, that breakwater or mole which does not work completely is imagistically connected to a failed bridge. A joke about disappointment certainly lurks behind the narrative's representation of Stephen's earnest emotions. By the time he teaches young men from wealthy families in Mr. Deasey's school, Stephen can make a joke about a pier as "a disappointed bridge" (*U* 2.39)—perhaps even remembering the tides of his past. We have noted that one feature of Joyce's comedy is its carrying over beyond one text to another—we might even say bridging one text with another. This may serve as an example where the joking in *Ulysses* has its unlikely origin in the somber moments of lyric expression in *Portrait*.

These comic touches of language do not arise without origin, any more than Stephen has no connection to his family; there must be something before this material that turns it to the comic, something not only before in time but to the side. In a similar moment in Stephen's family life (in *Hero* chapter 18), the narration gives this judgmental comment about a similar growing estrangement: "Stephen's home-life had by this time grown sufficiently unpleasant: the direction of his development was against the stream of tendency of his family" (*SH* 48). (The continued use of hyphenation in compound nouns shows the unworked earlier style.) This passage is highly narrative and seems objective—at least as regards its being external to Stephen—but it is freighted with a strained diction that makes it seem to belong to the economy of the marketplace. The tone here is brittle because weight is given unearned to words. The phrase "sufficiently unpleasant" has all the air of euphuism one would expect from a popular novel, and it strikes just the right note of demurral to soften the described adolescent rebelliousness. The second clause, working by way of defining that unpleasantness, is strikingly redundant in precisely the ways associated with common speech: "direction" and "tendency" are repetitive enough, but "stream of tendency" is tautological: one common synonym of "tendency" is "a course of action" or a "drift." The water imagery that is so prevalent and so poetic in *Portrait* here has overflowed. The implied image of Stephen as a young salmon is unescapable; one feature of common speech is the unrecognized comedy of its tacit metaphors, because it does not value words fully. Another occurrence of "tendency" in *Hero* equally shares the redundancy of this passage, describing a "tendency to oscillation in the soul of the free-spoken young student" who would be disciplined by the Church (*SH* 73). Here the inclination of tendency is repeated in the vacillation of "oscillation," a word rich with unwarranted scientism. "Tendency" is related to tendentiousness, so that the text, as it were, practices what it preaches. "Stream" likewise appears again in the early manuscript in a commonplace usage, "he had to listen to an inconstant stream of literary opinions" (*SH* 148), presumably about what is valuable in art.

While at first glance *Portrait* contains no such obvious and vulgar sentences, the economy of hoarding would show the dividends such phrases later pay, even when somewhat obscured and pushed behind. Much as Stephen argues that people use language ignorant of its etymological origin, so too *Portrait* uses phrases without acknowledgment of their origin in the earlier, more humorous, and hence more vulgar text. The "stream of tendency" of Stephen's life may well be the cause of, as well as being anterior to, so much of the particular figurative water of *Portrait* that seems to make it a different work from *Hero,* and about which there has long been critical comment.[25] While the events of Dedalus's wetting the bed and being shouldered into the square ditch establish the imagery of his thoughts, the disposition of the narrative to use diction regarding water might well go back to this phrase from *Hero;* if so, a view into the obscurity of the *ignotas artes* may lead to a comic view of the more poetic parts of the later text. Some of the most fervent figurative passages in *Portrait* may have a watery shadow of comic value.

Thus the repeated liquid imagery for emotions and sin found so frequently in *Portrait* is subject to a revaluation when its obscured comically vulgar origin is seen in the marketplace of *Hero's* common usages. A phrase such as this on Stephen's sin, as "the vital wave [which] had carried him on its bosom out of himself and back again" (*P* 103) seems to be a replaying of the overdrawn phrase "a tendency to oscillation in the soul of the . . . young student," with a residual, medial connection with the phrase "stream of tendency": an economy of language will hoard nearly everything. The vulgarity of the original phrases deflates the *Portrait* text, so that the earnest struggle with sin receives an obscure comic echo from the past behind the later text. That comedy is enforced by the metaphor hidden in a sentence in *Portrait* just a few after that about the wave, when we read that Stephen's "[d]evotion had gone by the board," swept over the side, no doubt, by those streams and tides.[26] There are actual streams in *Portrait,* most notably the one Stephen crosses after his interview with the director ("He crossed the bridge over the stream of the Tolka" [162]) and the one on the strand in which the girl stands ("A girl stood before him in midstream" "withdrew her eyes . . . and bent them towards the stream" [171]). While the later text actualizes events and objects, it seems to have done so merely by obscuring and reapplying the metaphors of the vulgar art of the earlier. To shift from metonymy to the literal is to revalue the currency of language; it is in fact to go from high to low, from the literary to the marketplace.

And sometimes the diction of the earlier text is not even obscured. From the "stream of tendency" of *Hero* we get in *Portrait* the following thoughts of Stephen about Emma:

> All day he had thought of nothing but their leavetaking on the steps of the tram . . . , the stream of moody emotions it had made to course through him, and the poem he had written about it . . . The old restless moodiness had again filled his breast . . . but had not found an outlet in verse . . . and all day the stream of gloomy tenderness within him had started forth and returned upon itself in dark courses and eddies. (P 77)

A passage such as this, of course, would seem to present all the features that make *Portrait* a different text: the immediacy of presentation, the emotional state of Stephen conveyed by free indirect discourse, the interconnected imagery of "stream," "outlet," "eddies." It seems to be a product of literary tradition alone. Yet the watermarks of the language of *Hero* remain. The coursing of tides and eddies is another tendency of "oscillating streams"; and the poem that Stephen seeks to write intending to give "outlet" to the "stream" of emotions that "filled his breast" would give them that liquid "direction" of his life (as *Hero* so vulgarly had it). Yet if the poetry fails Stephen within *Portrait,* the rewriting of *Stephen Hero* does not fail Joyce; he remembered his past and hoarded it: the "stream of tendency" of the earlier can be clearly seen, unobscured, in the latter's description of Stephen's "stream of gloomy tenderness." There is even the parsimonious saving of the initial five letters (*tende*). "Stream" when associated with "life" is of course a common cliché; its use in the phrase "the direction of his life went against the stream . . . of his family" in *Hero* is exactly prosaic. (As testimony, Bloom, that common man, thinks this very same cliché in "Lestrygonians," remarking on the Kino's signboard floating on the River Liffey: "Because life is a stream" [*U* 8.95].) One would never expect an artist like Stephen to use it. He does, however, and in *Portrait* too (Joyce makes him), in a diary entry: "5 April: Wild spring. Scudding clouds. O life! Dark stream of swirling bogwater on which appletrees have cast down their delicate flowers" (*P* 250). The apostrophe is Byronic, part of the profligacy of art, as it is when it occurs in his last entry; the scudding clouds are a poetic treatment of his thoughts of the dappled seaborne ones, and the bathos of the apple blossoms on the turf-colored water draws on stock images of literary tradition. Yet no amount of poetizing, however, can obscure that common origin of a cliché from the marketplace of life as a stream, a vulgar phrase from the earlier text that undergoes a redirection and revaluation by the artist's mind into obscure arts. What was the objective narration in *Hero* now belongs to the subjective character in *Portrait*, yet Stephen's youth and inexperience cannot cancel out the debt owed by the late text to the earlier through the economy that hoards the vulgar and the comic.

These examples from *Portrait* involve family, religion, and romance, crucial features in a novel of a young man growing away from parents, the Church, and into the calling of Beauty. In short, they are all the serious issues of *Kuenstlerroman*, the very essentials of *Portrait*. Yet all these contexts are colored and given an alternative comic lowering by the antic vulgar diction that resides just behind them. This comic undercutting, this tumbling of the serious, continues; the economy of the vulgar can be expected to spread to other features that belong to the novel's serious generic requirements. One such essential feature of the novel of development is the sensibility of its hero: his temperament as special, receptive, and poetic are the things necessary for the successful plotting of his superiority. From Werther on down, emotional acuity is required of the protagonist. Stephen displays this acuity in his heightened sense of smell and touch, his alertness to colors and language, and his morbid self-absorption. As he develops, so does that self-absorption, growing into an awareness of the injustices done to him by the callous outer world. In that encounter with the dean of studies, a battle in which Stephen seems to be easily victorious, he is checked in his own argument by such sensitivity. In the very exchange that establishes the idea of the marketplace of words, and immediately after the dean's amazement at "tundish," Stephen argues and as he debates, he uses a low phrase about art being made from "lumps of earth." The text notes that the little word "seemed to have turned a rapier point of his sensitiveness against this courteous and vigilant foe" (*P* 189). Here amid the imagery of a heroic duel, the word "sensitiveness" contrasts with the martial imagery and must be taken as relating to Stephen's artistic inner self, his punctiliousness, and sharp sensibility. However, as the entire subsequent exchange with the dean involves the use of words that belong to others before they belong to Stephen ("words that were his before they were mine"), the *hapax legomenon* "sensitiveness" should expectedly have another source where it had been hoarded long enough to be invested with a common, comic value.

Hero has the following sentence about the protagonist which, because it has in abundance the vulgar qualities of bathos and sentiment (the currency of marketplace conversation), it therefore seems to deserve obscurity: a "young man, specialized by fate or her stepsister chance for an organ of sensitiveness or intellectiveness"(*SH* 168). So directly judgmental a sentence would never appear in *Portrait,* not only because such narrative objectivity is to be avoided, but also because the ignorant and ignoble diction of such a word as "intellectiveness" would have to be reworked. It, tied with "sensitiveness" by repetition of the suffix and by combining mind and emotion, makes a monotonous word choice (although the latter word is used in part for its sense of morbid self-consciousness or touchiness). Thus "sensitiveness" in *Portrait* has its origin in *Hero*. To call the protagonist an "organ" of these qualities borders on the grotesque; the fragmentation of the main character is laughable enough by itself, but "sensitiveness" is a term that can mean, in the first definition in the O.E.D., the "power of sensation" in particular reference to plants and their capacity for stimulation by light. Thus the phrase about Stephen is comical, with the metaphors implied by the vulgar language operating much in the way as the example of the "stream of tendency" of Stephen's life suggest he was a metaphoric salmon; here the passage suggests he is a weak and sensitive flower, buffeted by the organic and familially related forces of fate and "stepsister" chance.

The open tone of *Hero* would allow this sort of exaggeration to be foregrounded, yet it would not surprise to find that *all* the features of this sententious sentence reappear, slightly obscured but still current in the text of *Portrait:* the allegorical "stepsister chance," the word "sensitiveness," and the narrative judgment it conveys—even that overdrawn "organ." The obscured origin of "sensitiveness" in the argument with the dean we can now clearly see. The strained family relationship of chance as the stepsister of fate, an allegorical designation of fatuously epic proportions, is echoed again in the more complicated legal and mystical notions of "fosterage, fosterchild and fosterbrother" (*P* 98), which we have seen is subject to other comic capering. Ideas that have important resonances for the concepts of generation and filiation for Joyce in *Ulysses* and *Wake* may well proceed from the inflated commonplaces of the earliest texts, applied to pay dividends.

Because any economy commodifies body parts and dissolves the subject, even that of vulgar language, the grotesqueness and obviousness of the separated "organ" remains in the later text as well, still coupled with a narrative comment making a judgment about the protagonist. Invited to confess yet fearing confession, Stephen responds: "A tremulous chill blew round his heart . . . , and yet, listening and suffering silently, he seemed to have laid an ear against the muscle of his own heart, feeling it close and quail, listening to the flutter of its ventricles" (*P* 126). This is an odd mixture of the precise and scientific ("ventricles") and the vague and suggestive ("feeling" and "flutter"); of Latinate and colloquial diction, "tremulous" and "close." Stephen would have to be an organ of some considerable "sensitiveness" to feel these sounds. Withall the vulgar anatomization of Stephen remains in the second version; the "organ" of the first is specified now as "ear" and "heart," and the particular formidably contortionist image of laying the one on the other continues the comic grotesquery of the earlier, separately denoted organ. The very essential nature of the artist, his sensitiveness, is taken for a comic fall by the reinvestment of a vulgar language from *Hero*.

The earlier text has an appeal to an audience that might have valued its novelistic turns and suggestive moods of the sensitive soul; those are, after all, appeals to the vulgar and commercial appetites. It is filled with such overwritings as "Stephen was still a lover of the deformations wrought by dusk. Late autumn and winter in Dublin are always seasons of damp gloomy weather" (*SH* 178). This first is a sentence filled with the sort of "sensitiveness and intellectiveness" which characterizes Stephen by a fin-de-siècle languorousness and an echo of Wordsworth (*Tintern Abbey:* "am I still/A lover of the meadows and the woods"); yet it has a vulgar character evident in its striving for effect, a characteristic continued by the second sentence's notation of the weather in a preachy, guidebook tone (like Homais and his praise for Yonville). Yet even so poor and unpromising an example as this is hoarded for later use. Because the economy of vulgarity demands a reapplication, a dispersal, of the vulgar language of *Hero* into the obscure arts of *Portrait,* this sort of passage works its own remembered changes on the later text. These examples are, moreover, less deformations or variations than they are uses of equal currency. There such "poetic" phrases as "a spectral dusk" (*P* 67) and "the sad quiet greyblue glow of the dying day" (*P* 163) have their effects undercut by their sententious origin in the "deformative dusk" of *Hero*. A usage of "dusk" in a simile reinvests the original: "A dusk like that of the outer world obscured his mind" (*P* 64). And this last sample is particularly apt, as it illustrates the economic force of vulgar language whereby small coinages from the earlier text are saved for subsequent investment in the later. While the "dusk" is here incorporated into Stephen, thereby paralleling the movement from the objective *Hero* to the subjective *Portrait,* its value is increased by the addition and reapplication of the very terms of obscurity and mind that are denoted by *ignotas artes* and *animum* in the epigraph—that statement which serves to post the exchange rate of the economy of vulgar language.

That dusk, however, is suggestive not of poetic Byronic posturing, but of the dusk that tumbles clownishly. It is the place where the presentation of the concept of antic misrule first appears from behind the somber *Portrait* to offer an alternate light to generic purpose. So the dusk shades not only the lighter forms of comedy that tumble in contrast to *Portrait's* somber direction, but the dusk also hides the comic elements from an earlier text which have been dismissed in the turning to obscure arts in *Portrait* but which are recoverable through an economy that invests common things with the persistent power of humor.

5

The Portrait Alternately Portrayed

Early in *Ulysses,* Stephen, taking the shaving bowl that Mulligan leaves behind on the parapet of the Martello tower, thinks of his past: "So I carried the boat of incense then at Clongowes. I am another now and yet the same. A servant too. A server of a servant" (*U* 1.310–12) True to his self-absorption, Stephen continually considers the inferiority of his position and, in the event, *Ulysses* shows him to be much "the same" as in *Portrait:* self-obsessed, still in a subservient role, still to the side of events and actions.

His memory of being a boat-bearer at Clongowes is not the wholly rueful experience he recalls so subjectively: then he "remembered the summer evening . . . dressed as boatbearer" (*P* 41). What he then remarks of the experience are those features which are most sensate and intense: the burning incense, its hissing sound and sour smell, as "he had stood holding out the boat to the rector"(*P* 41), as ever to the side of the essential action. The place is what calls the incident to mind, the sacristy "dark silent" (*P* 40) where the reprobate students had been caught in license by drinking the sacramental wine. Even out on the parapet of the tower, with the expanse of Dublin Bay and sky around him and Mulligan singing of drinking beer and wine, Stephen cannot be open but only private and closeted, concerned not with the real but with the self. It was summer then at Clongowes, as it is summer now in Dublin in June 1904, and, because a sad tale's best for winter, so summer is the time for comedy and laughter. Stephen, rather, wrongs the season with his grief, closed in the darkness of his guilt at his mother's death and of his intense self-pity.

Yet Stephen, however, is not only the same but "another now" because he is in a different text, one in which a sunny lightness contrasts with the restricted brooding intensity of much of *Portrait. Ulysses* is unabashedly overt in its humor; no longer closed up, closeted away, it is out in the open, just as Stephen's memory of an enclosed, dark space occurs under an open sky. As proof of this difference, the very first scene, a private moment of the toilet, is outdoors, the opposite of the etymological sense of closet. So intense is the sunlight of *Ulysses* in contrast to the dull darkness of *Portrait* that it even enters Bloom's kitchen half below grade. Stephen is always solemn, private, enmured within the walls of himself; he still seems to be within the confines of the directed, somber text that first portrays him when he is in another.

Stephen's memory of his past is subjective and subject to revision, but all memory is a backward glance, and backward glances reveal what is behind. *Portrait* is anterior to *Ulysses,* so Stephen's memories there of his past are all reflections on the earlier novel that presented his life; when he remembers something in *Ulysses* of his childhood, his memory makes an alternate look at what is portrayed by *Portrait.* There are few such memories, as if Stephen wishes not to remember or as if *Ulysses* chooses not to dwell on seriousness and solemnity: Stephen remembers times in which someone lit a fire for him, including Father Butt in the physics theatre (*U* 17.144), and thinks of his own enfeebled childhood when he observes the student Sargent at Deasy's school (*U* 2.169). What is continuous in Stephen's mind is less his memories than his moroseness. He can, however, refer to his past, often to measure again his own failings against it. Thinking of Mulligan saving a man from drowning, and his own fear of water, he thinks: "When I put my face into it in the basin at Clongowes. Can't see! Who's behind me? Out quickly, quickly" (*U* 3.325); he remembers an experience not directly represented in *Portrait,* but one clearly connected to Stephen's being pushed into the square ditch. The water does not permit him to see, which strikes fear in him (although he has voluntarily shut his eyes to see when walking on the Strand), yet that fear for Stephen is articulated as something "behind" him; what he fears is the exposure of his own inadequacy and failure. Yet what is behind him in time are the years of *Portrait,* and the place behind—of which he is so afraid—is the space of comedy. The comic lightness to be found there has a tone and a focus that are the strongest exposure of Stephen's character and failings; what is always behind are the comic elements of life Stephen resolutely refuses to face. If in *Ulysses* he is the same as he was in *Portrait,* the reader finds him in another text that illuminates this comedy by bringing it to the fore.

As *Portrait* itself displaced and obscured the comedy of the earlier *Stephen Hero,* so the solemnness and closeted focus of *Portrait* are put behind by the openness of *Ulysses.* Although related to it by consistency of place in Dublin and most particularly by Stephen's character as consistently morose, *Ulysses* is in every way an alternate to *Portrait,* and an alternate for *Portrait* is always something comic. It is in contrast as other to everything that *Portrait* is: open where the earlier is closeted; it is tripping and halting where the other is driven teleologically; its humor is in the forefront when the other has its humor behind. In short, *Ulysses* can be seen as the alternate *of* the *Portrait* itself, the other portrayal of the biographical novel. *Ulysses* has put the past behind it, as regards *Portrait,* so that the comic elements of the earlier text are directly seen in it. The open gaiety of *Ulysses,* its very sunniness, is the expression of the displaced humor of *Portrait* in *Portrait*'s very own terms. The overt tone and manner, focus and method of *Ulysses* give back another version of the biographical text, a version so marked as alternate and open that it fulfills all the characteristics of comedy, making tumble the serious earlier text, deflating the high purpose and poetic tone.

Ulysses presents this comic portrayal because what has been placed behind must come to the open. Bowen traces the comic trajectory of Joyce, which he considers as a continuous development, by noting that Joyce's "propensity to parodic comedy hinted at in *Dubliners,* which turned to irony in *Portrait,* returns to its ancient roots in *Ulysses.*"[1] While this acknowledges first off Joyce's continual comic temperament (a fact that prompted this study's look for the comedy of the biographical novel), and then stresses the inherent comic nature of *Ulysses,* it presents *Portrait* as a side road, a divarication, "turned" from Joyce's habitual comic ways. One might say that *Ulysses* makes fun of *Portrait,* taking the comic elements displaced and obscured in it and opening them up, throwing open the curtained and closeted seriousness. While not parodying *Portrait,* a move that would involve more censure than a related text of one's own would merit, *Ulysses* brings the comic shadows and displacements of *Portrait* to the fore, out of the somber absorption of Stephen and the narrow focus of the text that presents him.[2] This openness should come as no surprise, humor being irrepressible; the displacement and obscuring in *Portrait* in the service of irony or seriousness—or both—cannot be sustained for long. Joyce early on recognized his comic genius, and realized as well that he could not, and would not, resist its temptations; his temper, despite the obscure arts of *Portrait,* was comic. As early as work on *Dubliners* he speaks of "the spirit directing my pen" as "so plainly mischievous"[3] and that "the perverse devil of my literary conscience sit[s] on the hump of my pen."[4] "Mischievous" and "devil" are the descriptions of Joyce's character by classmates, "impish" and "elfish": he and his pen are of the same character.[5] The devil is the figure of carnival and comedy, and Joyce aligns himself with that spirit. The licentious and differently "perverse" quality of this spirit has been cabined and confined in *Portrait,* glimpsed behind but not dominant; it comes out fully in *Ulysses.*

This process of becoming explicit begins immediately. *Portrait* ends (as we have noted) with Stephen's comic conflation of a word pair in the diary notice of his mother's setting out his "new secondhand clothes"(*P* 252). Yet this humor, subtle and oblique in the text, is made even more open at the very start of *Ulysses* where the irrepressibly humorous Mulligan gives Stephen some castoffs and recognizes the comic absurdity of "secondhand" trousers by remarking to Stephen: "The mockery of it... Secondleg they should be" (*U* 1.116). Mockery is Mulligan's manner, as moroseness is Stephen's. We have noted that it is Mulligan who, as a mock prelate, opens the novel with a comic mass, and thus actively presents those cavorting priests of which *Portrait's* Stephen has only a brief, momentary glimpse. Yet that glimpse in the physics class, we have seen, opens up "the cloister of Stephen's mind," so that the "limp priestly vestments" of his somber life are shaken into gay life, set to sway and caper in a "sabbath of misrule." The place in his mind where those vestments are kept is much like the sacristy of Clongowes, "where the crimpled surplices lay quietly folded" (*P* 41); thus it is a "dark silent" place, where humor only occasionally emerges and is often silent like a surd. The cloister is the place away from the world, and thus away from the ordinary sources of humor, and it is the place where Stephen keeps his comedy closeted away. His somber dress is like the somber address of the novel. Yet in *Ulysses* if he is "the same," he is in another text, one where that sheltered world is opened and made lighter. The images Stephen has hidden away in the back of his mind in a closed space are out in the open in *Ulysses.* Mulligan the mock prelate is actual, not a figment of Stephen's imagining; he is capering and vested in an "open gown"; he is outside, not closeted away (despite his personal grooming). Mulligan blesses "gravely thrice the tower, the surrounding land and the awaking mountains" (*U* 1.10–11), thus continuing those alternates expressed in *Portrait* that configure its comedy, the pairing of "gravely" with "gayly." In contrast to his grave gesture is his gay vesture: his clothing is a gay array, not somber vestments; his wish for "puce gloves" and his "primose waistcoat" are not only dandyesque fashion but are also a parody of episcopal garments.

"Telemachus" is, of course, another chapter in the story of a young man, and in its opening, Stephen twice is aware of something "behind him." Each time it is something markedly different from him and his melancholic accustomed atmosphere: the comic figure of Mulligan and the brighter environment of the text, both of which contrast to the tenor of *Portrait* as a signal of the shift from displaced to direct humor. Stephen "heard warm running sunlight and in the air behind him friendly words.— Dedalus, come down like a good mosey" (*U* 1. 283–84); the words Stephen hears here, in contrast to those voices he ignores in *Portrait,* are friendly, and they treat Stephen much more lightly than he ever can treat himself, as a mosey, a sluggard, or an idler. (Such a comment was made to Stephen more seriously in the past [as we shall discuss below]; it is what Dolan calls Stephen when he punished him in *Portrait,* lazy and idle, yet in *Ulysses* it is only friendly banter in an invitation to eat.) Even the request to "come down," true because Stephen should descend from the parapet to the room where Mulligan has prepared breakfast, seems like a change from *Portrait,* where Stephen is constantly "soaring," striving for the elevation of development; to lower is the purpose of the comic. Somewhat later in "Telemachus," Stephen is again aware of Mulligan's presence, again by sound: "Behind him he heard Mulligan" (*U* 1.534), who, before bathing, plays at an epic-like slaughtering of enemies by hitting ferns and shoots with his towel. Mulligan behind Stephen is the actualization of the comic Irishman Stephen thought of in the *Portrait* physics theatre; but if Stephen still wants to situate that sort of figure behind him, the narration of this alternate text puts him right out in front.

When the ribaldry of another student's comment in that physics theatre airs out "the cloister of Stephen's mind," and he envisions the usually solemn priests cavorting and capering from the somber vestments, he thinks "the forms of the community emerged" (*P* 192). By "forms" he means the various types, the tall and short priests, the high president and the lowly instructors, of the fellowship of college and clerisy, yet the liberating energy of comedy suggests that what emerges, what comes to view, are the forms of community in another, alternate sense. For form, there is the philosophical and esthetic sense of the various possibilities in the Aristotelian sense of *eidos:* it is the potential for art such that what Stephen envisions momentarily in *Portrait* is what happens to the fullest in *Ulysses.* "Community," a sense of common purpose, suggests something common, something everyday, which is the source of humor and also of the community of the village that makes comedy a shared experience. In the somewhat scholastic setting of the National Library in "Scylla and Charybdis," Stephen argues that a man of genius makes no mistakes, that his errors are portals of discovery. Whatever the merits of that argument, one could say that *Ulysses* is a work that throws open the doors of possibility (not only of narrative and psychological representation) but particularly of humor.

Backward glances from the perspective of *Ulysses,* much like Stephen casting back his memory, allow us to engage the comedy which in *Portrait* is always located behind, over the shoulder: in the comic Irishman in his bench, in the contexts around Joyce's writing, and in the earlier version of *Stephen Hero.* As *Portrait* is closed, its humor displaced, and as the humor of *Ulysses* is open, we would expect to find that when the former refers to the latter, it does so in ways that open up what *Portrait* has been at pains to obscure and close off. *Portrait* is behind *Ulysses,* and when it is alluded to by memory, it forms some of the ludic features of the longer later novel. The surest way to determine that something is comic in Joyce, as we have noted from the outset, is to see how it connects to another site and text of his own; thus the appearances of parts of *Portrait* in *Ulysses* are confirmation of the comedy that is in that solemn text.

Ulysses, then, more open than *Portrait,* has as its most open and least restricted chapter "Circe"; Stephen's momentary glimpse of the "sabbath of misrule" in *Portrait* might well be a definition of the practice of the entire chapter. "Circe" is not only the liberation of libido, but the license of the carnivalesque;[6] it is slapstick, antic, playful, and play-like. Its oneiric quality, its masked postures, seem to define the revelry (κῶμος) that is at the heart of comedy. This chapter is itself a capering within the verisimilitude of the novel, and within *Ulysses* it performs a function that liberates the text from the realism of the rest; in a similar way, it plays with elements from *Portrait,* so much so that it could be seen as a comic rewriting of it, in which things that were more displaced in their humor and more serious are now opened and comical. Nearly every disjointed action and ludic mayhem that pertains to Stephen's past, what is behind him by June 1904, is in "Circe" as a playful treatment of the crucial elements of the novel of development, a comic series of misrule and misadventure contrasting completely with the direction and purpose of the novel of development.

If one could designate the disjointed and chaotic events of the chapter as scenes, the one most connected to Stephen's past is where he again remembers something that was depicted in the earlier text, the memory of the crucial pandying. In the context of *Portrait,* that incident is full of intense feeling and pain. What is in the foreground of that novel, however, is always treated as crucial and solemn; what humor there is, is always behind. So the "Circe" scene replays that of *Portrait:* "replay" is the correct word, as it reenacts the earlier incident with an overtness that brings out the comedy of *Bildungsroman.* What we find in the brief compass of a few lines of "Circe" is a comic compression of *Portrait* as a whole, of the major elements that make it such a directed, focused text. "Circe" playfully and somewhat chaotically presents the very issues against which the comedy of *Portrait* must covertly work: the telos of the genre, the inner focus, the intensity. There are alternate versions in this brief incident of Stephen and his memory that refer to *Portrait's* solemn themes of artistic freedom (essential to the plot of the development of an artist), of instruction (crucial to the novel of development), sexuality, and appetite. One might say that, as regards those moments when Stephen's past are presented in "Circe," they are the stuff of parodic comedy that Bowen says characterizes the development of Joyce's comic bent.

The scene begins with Stephen drunkenly attempting to light a cigarette; this passage specifically connects to *Portrait* by Stephen's use of a cigarette pack to endite his vaunted villanelle and by mention of his eyesight, evoking the "sixteen years" since the time of the first Clongowes classroom. Further, if brief, evocation of *Portrait* and its artistic purpose is to be found in the actual woman Zoe, representing in one person both the woman and the "life" that *Portrait* only generally but repeatedly claims to go to encounter. True to his unchanged nature, being "the same" as in the earlier text, Stephen only distantly engages the actual woman in this scene. Stephen's drunken state, itself a licensed contrast from the excessive soberness and solemnity of *Portrait*, moves Bloom to look after money Stephen has so carelessly dispersed in the brothel, where he is as profligate with his wages from teaching as he was earlier with his prize money from scholarship.

The smallest events in "Circe" recall the largest issues of *Portrait;* such tumbling disproportion is an essential move of comedy. As Stephen attempts to put away his returned money, he drops a box of matches. The acknowledgment, "That fell," and then "Lucifer" (*U* 15.3595, 3599), together make not only a realistic detail (about matches as "lucifers") but also an encapsulation of the major theme of Stephen's development in *Portrait*, that of moving to the end of his luciferean declaration that he will not serve (*P* 239). So what is most necessary in the novel of development, the liberation of the protagonist, is reduced to a clever joke by an inebriate, fumbling in slapstick in the simple act of trying to light a cigarette. This is a move of economy, where the details of *Portrait* are hoarded to pay later comic dividends. The *Wake* will continue this comic devaluation when, among the trash in Shem's house *Quivapieno,* there are "fluefoul smut" (Stephen's pornographic pictures hidden in the chimney) and "fallen lucifers, vestas which had served" (*FW* 183.16), the matches another of Stephen's various shortcomings and the vestas echoing these "virgins" in the brothel.

The pedagogical aura of *Portrait* is likewise caperingly encapsulated when during the exchange Stephen says his riddle of the fox and the grandmother; this is another backward glance because it makes a repetition with the scene earlier in the text when he taught. The classroom in "Nestor" is a variation of those classroom settings in *Portrait* which frequently afforded glimpses of humor and the license within the strictures of authority. So the riddle evokes not only the pointless humor of its unsolvability, but the asking of it also recalls the classroom strictures whose moments in *Portrait* of antic behavior offered a sabbath of comic respite. Those scenes in classrooms of license within order were themselves emblems of the novel's occasional comedy within the purposeful direction of its generic demands. Moreover, that the riddle is unsolvable means that it cannot be told, like a surd, so the scene reflects the Belvedere mathematics class in which the two-headedness of language and the tumbling clownish movement are first glimpsed behind the pedagogical insistence of the *Portrait* classrooms. The word "proparoxyton" is itself scholastic, continuing the air of pedagogy; it is temporal (from προπαρ, before) as regards metrical feet, but the notion of coming before suggests logically something that will also be behind, so it functions as a reminder of the elements of *Portrait* that are behind "Circe." The fact that Lynch playfully hits Florry "behind twice" brings to the forefront the placement of comic misrule.

The only incident that seems not to reflect *Portrait* directly is the palm reading which Zoe performs on Stephen, merely a parlor game in keeping with the party-like dimension of the chapter. Yet what is lightly rendered in Joyce is often full of context. Parlor games have been part of Stephen's youth and were for him not amusements but rather the means to measure his distance from his peers. In *Hero,* there is a long scene (42–47) in which Stephen plays charades, both keeping his distance and yet engaging in the play; both the length of the scene and Stephen's engagement with the games are again a measure of the different tenor of that text. It is at that party Stephen meets Emma Clery, who tells him later that she has had her hand read (*SH 67*). *Portrait,* of course, presents another version of Stephen's partygoing: at the Sheehy's "he took little part in the games," feeling himself a "gloomy figure amid the gay cocked hats" and he withdraws to "taste the joy of his loneliness" (*P 68*). The gay party favors he rejects, like those unmentioned at the family Christmas dinner in chapter 1, resemble the gay vestments of Mulligan in "Telemachus" or the cavorting priests in *Portrait's* chapter 4 who enjoy their fun and appetites; whereas Stephen likes only the savor of his moody separateness. In "Circe" others are adorned with changed vestments and other hats; Stephen is never so transformed. At a party for adolescents, or at "the feast of the world's culture"(*P* 180), Stephen is at least true to his moroseness, and he continues to be so even in a brothel.

The very nature of divination that Zoe offers to perform in playfulness has, moreover, another reflection pertinent to the earlier work. Such carnival divination treats comically and lightly the directional drive of the genre of *Bildungsroman* heavily weighted to purpose, the "prophesy of the end he had been born to serve and had been following" (*P* 169). Zoe's final reading, "Thursday's child has far to go. . . . Line of fate. Influential friends" (*U* 15.3687–8), is only a comic treatment of the solemnity of Stephen's own "divination" in the last diary entry, which has a calendar date, if not a day, of his going forth aided by that rather "influential friend," the artificer.

When Lynch asks Zoe who taught her palmistry, he brings up again the pedagogy that is so central to the plot of *Portrait*, and when Zoe responds, "Ask my ballocks that I haven't got" (*U* 15.3663), her ribald answer, somewhat appropriate to a brothel, is an open reference to the less appropriate joke about ellipsoidal balls in the instructional hour of the physics lecture, that comment which set off Stephen's image of the momentary sort of carnival of misrule which is fulfilled in the long chapter of "Circe." As we have seen, Joyce's humor always extends throughout a work and also between works, as a measure of its persistence, its endurance, and its importance. The "ballocks" that Zoe claims comically to have refers also to another part of *Portrait*, to the comment by Temple, during the comic exchanges in the scene at the signing of the petition for the Czar, when he claims to be a "ballocks." Temple himself, slight and "olive eyed," is feminized as well despite this distinction. Similarly, the persistence of gender confusion about women's hands (Stephen's being like a woman's) is not merely a challenge to traditional roles but also creates a confusion that is a source of comic hilarity. Gender transgression is something ludic, the stuff of the panto, and so it is something essentially humorous. "Circe" is, after all, the chapter in which Bloom becomes a woman, and Bella a man, to great comic effect.

The brothel, the entire setting of "Circe," is of course instituted for transgression and for the relief of appetite, and even in the brief vignette under consideration there is mention made of various needs: the unfulfilled desire for sex, the handling of money, Stephen's request for stimulation ("Cigarette, please"), Bloom's concern with Stephen's diet ("you ought to eat") as well as Zoe's ("Is he hungry?"). The fact of Stephen's smoking in *Portrait* is presented obliquely (as are so many of Stephen's actual habits or needs), most noticeable in the creation of the villanelle, which is composed, along with its suggestions of autoeroticism, on an opened cigarette packet (*P* 218). What makes for the production of art in *Portrait* is merely the consumption of appetite in *Ulysses*.

The pandying itself, the signal, most overt connection to the earlier text, is here completely changed. It is introduced (we have noted) when Lynch, that companion of Stephen's wandering in *Portrait,* slaps Kitty behind, "Like that. Pandy bat" (*U* 15.3667). (This rhyme evokes the doubled language of comic effect.) Both that rhyme and the location of the slap indicate that the comedy that is only an alternate in *Portrait* is here present. As well, the phrase recalls the young Stephen's question, "Why did Mr Barrett in Clongowes call his pandybat a turkey?" (*P* 30), with its sexual suggestiveness. Dolan appears as if summoned, but his entry here in this text elicits no fear; the serious appearance in *Portrait* is completely transformed. He has features similar to those highlighted in *Portrait,* such is the persistence of Stephen's memory for pain and difficulty: Zoe's observation of Stephen's hand as being like a "woman's hand" (*U* 15.3679) recalls Stephen's reaction to being touched by Dolan just before the beating (whatever else it provides by way of gender confusion). As well, what Dolan says in Stephen's vision is a compression of all that he said in the actual incident in the classroom of Clongowes: when he directly addresses Stephen, he calls him "lazy idle little loafer" (*P* 50) although when he first threatens Fleming, he says, "We want no lazy idle little schemers." In "Circe" he says, "Lazy idle little schemer" (*U* 15.3671). Just as the threatening charge of "lazy" is turned to the genial "mosey" of Mulligan in "Telemachus," the Dolan of *Ulysses* can no longer be a frightful figure, because the text he is in is changed: he becomes a plaything, a toy that might temporarily frighten children but ultimately makes them laugh. His appearance is pure carnival, the jack-in-the-box invariably dressed as a clown; he is like the Punchinello figure of feasts and fairs, popping up with his stick. The injustice and achievement of *Portrait* are reduced to *commedia dell' arte,* a tribute the open *Ulysses* pays to the tightly virtuous novel of development.

Father Conmee's comment—"I'm sure that Stephen is a very good little boy" (*U* 15.3676)—does not function as does his initial reaction to Stephen's claim of mistreatment in chapter 1 of *Portrait,* but is rather more like his anecdotal comment to Simon in chapter 2 (*"Manly little chap!"* [*P* 72]); that is, the first incident is tragedy, the second comedy, and the third, here in "Circe," is farce.[7] Conmee is also a figure of carnival, a Don Juan of licentiousness rather than rectoral rectitude; he, too, is different in another text. His comment about "a very good little boy" is another reference to the entire focus and form of *Portrait* itself, a comic description of the studious representation of the ascent of the protagonist, as any *Bildungsroman* is the story of the little boy who makes good.

The culmination of Stephen's morbidity and *angst* in *Ulysses* is the vision of his mother returned from the grave; the climax of the humor so long put off by him occurs immediately before. (This tight juxtaposition should be no surprise; in Joyce whenever there is something tragic, something comic should be close by, if not behind.) Before his mother appears, Stephen dances; this is an activity so alien to his nature in this novel and the one before that it is itself remarkable. He dances in turn with Zoe, Florry, and Kitty, the whole emblematic panoply of life, flora, and fauna he now embraces in a physical, not intellectual way. His noble claim in *Portrait's* chapter 4 to engage the "vegetable life" is here presented in comic play with Zoe and Florry. His dancing, while unique, has familiar patterns; he "waltzes," "wheels" in "a looser swing," "cumbrously" (with the heavy Florry). The motion is repetitive, circularly undirected, making as the pairs weave "a pattern on the floor," a text that is an alternate to the direction and telic drive of the biographical novel, and the "pair" a figure of the yoking opposites of humor. Stephen's dancing is the motion of capering and tumbling, of that exuberance and vegetable life (Zoe and Florry) which he claims in *Portrait* but never possesses. The loveliness he says he desires to press in his arms "which has not yet come into the world" (*P* 251) is here represented comically by two actual and rather cosmetically enhanced beauties.

Stephen, always the self-absorbed egotist, then dances by himself, with a motion which is his alone. This dance is unique, not only because nothing like it has been seen in Stephen's textual life, but it is unique because it was a dance of Joyce himself in his actual life—the "spider dance": "flinging his loose limbs about . . . , the effect accentuated by his tight trouser legs and . . . diminutive hat."[8] When Stephen dances even in the hallucinatory "Circe" there is something particular; he resembles the actual Joyce more than at any other part of *Portrait* or *Ulysses;* the gap between the morose Stephen and the lively Joyce is closed.

More openness: Stephen "frogsplits," with "highkicks with skykicking mouth shut hand" (*U* 15.4124)—all actions in themselves uncharacteristically *infra dignitatem,* the stuff of burlesque, and overtly funny, when Stephen is usually reserved. The odd gestures, and the unrestrained spontaneity with which they are performed, reflect something from Stephen's past, the final emergence of what has been so long immured, personally and textually: it is his image of the priests cavorting in the "sabbath of misrule." Stephen actually performs what he imagined before, the gestures parallel: his "frogsplits" with the priests' "leap frog"; his "shut mouth hand" with their "whispering... behind their hands"; his "highkicks with skykick[ing]" with their "stumbling, tumbling"—with both near rhyme pairs ("high/sky" and "stumbling, tumbling") another glance at the doubled comedy of language, voiced as sound. Stephen in the openness of *Ulysses* and in the carnivalesque of "Circe" has become what he had only thought—the comedy which is behind the earlier text of his life. Now active and outgoing, playful, he has become himself the literal embodiment of the comic other, stepping—or rather leaping—out from behind the text of *Portrait*. After alternate views of that text through displaced comedy, the doubleness of language, through the contexts of other works and that of earlier version, we now have an image of the alternate Stephen himself, different, other, in his full-length comic portrait.

Notes

Introduction

1. Page numbers refer to the *Viking Critical Edition*, edited by Anderson (1968); where the discussion also refers to other texts such as *Hero* or the essay "Portrait," a *P* will indicate this edition.

2. Scholes and Kain, *The Workshop of Dedalus*, 60.

3. It is axiomatic that *Portrait* is considered a *Bildungsroman*. Critics as separated by time and by critical temperament as Harry Levin (*James Joyce*, 41–43) and Enda Duffy *(Subaltern "Ulysses,"* 26, 30, 41) make this unquestioned claim. Breon Mitchell traces a literary history in his "*Portrait* and the *Bildungsroman* Tradition" in Staley, and notes pertinently that the novel is a "path . . . traced" (70) and that the genre is, "by implication and in fact, programmatic" (73). Jerome Buckley discusses the *Portrait* in his *Seasons of Youth* (Cambridge, Mass.: Harvard University Press, 1971), 230. Weldon Thornton discusses *Portrait* in this genre in great detail (also drawing connections to the corollary *Entwicklungsroman* and *Erziehungsroman*), although the focus of his treatment is to discuss the fundamental antimodernism of both that genre and consequently *Portrait* (*The Antimodernism*, chapter 4). Buttigieg considers the novel's tradition as a way to distinguish the critical approaches it elicits (8). Other full considerations include Lanham, "The Genre of *A Portrait* . . . and 'the rhythm of its structure,'" and Gregory Castle, "Reading Joyce's Bildungsroman." Castle pertinently notes that *Portrait* is an alternative to the exhausted cultural convention of the "general transmission and critique of cultural values without [its] having to conform to any . . . narrative authority' (24), yet for all that he still considers the novel as a *Bildungsroman*. In his *Ulysses as a Comic Novel*, Bowen notes that Stephen's position "in a *bildungsroman* search for personal truth . . . sets the tone and direction of the novel as a . . . solemn work" (4). I take no quarrel with these definitions, as they seem to be true of the novel; the point at issue is that, as such a work, there is an overdetermined telos intrinsic to the narrative and a correspondingly solemn cast, against which, I will argue, there is a countermovement and tone.

4. Ellmann, *James Joyce*, claims that Joyce at Clongowes was "happy and well" (27) and "laughed easily" (31). Costello remarks that "others around [Joyce] at

the time had the impression of a lively, contented child" (*Joyce: The Years of Growth*, 85). Bradley cites contemporaries who saw Joyce as "blithe and happy" (*Joyce's Schooldays*, 83). Lyons (*Joyce and Medicine*, 15) cites a contemporary at UCD who found that Joyce's "humor was impish." Robert Bell notes the differences between Joyce and Stephen in *Jocoserious Joyce*, "[Q]ualities in James Joyce, although well-documented, are too rarely remembered in connection with Stephen Dedalus" (33). Those qualities, and their documentation, can be found in Scholes and Kain, *The Workshop of Dedalus*, where several accounts of Joyce's contemporaries are anthologized, and all concur: Eugene Sheehy says, "Joyce had an impish humour" (176); Thomas Kettle notes that Joyce was "a lover of elfish paradoxes" (164); J. F. Byrne notes that Joyce "had a fine sense of humor, but his definitely favorite mirth rouser was when anyone pulled a boner" (140). "Elfish" and "impish" are terms one would not immediately chose to characterize Joyce, yet we shall find a certain puckish quality peering out from behind the serious foliage of the novel. Kenner calls Stephen "priggish, humourless" in *Dublin's Joyce*, 112.

5. Costello notes that Joyce wrote such a postcard to Vincent Cosgrave on December 15, 1902, 201, but does not give the text.

6. Ellmann, 12; Gorman, 8.

7. Kenner remarks that Joyce "excised the diphthong from the hero's surname so that Dedalus chimed with 'dead'" (*Dublin's Joyce*, 38).

8. Thornton in *The Anti-Modernism* discusses the text in contradistinction to its time; Buttigieg, in his *Portrait in Different Perspective*, treats the novel in contrast to the epistemological assumptions of criticism. Gillespie, *Reading the Book of Himself*, considers a dialectic of revision and response to *Portrait* which he sees mainly operating under the aegis of a novel that moves to a "goal" (102) and hence is still directed and purposeful.

9. Bakhtin discusses "the life of the belly" as a fundamental feature of the world of carnival in his *Rabelais and His World*, cited by Bowen, 80.

10. Kershner (*Joyce, Bakhtin, and Popular Literature*, 18) notes that Stephen is "briefly . . . visited" by the carnival muse; his choice of adverb acknowledges that way in which the context of comedy is temporarily glimpsed in the text. Kevin Dettmar discusses the carnivalesque in detail with reference to *Ulysses*, *The Illicit Joyce*, chapter 7.

11. Bakhtin notes that carnival "celebrated temporary liberation from the prevailing truth and from the established order" (*Rabelais and His World*, 10). This image of Stephen's has several further liberating features, most notably that of providing a definition of comedy within the text.

12. Monastic life was also the source of Lenten carnival; Bakhtin discusses monkish pranks (*Joca monacorum*) ibid., 13. See also Krause, *The Profane Book of Irish Comedy* for a discussion of the historical role of humor of "comic profanation that develops from the medieval to the modern period" (44) in "a socially and religiously conservative country such as Ireland [which] creates a favorable climate for the dangerous risks and rewards of comic rebellion" (53).

13. Fortuitously, but as if in confirmation of Joyce's signaling the comic impulse in his work, Suzanne Langer discusses the necessary action of "tumbling" in humor (*Feeling and Form,* Scribner's, 1953, 342): "the indomitable living creature fending for itself, tumbling and stumbling . . ."

14. Dettmar, in his perceptive and inventive readings of Joyce, considers *Portrait* to be beyond the possibilities of humor, arguing that it "cannot be fruitfully discussed in terms of its post-modernism" (*The Illicit Joyce,* 9) and thus in terms of the humor such a theory affords. He considers a further cause: "Given his early predilection for autobiography, and his unwavering youthful sense of his own importance, the comic exuberance that would break through years later in *Ulysses* was at this point perhaps beyond Joyce's scope"; 114. Exuberance may have been but humor is never beyond Joyce's reach, only occasionally it is just behind his text.

15. Kenner, usually quick to perceive irony at Stephen's expense, sees this juxtaposition rather as "dramatically" making the point about the vitiation of the Irish clergy (*Dublin's Joyce,* 126).

16. Maureen Waters discusses the tradition of the comic rural figure in *The Comic Irishman,* especially chapter 1. Declan Kiberd gives a more nuanced reading of this figure of Joyce's in political terms as an "impossibility" posed by nationalist rhetoric, *Inventing Ireland* (Cambridge, Mass.: Harvard University Press, 1995), 337.

17. Susan Stanford Friedman, "(Self)Censorship and the Making of Joyce's Modernism" (36–44) discusses the removal of the female figures, especially Stephen's mother, in psychoanalytic terms.

18. *Dublin's Joyce,* 132.

19. Dettmar, who reads postmodernism as "textual play over high artistic purpose" (10) cannot see such play in *Portrait,* which "I treat more skeptically, for I am convinced that it cannot be fruitfully discussed in terms of its postmodernism in the way that *Dubliners* and *Ulysses* can" (9).

20. Edited by George Sampson (London: Cambridge University Press, 1965), 992. Robert Bell makes the claim in *Jocoserious Joyce* that *Ulysses* is read too solemnly and not recognized for its humor; this claim seems even more pressing in the case of *Portrait,* although the comedy in it will be more oblique than that in *Ulysses.* There has been only one article among the many to see any humor; that is Ronald Wallace's "'Laughing in Your Sleeve': James Joyce's Comic *Portrait.*" Remarking that Joyce is a comic writer, Wallace claims that "the intrinsic genre of *A Portrait* is comedy, and the novel is structured on the two archetypal patterns of integration and exposure"(68): the former he finds in Stephen's marriage-like making and merging images of women to create a "society" of art (63); and the latter the society to be ridiculed in Joyce's "social satire," "aimed at the institutions of Dublin society, particularly school, state, and church" (64). Apropos his title, Wallace claims that "Joyce is laughing in his sleeve at Stephen; part of the reason that Joyce is laughing is just that Stephen isn't" (65). As the major claim about

archetypes demonstrates, Wallace has taken his terminology from Northrop Frye.

21. Despite his reading of the postmodern freeplay and humor of Joyce, Dettmar can find no such qualities on *Portrait:* it is "the Joycean text that fares least well in the postmodern age. Because the novel is the spiritual autobiography of a would-be Byronic artist/hero, and Joyce doggedly adheres to the tenets of imitative stylistics, the subject and subject matter are inherently serious and self-important . . ." (10), and that, at best, there is only "Joyce's irony [which] was too little, too late." (11).

22. Ellmann, 26.

23. The issue of irony in *Portrait* is central to its reception, as irony forms the counterreading to the novel as successful artistic development. Gillespie, in his *Reading the Book of Himself,* gives a perceptive overview of the issue of irony as it causes different assumptions of the text of *Portrait* by the reader (see especially pages 83, 89, 152). Staley, in his "James Joyce" in *Anglo-Irish Literature,* edited by Richard Finneran, has a full discussion of the critical issues; as does Sosnoski, "Reading Acts and Reading Warrants: Some Implications . . . ," who uses the conflicting interpretations of irony to call for a reader-oriented poetics. He attributes the ironic, detached readings of *Portrait* to the effects of *Bildungsroman.* Likewise, Thornton also discusses the "inherently ironic mode of presentation" of *Bildungsroman* (79, also footnote 16) stemming from the disparity of narrator and character. In a post-structuralist view, Stephen Heath discusses the antitraditional "irony of suspended sense" in the *Portrait* narrative, that is, the "absence of the sense to which the irony could be reduced" (37), leading to a strategy of hesitation in the bafflement and confusion of the text ("Ambiviolence").

24. In discussing Stephen's esthetic irony, Buttigieg correctly notes Stephen's disdain for experience and aloofness from the material world (73). Experience and the material world are those places, of course, that form the sources of comedy.

25. Dettmar discusses the modernist impulse of "faithfully representing the signified," 21.

26. See Hancock, *Word Index to James Joyce's "Portrait of the Artist."*

27. Wallace cites this passage as demonstrating Joyce's comic focus and goes on to note that Lynch makes comic interpolations in *Portrait,* when in *Hero* (rather uncharacteristically we shall come to find), Cranly only listens (70).

28. It is depicted in Kenner's *Joyce's Voices,* 46.

29. Buttigieg notes that Lynch undercuts Stephen's theorizing (74).

30. Ellmann notes pertinently that "Joyce allowed the Stephen of twenty to display a sense of humor" in chapter 5 (355).

31. Robert W. Corrigan, "Introduction," *Comedy: Meaning and Form* (New York: Harper and Row, 1981), 8, 12.

32. James Feibleman, *In Praise of Comedy* (New York: MacMillan, 1939), 178.

33. For the ways in which feminist humor challenges universal (and masculine) assumptions, see Regina Barreca, introduction to *Last Laughs* (New York: Gordon and Breach, 1988) 8; the quotation cited comes from her *Untamed and Un-*

abashed (Detroit: Wayne State University Press, 1994), 15.

34. Barthes from *The Pleasures of the Text,* Kristeva from *Revolution;* cited by Dettmar, 21 and 41, respectively.

35. Anderson, in the notes to his edition, remarks that "the expression is a tautology" (517).

36. In discussing the diversionary aspect of feminist humor, Barreca cites Mary Ellmann (commenting on Schopenhauer's sense that women see only what is before them); Ellmann's location of humor seems particularly apt: "if a person does not see an object, it must follow that he sees something beyond or above the object" (cited in introduction to *Last Laughs,* 6).

1. "The Comic Irishman in the Bench Behind": The Portrait with Two Heads

1. *Ulysses* 2.166, whose mother had fed him with her "wheysour milk."
2. Kershner, in his essay "The Artist as Text: Dialogism and Incremental Repetition in *Portrait,*" suggests that when Stephen disavows the comment on MacAlister, the reader recognizes that it comes "from Simon Dedalus, whose language Stephen so reluctantly shares" (in *Critical Essays on James Joyce's A Portrait,* edited by P. Brady and J. Carens [New York: G. K. Hall, 1998], 241). Simon as a comic figure is similarly eclipsed and replaced in *Portrait.*
3. *James Joyce,* 355.
4. Krause: "In an insular and parochial country such as Ireland . . . comic renewal has often been greeted with suspicion, violence, or censorship" (20). He also speaks of the antagonism of the jester with the priest (54).
5. In discussing the political effect of subversive humor, Dettmar claims that, in order to "destroy Stephen's aesthetic [of Romanticism], Joyce needed to adopt a guerilla position. This he doesn't do in *A Portrait.* . . . Thus *A Portrait* has a difficult time laughing at Stephen" (136). I would argue that the humor, literally subversive and to the side, is in fact the guerrilla activity, the laughter of the suborned of the text, and does laugh at Stephen to the political end of undermining all the novel's authoritative orders. Dettmar finds the humor of "Telemachus" as "the carnivalization of *A Portrait*" (136). He notes, with respect to "Aeolus," that the changing polyphony of *Ulysses* is "a guerrilla action, from the outside" (187). As demonstrated, this study finds such polyphony in *Portrait,* so that there is this sort of political action within but just behind that text.
6. *Jokes and Their Relation to the Unconscious* (Norton, 1963), 200.
7. In his discussion of whether *Portrait* is ironic, Scholes considers the tension between serious and satirical in terms of Frye's patterns of comedy, where the tendentious part of the text functions as the *alazon,* the humorous as the *eiron.* Scholes's main point is that the balance of these features is to be found in Stephen, "himself as both *eiron* and *alazon*" in *In Search of James Joyce,* 10. The places where I claim comedy is to be sought and found extend beyond Stephen even to the countermovement of the genre itself, such as here.

8. That figure, as Maureen Waters discusses, is a convention of the late nineteenth century; see especially her chapter 3.

9. From Booth onward, the distance between Stephen and the narrative (or the world around him) is seen as an esthetic one exclusively in the service of irony. Staley gives an overview of the criticism in his "Sixty Years with Joyce's *Portrait*," as does James Sosnowski's review of esthetic distance in "Reading Acts and Reading Warrants." Buttigieg (40–41) sees irony as a means to assert the novel's autonomy as a work of art and the necessary demand for stasis that made it so appealing to New Critical approaches (such as Sharples, "The Stasis of Pity," reprinted in Schutte, 96–106). Gillespie finds that there is a polyphony in the "sophisticated reading of *Portrait*," and that the "emphasis given to irony will vary from reader to reader [as] . . . the tones of Stephen and the narrator become implicit commentaries on one another" (153). Yet that distance need not be bridged by knowing, purposeful irony but rather capering humor.

10. Kershner, 6; Ellmann, 50.

11. *Ulysses* 16.362.

12. Thornton, 126, gives a very original analysis of the way in which Stephen's mind is affected by what is going on around him, although Stephen resolutely fails to acknowledge that anything is: "Consider how subtly Stephen's 'inner' psychic processes reflect his sensations and his perceptions of the outer world . . . images and metaphors . . . are engendered in Stephen's mind by the public objects and events in the scene before him"; for example, how the candles the dean lights makes Stephen think, "His very body had waxed old in lowly service."

13. For the relationship of Stephen and Cranly, see Joseph Valente, "Thrilled to His Touch: Homosexual Panic and the Will to Artistry in *A Portrait*," *The James Joyce Quarterly* vol. 31, no. 3, spring 1994, particularly 184–186.

14. See Waters, 4: "The children in some districts wore sticks, suspended from their necks, on which notches were carved to indicate any lapse into Irish, for which punishment was duly meted out." Humor in Joyce can always gesture to political oppression.

2. The Surd and the Absurd: The Conflated Language of Comedy

1. That is, as noted in the last chapter, the prohibition of Gaelic and the stick used to record such lapses, cf. Waters, 4.

2. Doubling is a long-recognized feature of comedy, especially in parallel scenes of figures; Ronald Wallace, in his "'Laughing in Your Sleeve'" quotes Bergson on repetitious symmetry: "Any arrangement of acts which gives . . . the distinct impression of a mechanical arrangement" (67). Doubling of words, such as these in *Portrait*, is less often recognized. A more contemporary critical view suggests the subversive power of comic language: "Language explodes with meaning and by doing so explodes the structures of the system from within. This process is in itself duplicitous in that it destroys and creates simultaneously." (R. Barreca, introduc-

tion in *Last Laughs: Perspectives on Women and Comedy* [New York: Gordon and Breach, 1988], 17).

3. "The repressive activity of civilization brings it about that primary possibilities of enjoyment, which have now, however, been repudiated by the censorship in us, are lost to us. But to the human psyche all renunciation is exceedingly difficult, and so we find that tendentious jokes provide a means of undoing the renunciation and retrieving what was lost." *Jokes and Their Relation to the Unconscious* (New York: Norton, 1963), 110.

4. See Riquelme, 68: "Because telling and tale, process and product, are both suggested to the reader at once, there are always two Stephens to be experienced and judged." While this comment perceptively suggests the doubled nature of the text, its insistence on judgment ("judged") still retains a sense of the purposefulness of reading, rather than its comic playfulness. Riquelme does acknowledge the "the language of the book casts two shadows, projects two images . . ." (64).

5. *The Dialogic Imagination* (Austin: University of Texas Press, 1981), 324.

6. See particularly Kershner, chapter 4, 165–185.

7. Compare Zack Bowen's analysis of plot in *Ulysses* and his quotation from Northrop Frye that "not going anywhere belongs to comedy," cited on 27.

8. *Joyce's Voices*, chapter 2.

9. The chiasmic structure of the language, which is a doubling and turning, is pertinent to this sense, if not directly related to it. Riquelme (80) speaks of language being "duplicated," while, according to Elliott Gose, this is a balance of inner and outer and is said to produce a stasis, in which "one phrase mirrors another" (260). Yet this doubling may be something more than rhetorically artistic word order; it is a function of a diction that dynamically unbalances the text toward the humorous.

10. Kenner finds that the "indulgence in *chiasmus*" "leaves after-vibrations of sententiousness by which the young man does not seem to be troubled," *Ulysses*, 7; he concentrates particularly on the description of the girl in chapter 4.

11. Thrane, in his discovery of the sermon from which Joyce derived Arnall's, notes that what Joyce had "taken from his model he has made his own." "The sermonistic parallelism, balance, and suspensions of the original [were] made more telling" (188). Pertinent here is the fact that the various doubled diction that Joyce gives to Arnall has no source in another text, but is uniquely and comically Joyce's own.

12. See *Romans* 3:9, "for we have before proved both Jews and Gentiles that they are under sin"; and 3:29, "is he God of the Jews only? is he not also of the Gentiles?"

13. It should be remarked in passing that this infernal vision is an intense, alternate version of the comic capering and Sabbath misrule that Stephen envisions in the physics theater: there is the same whispering and soft language, the same repetitive and pointless motion. The one is solemn, although conflated with the comic; the other is comic, although touched with a serious appreciation. Reflec-

tion will suggest other scenes in *Portrait* that are paralleled to provide alternately solemnity and humor (as discussed, for example, the pandy scene and Conmee's comic account of it).

14. *James Joyce,* 49.

15. With thanks to Zack Bowen, who brought this point to my attention.

16. According to the *Word Index, shadow* appears three times; *shadowed,* once; *gravely,* twice; *grave,* once, all in the space of a page.

17. As regards Stephen's overlooking the world outside him, Thornton notes that "Joyce's third-person presentation in *Portrait* facilitates his presenting dimensions . . . that Stephen is not himself aware of" (120). Richard Peterson notes that in Stephen's esthetics, there is a lack of "an attempt to define reality in terms of human experience" and goes on to argue that were Stephen to admit that experience "would be to leap into a sea of poverty, dogma, and censorship" (432). One could argue that *Portrait* is already steeped in those miseries or one could say that Joyce would and did easily turn them into art, and humor.

18. The epiphany recognizes the transcendent moments that arise artfully from the commonplace. But as is the case with everything Stephen considers, he stresses the serious intellective side of what the epiphany achieves and neglects the place from which it comes, a place he puts beside him. Pertinently, the entire notion of the epiphany is directly developed in *Stephen Hero* but displaced behind *Portrait.* Joyce will exploit the way in which the banal comically connects with the sublime (see, for example, the epiphany written to Stanislaus about the Coliseum and Rome falling, the banal exit of the inferior British visitors, "Kemlong, 'ere's the way aht" *Letters* II, 146). The epiphany will seek to manifest the higher things, but it does so from the very simple and silly (in the etymological sense of the words) that lie just beneath or behind what shines forth. Scholes and Kain note that the epiphanies are of two kinds, one in which the mind of the writer is important, and the other which focuses on some "vulgarity of speech or of gesture," *Workshop,* 4.

19. In the long and often acrimonious exchange between Joyce and Grant Richards about the publication of *Dubliners,* Joyce defended his subject matter by noting the sort of details that Stephen overlooks: "the odour of ashpits and old weeds and offal hangs round my stories" (*Letters* I, 64).

20. F. L. Radford notes, in his "Daedalus and the Bird Girl: Classical Text and Celtic Subtext," that "the theme of fosterage . . . that runs through *A Portrait* is as much Irish as classical" (256); it is also comic.

21. Edmund L. Epstein remarks that this word pairing "is not inconsistent. The sacred and the profane here join" (*The Ordeal of Stephen Dedalus,* Carbondale: Southern Illinois Press, 1971, 99–100). Yet surely the combination is, if not inconsistent, incongruous.

22. Bowen notes in *Ulysses as a Comic Novel* that the *alazon* is the profaner, the outsider to the mysteries (37); perhaps Stephen's tediousness here is a reflection of that type.

23. Marguerite Harkness notes the similarities of the two disparate figures, *Voices of the Text,* 85–86.

24. Culleton calls them "onomastic caricature," *Names and Naming*, 33.

25. Most critics tend to see the villanelle as serious and accomplished. Scholes claims that "the inspiration and the poem are both intended to be genuine" ("Stephen Dedalus; Poet or Esthete?" 289). Even a critic attuned to the differences in the texture of the narrative such as Riquelme finds the poem an "astonishing and successful attempt to make thought, speech, writing, aesthetic response, and sexual fulfillment all appear to commingle in the language and the processes of a single text" (75). Surely in that catalogue of achievements there might be room for some element of humor.

26. For a discussion of the bull imagery, see Benstock, "A Light from Some Other World," in *Approaches to "Portrait,"* edited by Staley, 211.

27. Riquelme discusses this pairing as a function of the novel's complex temporality, rather than its humor (67).

28. Michael Levenson, in his "Stephen's Diary: The Shape of Life" (in *Critical Essays on Joyce's "A Portrait,"* edited by Philip Brady and James Carens [Boston: G. K. Hall, 1998]), remarks on how the diary's language "plays a comedy," 45, and how one possible effect of the diary is to recast "momentous incidents in a parodic mode." This claim, while certainly a welcome corrective, accounts only for those portions in which Stephen is conscious of his tone.

29. That the word "stead" may be a joke on the journalist Stead, mentioned at the university, cannot be ruled out. The next chapter will consider popular publications and some reference to Stead himself.

3. Two Comic Contexts

1. Kershner: "Joyce by no means spent his reading life closeted with Flaubert, Ibsen, Bruno and Vico" (7); among the periodicals Kershner notes are several low cultural ones from Ireland, such as *Dublin Opinion*, a comic paper.

2. Gifford, 178.

3. Anderson, 510.

4. Ellmann, 50.

5. "A monthly illustrated paper, edited by H. Easom/Hudson"; vol. 1, no. 1; vol. 6, no. 63; Dublin, January 1894-December 1899. As far can be determined, the only extant copies are in the National Library of Ireland (which is missing numbers of vol. 1 for May 1894), and the British Library.

6. Costello claims that "a photograph of the school taken at this time shows him . . . on the end of a front row" (130), and displays it in his set of illustrations, attributing it to the *Illustrograph*.

7. Both Ellmann, 40, and Costello, 129 say that Joyce attended "Araby" in that year 1894. Costello reproduces a photograph of the stall "Algeciras" in his illustrations.

8. *Illustrograph*, vol. 1, no. 6, July 1894, 142.

9. Letter of October 15, 1906; *Letters,* II, 122.

10. Vol. 6, no. 63, 21.

11. *The Irish Comic Tradition* (Oxford: The Clarendon Press, 1962), 36.

12. "American novelties took time to affect the diet [in the late 1700s]. Turkeys caught on easily with nobles used to devouring . . . storks, swans, and peacocks": review by Eugen Weber of Flandrin and Montari, *Histoire d'Alimentation, Times Literary Supplement,* January 31, 1966, no. 4896, 9.

13. Jonathon Green, *Slang Through the Ages* (Lincolnwood, Ill.: NTC Publishing Group, 1997), 58.

14. Gifford, in *Ulysses Annotated* (Berkeley: University of California Press, 1988), glosses the phrase a slang for sexual intercourse; his bibliography lists Partridge as a source.

15. *James Joyce,* 34.

16. Partridge notes that it is late eighteenth to early twentieth centuries; he also gives the less common Catholic counterterm of "parson's nose." (*Dictionary of Slang and Unconventional English* [New York: Macmillan, 1950]).

17. For a discussion of the evolution of Joyce's writing in this crucial time frame, with emphasis on the change from *Hero* to *Portrait,* see Gillespie, 48–57.

18. Kershner describes the wide-reaching effect of Harmsworth's journalistic empire, beginning with his publication of the "penny dreadfuls," 5–6.

19. The standard biography of Wallace is *The Biography of a Phenomenon,* by Margaret Lane (London: Heinemann, n.d.). Wallace, a self-taught writer, transferred out of the army in South Africa on the eve of the Boer War, to become an independent journalist. Through a fortuitous chance, he was hired by the *Daily Mail* first to be its auxiliary war correspondent and, following a scoop of reporting on the details of the peace talks, hired permanently in London in 1903. He was often sent abroad for reporting, as far as Canada or Algiers. After 1906, Wallace became a self-supporting writer (and Joyce takes no notice of his novels).

20. His biographer notes that in reporting "he brought a freshness of imagination and a descriptive skill . . . He approached the writing of each article as he might have done the construction of a short story—with a sharp eye for an interesting opening, an amusing or dramatic development, and a neat end" (*ibid.,* 140).

21. David Glover, introduction to *The Four Just Men,* by Edgar Wallace (Oxford: Oxford University Press, 1995), xv.

22. "I: Peter's Beginnings," *The Daily Mail,* Tuesday, November 21, 1905, 8; the series was entitled "Red Pages from Czardom."

23. Gillespie remarks of Joyce's use of predecessors that "his interest in other authors mirrored his own evolving artistic consciousness," and that he was influenced by a "range of artists" (80). Gillespie focuses on Joyce's technical development, not on that of his humor.

24. *The Daily Mail,* Thursday, May 17, 1906, 6.

25. For a further discussion of the parodic elements of *Dubliners* but in terms of the literature of the Irish Revival, see my "'Scrupulous Meanness' Reconsidered: *Dubliners* as Stylistic Parody" in *Joyce in Context,* edited by Vincent Cheng and Timothy Martin (Cambridge: Cambridge University Press, 1992), 153–169.

26. *Madam Bovary,* translated by Paul De Man (New York: Norton, 1965), 107.

27. Dettmar makes a great deal of the importance of the funeral to the postmodern and carnivalesque sensibility of the novel in his *The Illicit Joyce*, chapter 7.

28. "Where France Meets Germany. The Comedy of the Morocco Conference." *The Daily Mail*, Monday, February 26, 1906, 6.

29. For a reading of the nationalist rhetoric of "Cyclops," see Enda Duffy, *The Subaltern "Ulysses,"* chapter 3, "The Spectacle of the Native," especially 109–129.

30. *The Daily Mail*, October 12, 1906, 5.

31. *The Daily Mail*, Tuesday, June 25, 1906, 6.

32. "A Day in Switchback Lisbon," *The Daily Mail*, Tuesday, July 3, 1906, 6.

33. *The Workshop of Dedalus*, 61.

4. Obscure Arts and the Economy of Vulgar Language

1. This misinformation comes from Gorman, 196; Ellmann states that what was burned was an early draft of *Portrait*, 314. The wish that *Hero* was eradicated is father to the fact that it is seen as radically other than the canonized *Portrait*.

2. Viking critical edition, 484. The Loeb edition has "he sets his mind to work upon unknown arts" (translation by Frank Justus Miller [Cambridge, Mass.: Harvard University Press, 1984]). The sentence in Ovid concludes *naturamque novat*, "and changes the laws of nature"; this change of what is natural is also pertinent to the ways in which *Portrait* changes the nature of *Hero* and also of Joyce's own characteristic writing.

3. Fritz Senn has examined the epigraph with characteristic minute acuity in "The Challenge," although his final judgment is that it refers to the text as the "gropings of a developing mind at crucial stages" (128).

4. Ellmann, 196.

5. *Letters*, II, 87.

6. *James Joyce*, 264.

7. A. Walton Litz notes that "the richness of the earlier work was sacrificed in favour of intensity" and Joyce discarded "multiple events and elaborate expository passages . . . in favour of a few scenes" (*The Art of James Joyce*, New York: Oxford, 1964, 35). Fortuitously, Litz uses as his epigraph the same quotation from Ovid.

8. There is considerable latitude in finding the focus to the elliptical quality of the epigraph; Senn, *op. cit.*, suggests that the subject of the epigraph is the artist, the author, or the reader (124); similarly, Gillespie suggests that it refers to Joyce, Stephen, or the reader (82).

9. Harry Levin in *James Joyce* notes that as Joyce rewrote *Hero* he seemed to have transferred "the social into the psychological sphere" (48); another way to say this is that he moves the focus interiorly leaving the active, actual, and potentially comic world behind.

10. Gabler, in his "The Seven Lost Years," notes how Joyce's revisions alter the "episodic pattern" of *Hero* into the "evolving narrative principles and techniques" of *Portrait*, in Staley, 41.

11. For a discussion of this sort of censorship, see Susan Stanford Friedman,

"(Self)Censorship and the Making of Joyce's Modernism" in *Joyce: The Return of the Repressed*, 21–57.

12. Gillespie notes how *Portrait* "obscures [apt word choice] the features that in *Dubliners* allowed one to distinguish unambiguously the sources of specific voices" (13).

13. Gillespie, for example, remarks on how the *Portrait* scene at the Sheehy's house "discards the declamatory asides of the longer version" (51); these sorts of narrative comments in the expanded earlier text, thrown away, are the obvious comic elements of *Hero*.

14. This demon is also Joyce's literary daemon, as is substantiated in a letter to Stanislaus where Joyce describes "the perverse devil of my literary conscience" (*Letters*, II, 166). This is the devil in Joyce's inkwell, who, indelible, can never be wholly erased. See also Krause, 35–38, for the presence of the devil in Irish comedy.

15. Surprisingly, Connolly suggests the narrator "does not usually comment in any way, favorably or unfavorably, on Stephen's actions" (233), but rather presents scenes "with astonishing objectivity" (234).

16. κῶμος is revelry, but the O.E.D. suggests that it derives from village, κώμη.

17. This passage is connected to another part of *Hero*, with the connection reinforcing the same parallel of high art and low subject that Wallace employed. During the debate about Stephen's paper "Drama and Life," an interlocutor, deriding Stephen's assumption that literature may have a less than lofty focus, remarks: "If this was drama he did not see why some Dublin Shakespeare should not pen an immortal work dealing with the new Main Drainage Scheme of the Dublin Corporation" (*SH* 102).

18. Bradley, 37 (he reproduces the punishment book, 38); Ellmann, 30.

19. Gillespie discusses the parallel sections as enhancing the reader's "creative participation in the formation" of the text of *Portrait*, "especially when compared with the alternative[s] offered by *Stephen Hero*" (55). He argues that the discussion on the character of language foregrounds "the ambivalence with the consciousness of Stephen as it appears in *Portrait* from the certitude that had been depicted in the earlier work." That certitude, especially as regards the value of vulgar language, is one of the ways in which *Portrait*, renouncing its earlier version, maintains its serious tone.

20. Wayne Booth had a different view of the effect of the original *Hero* on *Portrait*, one pertinent to the discussion here. Booth claimed that "ironic readings did not become popular, in fact, until after the fragment of *Stephen Hero* was published in 1941" (333). He argues that ironic reading of the later text is imported from external factors, and not internal to it. The argument I make here suggests that humor, not irony, in *Portrait* is beside the text, and may be glimpsed by external factors such as *Hero* or Joyce's comic contexts.

21. Hancock notes that the text of *Portrait* contains 909 compounds; such elision marks Joyce's style, yet it might be argued that the very method of

enjambing words will have the effect of bringing their possibilities for comic conflation into a violent conjunction. The word "marketplace" is certainly a word with important meanings.

22. In *Rabelais and His World,* Bakhtin speaks of the special "forms of marketplace speech," being "frank and free," cited by Bowen (18).

23. Oxford: Clarendon Press, 1882.

24. Gillespie notes that "prosaic segments" in *Hero* "become the kernel for elaborate lyrical descriptions underscoring Stephen's emotional turmoil" (52); just this substitution, however, makes the more elevated language that much more subject to comic tumbling.

25. For a survey of the imagery of water, see Carens in *A Companion to Joyce Studies,* edited by Bowen and Carens, 306–308.

26. That "to go by the board" also has metaphoric suggestions of the loss of playing pieces in a game adds to the ludic possibilities latent in the language.

Conclusion: The Portrait Alternately Portrayed

1. *Ulysses as a Comic Novel,* 116.

2. Dettmar has perceptively noted that, "The 'Telemachiad' is . . . the carnivalization of *A Portrait,* especially embedded as it is in the context of the rest of *Ulysses*" (136); but he does not focus, in his treatment of *Ulysses,* on those places where it recalls the earlier autobiographical novel. He rather discusses the carnivalization of *Ulysses* extensively in terms of the "Hades" episode, in his chapter 7.

3. *Letters* II, 99.

4. *Letters* II, 166.

5. As noted previously, *The Workshop of Dedalus* cites Sheehy as noting Joyce's "impish humour" (176) and Kettle, his love of "elfish paradoxes" (164).

6. Bell, discussing the various forms of play in the chapter, notes that it "takes form as a kind of carnival" (161). He also notes the continuity of *Portrait* and *Ulysses* mentioned earlier: "In several compelling but inconclusive ways, *Ulysses* . . . conveys Stephen's traditional notion of personal identity, though now the possibilities are comically multiplied and contradicted" (179): exception taken only to the "inconclusive."

7. By contrast, even Kenner, who is inclined to read Stephen always skeptically and comically, sees the scene in *Portrait* and *Ulysses* as "associated with the hangman-god and the priestly denial of the senses, . . . one of Joyce's standard images for Irish clericalism—hence the jack-in-the-box appearance of Father Dolan in Circe's nightmare imbroglio, his pandybat cracking twice like thunder." *Dublin's Joyce,* 123.

8. Ellmann, 430.

Selected Bibliography

Works of James Joyce

The abbreviations following the citation indicate the designation used within the text.

Critical Writings. Edited by Ellsworth Mason and Richard Ellmann. New York: Viking, 1959. (*CW*)

Dubliners. New York: Viking, 1965. (*D*).

Finnegans Wake. New York: Viking, 1966. (*FW*)

Letters. 3 vols. Vol. 1 edited by Stuart Gilbert. New York: Viking, 1957; reissued with corrections, 1966. Vols. 2 and 3 edited by Richard Ellmann. New York: Viking, 1966. (*Letters* I, II, III).

A Portrait of the Artist as a Young Man. Edited by Chester Anderson. New York: Viking, 1977. (*P*)

Stephen Hero. Edited by Theodore Spencer. New York: New Directions, 1963. (*SH*)

Ulysses. Edited by Hans Walter Gabler. New York: Random House, 1986. (*U*)

Secondary Works

Anderson, Chester G., ed. *A Portrait of the Artist as a Young Man.* New York: Viking Press, 1964.

———, ed. *A Word Index to James Joyce's "Stephen Hero."* Ridgefield, Conn.: Ridgebury Press, 1958.

Attridge, Derek and Daniel Ferrer, eds. *Post-Structuralist Joyce.* Cambridge: Cambridge University Press, 1984.

Bakhtin, Mikhail. *Rabelais and His World.* Translated by H. Iswolsky. Cambridge, Mass.: MIT Press, 1968.

———. *The Dialogic Imagination.* Translated by Caryl Emerson and Michael Holquist. Austin: University of Texas Press, 1981.

Bell, Robert. *Jocoserious Joyce.* Gainesville: University Press of Florida, 1996.

Benstock, Bernard. "A Light from Some Other World: Symbolic Structure." In *Approaches to Joyce's Portrait,* edited by Thomas Staley, pp. 185–211. Pittsburgh: University of Pittsburgh Press, 1976.

Booth, Wayne. *The Rhetoric of Fiction.* Chicago: University of Chicago Press, 1961.
Bowen, Zack, and James F. Carens, eds. *A Companion to Joyce Studies.* Westport, Conn.: Greenwood Press, 1984.
———. *Ulysses as a Comic Novel.* Syracuse: Syracuse University Press, 1989.
Bradley, Bruce, S. J. *James Joyce's Schooldays.* New York: St. Martin's Press, 1982.
Buttigieg, Joseph. *A Portrait of the Artist in Different Perspective.* Athens, Ohio: Ohio University Press, 1987.
Carens, James F., and Zack Bowen, eds. *A Companion to Joyce Studies.* Westport, Conn.: Greenwood Press, 1984.
Carens, James F. "*A Portrait of the Artist as a Young Man.*" In *A Companion to Joyce Studies,* edited by Zack Bowen and James F. Carens, pp. 255–359. Westport, Conn.: Greenwood Press, 1984.
Castle, Gregory. "The Book of Youth: Reading Joyce's Bildungsroman." *Genre* 22 (spring 1989): 21–40.
Connolly, Thomas E. "*Stephen Hero.*" In *A Companion to Joyce Studies,* edited by Zack Bowen and James F. Carens, pp. 229–253. Westport, Conn.: Greenwood Press, 1984.
Costello, Peter. *James Joyce: The Years of Growth.* New York: Pantheon Books, 1992.
Culleton, Claire A. *Names and Naming in Joyce.* Madison: University of Wisconsin Press, 1994.
Dettmar, Kevin J. H. *The Illicit Joyce of Postmodernism: Reading Against the Grain.* Madison: University of Wisconsin Press, 1996.
Duffy, Enda. *The Subaltern "Ulysses."* Minneapolis: University of Minnesota Press, 1994.
Ellmann, Richard. *James Joyce.* New York: Oxford University Press, 1982.
Friedman, Susan Stanford. "(Self)Censorship and the Making of Joyce's Modernism." In *Joyce: The Return of the Repressed,* edited by Susan Stanford Friedman, pp. 21–57. Ithaca, N.Y.: Cornell University Press, 1993.
Gabler, Hans Walter. "The Seven Lost Years of *A Portrait of the Artist.*" In *Approaches to Joyce's Portrait,* edited by Thomas Staley, pp. 25–60. Pittsburgh: University of Pittsburgh Press, 1976.
Gifford, Don. *Joyce Annotated.* Berkeley: University of California Press, 1982.
Gillespie, Michael. *Reading the Book of Himself: Narrative Strategies in the Works of James Joyce.* Columbus: Ohio State University Press, 1989.
Gorman, Herbert. *James Joyce.* New York: Rinehart and Company, 1939.
Gose, Elliott B., Jr. "Deconstruction and Creation in *A Portrait of the Artist as a Young Man.*" *James Joyce Quarterly* 22 (spring 1985): 259–270.
Hancock, Leslie, ed. *A Word Index to James Joyce's "Portrait of the Artist."* Carbondale: Southern Illinois University Press, 1967.
Harkness, Marguerite. *"A Portrait of the Artist as a Young Man": Voices of the Text.* Boston: G. K. Hall, 1990.

Heath, Stephen. "Ambiviolences: Notes for Reading Joyce." In *Post-Structuralist Joyce*, edited by Derek Attridge and Daniel Ferrer, pp. 31–68. Cambridge: Cambridge University Press, 1984.
Kain, Richard M., and Robert Scholes, eds. *The Workshop of Daedalus*. Evanston, Ill.: Northwestern University Press, 1965.
Kenner, Hugh. *Dublin's Joyce*. Boston: Beacon Press, 1962.
———. *Joyce's Voices*. Berkeley: University of California Press, 1978.
———. *Ulysses*. London: Allen and Unwinn, 1980.
Kershner, Brandon. *Joyce, Bakhtin, and Popular Literature: The Chronicles of Disorder*. Chapel Hill: University of North Carolina Press, 1989.
Krause, David. *The Profane Book of Irish Comedy*. Ithaca, N.Y.: Cornell University Press, 1982.
Lanham, Jon. "The Genre of *A Portrait of the Artist as a Young Man* and 'the rhythm of its structure'." *Genre* 10 (1977): 77–102.
Levin, Harry. *James Joyce*. New York: New Directions, 1960.
Lyons, J. B. *James Joyce and Medicine*. Dublin: Dolmen Press, 1973.
Mitchell, Breon. "*A Portrait* and the *Bildungsroman* Tradition." In *Approaches to Joyce's Portrait*, edited by Thomas Staley, pp. 61–76. Pittsburgh: University of Pittsburgh Press, 1976.
Peterson, Richard. "Stephen's Aesthetics: Reflections of the Artist or the Ass?" *James Joyce Quarterly* 17 (summer 1980): 427–433.
Radford, F. L. "Daedalus and the Bird Girl: Classical Text and Celtic Subtext in *A Portrait*." *James Joyce Quarterly* 24 (spring 1987): 253–274.
Riquelme, John Paul. *Teller and Tale In Joyce's Fiction: Oscillating Perspectives*. Baltimore: The Johns Hopkins Press, 1983.
Scholes, Robert. "Stephen Dedalus: *Eiron* and *Alazon*." In *In Search of James Joyce*, edited by Robert Scholes, pp. 7–15. Urbana: University of Illinois Press, 1992.
———. "Stephen Dedalus: Poet or Esthete?" *PMLA* 79 (September 1964): 484–489.
———, and Richard M. Kain, eds. *The Workshop of Daedalus*. Evanston, Ill.: Northwestern University Press, 1965.
Schutte, William M., ed. *Twentieth Century Interpretations of "A Portrait of the Artist as a Young Man."* Englewood Cliffs, N.J.: Prentice-Hall, 1968.
Senn, Fritz. "The Challenge: '*ignotas animum*' (an Old-Fashioned Close Guessing at a Borrowed Structure)." *James Joyce Quarterly* 16 (fall 1978/winter 1979): 123–134.
Sharpless, F. Parvin. "Irony in Joyce's *Portrait*: The Stasis of Pity." In *Twentieth Century Interpretations of "A Portrait of the Artist as a Young Man,"* edited by William Schutte, pp. 96–106. Englewood Cliffs, N.J.: Prentice-Hall, 1968.
Sosnowski, James J. "Reading Acts and Reading Warrants: Some Implications for Readers Responding to Joyce's Portrait of Stephen." *James Joyce Quarterly* 16 (fall 1978/winter 1979): 43–63.

Staley, Thomas F., ed. *Approaches to Joyce's "Portrait."* Pittsburgh: University of Pittsburgh Press, 1976.

———. "Strings in the Labyrinth: Sixty Years with Joyce's *Portrait*." In *Approaches to Joyce's "Portrait,"* edited by Thomas F. Staley, pp. 3–24. Pittsburgh: University of Pittsburgh Press, 1976.

———. "James Joyce." In *Anglo-Irish Literature,* edited by Richard J. Finneran, pp. 366–435. New York: Modern Language Association of America, 1976.

Sullivan, Kevin. *Joyce Among the Jesuits.* New York: Columbia University Press, 1958.

Thrane, James R. "Joyce's Sermon on Hell: Its Source and Its Backgrounds." *Modern Philology* LVII (February 1960): 172–198.

Thornton, Weldon. *The Antimodernism of Joyce's "Portrait of the Artist as a Young Man."* Syracuse: Syracuse University Press, 1994.

Waters, Maureen. *The Comic Irishman.* Albany: State University of New York Press, 1984.

Wallace, Ronald. "'Laughing in Your Sleeve': James Joyce's Comic *Portrait*." *Essays in Literature* 3, no. 1 (spring 1976): 61–72.

Index

absurd: boundary marked by, 46–47; comic deflation in, 73; confession and, 65–66; as counterpart of surd, 49, 54–55; gaily/gravely combined in, 55–56, 57; inherent in language, 81–82; in interview with director, 68; in reaction to girl on the beach, 77–78; in word pairings, 62. *See also* surd
adieu/lane/rue: conflation of, 9, 122
admit/submit: pairing of, 35–36, 121
"Aeolus" (Joyce), 108, 109
afflict/inflict: pairing of, 61
"After the Race" (Joyce), 103–5
ale/master/home/Christ: wordplay and, 39–40, 133–34
Algeciras Conference, 107–8
alibi/disavowal: as doubling, 30, 165n.2
Alice in Wonderland (Carroll), 62
Anderson, Chester G., 118, 165n.35
anima: use of term, 119
anticlericalism, 96
antimodernism, 161n.3
"Araby" (Joyce), 86, 92, 129, 169n.7
Aristotle, 15, 21, 40, 129
arms: in artistic gesture, 80–81
Arnall, Father (char.): demonology of, 64; idle students and, 34–35; word pairings of, 61–63, 79
art: autogeneric type of, 75; comedy as just behind, 73–75; comic deflation and, 71–73; comic type of, 15–16; economy of, 138–40; esthetic discussion of, 16–19; gesture toward, 80–82; Joyce's understanding of, 53–54; language as, 51–52, 133–38; as mediation in portraits, 43; possibilities in, 152–53; religion replaced with, 66–71, 72–73; vision of, 76–77. *See also* esthetics
artists: characterized as "our young," 88; independence of, 113–14; value of language and, 136–38
Athy (char.), 49–50
authority: in classroom, 24, 34–36; comedy's function and, 31–33; countervoices to, 26–28; doubling as possibility in, 60–61; reading vs., 85; wordplay's stance against, 50–51. *See also* imperialism
autobiography: comic conflation in, 82; influence of, 2–3; resistance to burlesque in, 87–88

bad: repetition of, 56
Bakhtin, Mikhail, 51, 162n.9, 162nn.11–12, 173n.22
Barreca, Regina, 164–65n.33, 165n.36
Barthes, Roland, 21
bedroom: symbolism of, 63
before/behind: pairing of, 80
Bell, Robert, 161–62n.4, 163–64n.20, 173n.6
Bella (char.), 156
belladonna: use of term, 44–45
belly, 3–4, 72, 162n.9. *See also* carnival; commonplace
Belvedere College: Joyce's time at, 85–86, 169n.6
bench: doubling of, 28

Benstock, Bernard, 169n.26
Berard, Victor, 98
Bildungsroman (novel of development): comic suppressed by, 9; critical issues in, 144–45; direction in, 20, 71, 75, 82, 136; education in, 24; humor as other side in, 13, 15–16, 22–23, 30–31, 158; irony in, 15, 164n.23; liberation in, 31, 154; *Portrait* as, 1–2, 161n.3; rebellion in, 51; resistance to hegemony of, 32–33; soul and God in, 36; subject vs. family in, 140–46; utility of language and, 135–37. See also classrooms
birds, 62–63, 78
Bloom (char.), 144, 156
body: intellect vs., 3–5; as source of comedy, 32. See also belly; sexuality
Booth, Wayne, 166n.9, 172n.20
Bowen, Zack, 150, 154, 161n.3, 167n.7, 168n.22
bowstring: use of term, 29, 30
Bradley, Bruce, 161–62n.4
Buckley, Jerome, 161n.3
Bull: use of term, 76, 79, 169n.26
Burke, O'Madden (char.), 128
burlesque, 87–88, 158–59. See also carnivalesque
Buttigieg, Joseph, 161n.3, 162n.8, 164nn.24, 29, 166n.9
Byrne, J. F., 161–62n.4
Byron, George Gordon, 35, 76

>idx>Carens, James F., 173n.25
carnival: monastic life and, 162n.12; as outside *Portrait*, 12; party games and, 155–56. See also commonplace
carnivalesque: belly linked to, 3–4, 162n.9; brief visit by, 162n.10; "Circe" as, 153–59; farcical in, 124–26; liberation in, 162n.11; lists as, 62–63; masking of, 70; peasantry linked to, 87–88; tumbling linked to, 5–6; words in service of, 138. See also common language
Castle, Gregory, 161n.3
censorship: by Church, 31, 165n.4; of immediate, 121, 171–72n.11
chapel/church: pairing of, 65–66

"The Chauffeur" (Wallace), 103
chiasmus, 58–59, 167nn.9–10
children/pigs: pairing of, 62–63
Christ/ale/master/home: wordplay and, 39–40, 133–34
Christmas dinner, 56–57, 95–97
church/chapel: pairing of, 65–66
"Circe" (Joyce): as comic compression of *Portrait*, 4, 153–59; prostitutes in, 44; turkey in, 95
classmates: Joyce's attitudes toward, 89, 111–12; narrative presence of, 113; Stephen's distance from, 3–5, 8, 25
classrooms: common language in, 4–5, 26–27, 156; function of scenes in, 24–25, 33–34; heads in, 26–29, 45–46; intellect vs. physical in, 3–4; misrule in, 34–36, 45–47; pandying and heresy in, 35–38, 121, 153–54, 157–59; reader's missed attention to, 24–25; reading vs., 85; replayed in *Ulysses*, 155–56; wordplay's role in, 50–51
Clongowes (school): Joyce's language at, 130; popular publication on, 86; Stephen as bystander at, 25; Stephen's memories of, 148–49, 151. See also classrooms
Clontarf, 76, 80
comedy: alleged absence of, 163n.14; as alternative, 7–9, 22–23, 27–28; in art, just behind, 73–75; boundary marked by, 46–47; chronology subverted in, 25–26; as conservative and disruptive, 20–21; contexts' relation to, 83–84; critical discourse on, 6, 13–14, 20–21, 86–88; cunning type of, 80; direct vs. indirect, 91; displacement of, 26–28, 31, 33–34; of disproportion, 107–8, 154; doubling and, 6–7; in esthetic discussion, 16–19; historical role of, 162n.12; implications of, 2–3, 15; location of, 9–10, 12–13, 30–31; overt, in *Portrait*, 13–14; self-sufficiency of, 15–16; use of term, 16. See also humor; tumbling; wordplay
comic impulse: concept of, 92
comic Irishman: actualization of, 152; location of, 30–31, 38; as marginalia and

misrule, 31; nomad as, 139; Stephen's disdain/fear of, 11, 16, 32–33; stereotype of, 87–89, 166n.8; as symbol, 163n.16
comic journals. *See* popular literature; *specific titles*
common language: comedy in, 131–32; comic undercutting by, 144–45; economy of, 146–47; *Hero*'s link to, 129–30; hoarding of, 139, 142, 143–47; as outside *Portrait*, 12; revaluation of, 139–40; value of, 130–31, 133–44, 172n.19. *See also* commonplace
commonplace: art's origins in, 72–74; *Hero*'s link to, 129–31; opting for, 70; recognition of, 72–73; removal of, 121–23; as source of metaphors, 72–73, 76–77; Stephen's descent to, 152; Stephen's distance from, 65–68, 71–75, 140–41; transcendent moments based in, 168n.18; value of, 130–31; words in service of, 138. *See also* common language
communal sentiment, 127–30, 138–39
Communion: self-communion juxtaposed to, 70
community: meanings of, 152–53
Concise Cambridge History of English Literature, 14
Conmee, Father (char.), 37–38, 157–58
Connolly, Thomas E., 172n.15
contexts. *See* counterparts of narrative; cultural context
Cosgrave, Vincent, 78, 162n.5
Costello, Peter, 161–62n.4, 162n.5, 169nn.6–7
counterparts of narrative: concept of, 83–84; in *Hero*, 104, 111, 112–13, 115–16; Joyce's reading and, 84–86, 169n.1; Wallace's writing as, 97, 102, 103–5, 107–11, 114–16
Count of Monte Cristo, The (Dumas), 85
Crampton, Sir Philip, 17–18, 46
Cranly (char.): as another head, 42–45; appreciation of poetry and, 74; as behind, 27; "Bull's eye" of, 79; on Jesus, 81; name of, 78; Stephen's relationship with, 57, 76, 80, 129, 166n.13

Culleton, Claire A., 169n.24
cultural context: *Portrait* at odds with, 2, 162n.8
cunning: use of term, 80
Cunningham, Martin (char.), 105–6
"Cyclops" (Joyce), 108, 109

Daily Express (newspaper): review in, 102
Daily Mail (newspaper): Joyce's reading of, 99–100, 103, 108, 110; writers for, 100–101, 107–8, 170n.19
"Dead, The" (Joyce), 93–95, 104
dean: comic language for, 40–42; compared in *Hero* and *Portrait*, 132–37; Stephen as instructor to, 38–40; Stephen's sensitiveness in, 144–45; use of "detain" and, 57–58, 133–34; vulgar language and, 130
death: humor linked to, 53–54, 158–59, 171n.27; novelistic use of, 106
Dedalus, Maurice (char.), 37
Dedalus, May (char.), 75, 122, 148, 158, 163n.17
Dedalus, Simon (char.), 16, 37–38, 96, 165n.2
Dedalus, Stephen (char.): aloofness of, 54, 67, 71–72, 74–76, 164n.24; change to university, 9–10; as character and narrator, 51, 167n.4; comic and serious contrasted, 3–5, 16, 22–23; confession of, 64–66, 146; dancing of, 158–59; displacement of, 78–79; doubleness of, 28–30; family differentiated from, 140–46; habits of, 156–57; improvement/development of, 1–2; independent gesture of, 80–82; inner focus of, 2, 7–9, 15, 24, 33, 121, 124, 148–49; just behind and, 22–23, 34–36, 151–52; name of, 2, 162n.7; otherness of, 33–34, 38–40, 42–43, 54, 78, 113–14; other voices/heads as intrusions for, 27–30; pandying and heresy of, 35–38, 121, 153–54, 157–59; as priest/monk, 11–13, 21; reading of, 84, 85–86; sermons of retreat and, 61–64; theology of, 36, 114; unreal language of, 40–42
desire: Joyce's art and, 91–92

detain: use of term, 57–58, 133–34
Dettmar, Kevin: on carnival, 162n.10, 171n.27, 173n.2; on humor's absence, 163n.14, 164n.21; on postmodernist textual play, 163n.19; on signified, 164n.25; on subversive humor, 165n.5
devil: function of, 172n.14; use of term, 124–26, 150–51
diary entries: comic conflation in, 80–82, 169n.28
"Diary of a 'Special' In a Hurry, The" (Wallace), 109–10
dimitto: meanings of, 118, 120–21, 132
director: Stephen's interview with, 67–71
Dolan (char.), 34, 37, 157
doubling: alibi/disavowal as, 30, 165n.2; alternative created by, 51–55; of alternative heads, 28–30, 43–45; authority and, 60–61; critical discourse on, 166–67n.2; of earnest/comic, 28–31; function of, 46–47, 82; of names, 49–50; in rejecting priesthood for art, 67–71; in Stephen's pandying, 37–38; in surd/absurd, 48–51; of teachers/priests, 6–7; in villanelle, 79; as wordplay, 49–50, 52–53
drainage: humor of, 10, 106–7, 128–29, 172n.17
"Drama and Life" (Stephen/Joyce), 89, 124–25, 172n.17
Dryden, John, 138
Dublin: church/chapel in, 65–66; communal sentiment's source in, 128–29; use of real places in, 10, 75–76
Dubliners (Joyce): ceremonial carving in, 92–95; comic in, 104–6, 115, 150; communal sentiment in, 128; details in, 140, 168n.19; humor in, 12, 14; influences on, 102; parody in, 170n.25; *Portrait* compared to, 10, 11; source of, 86, 87; writing of, 97–98. *See also specific stories*
Dublin Illustrograph (periodical): comic articles in, 89–97; critical articles in, 86–88; extant copies of, 169n.5; Joyce's reading of, 85–88, 89
Dublin Opinion (periodical): Joyce's reading of, 85, 169n.1
Duffy, Enda, 161n.3

Dujardin, Édouard-Émile-Louis, 98
dull: use of term, 3, 14
dusk: use of term, 3, 147

economy: definition of, 138; revaluation by, 139–40; value of words in, 133–39, 146–47
elephant: use of term, 62–63
ellipsoidal balls, 4–5, 26–27, 156
Ellmann, Mary, 165n.35
Ellmann, Richard: on burning of manuscript, 171n.1; on comedy, 31, 164n.30; on *Hero*, 118; on Joyce and Araby, 169n.7; on Joyce's characteristics, 2, 161–62n.4; on Joyce's confession, 65
Emma (char.), 11, 123–24, 143
emotions: "curve of," 1; of hero, 144–45; Joyce's removal of, 11; water imagery for, 142–44
Ennis (char.), 45–46, 48–50
Epictetus, 40, 41
epigraph: concept of, 117
epigraph to *Portrait*: alternatives in, 117–20; commonplaces and, 129–31, 147; critical discourse on, 171n.3, 171n.8; effects of, 120–23, 125; etymology of, 121, 130; as renunciation, 119–21
epiphany, 110, 137, 168n.18
Epstein, Edmund L., 168n.21
Erzeihungsroman (novel of education): comic as respite in, 7–8; lightness present in, 69; *Portrait* as, 1–2, 5; reading in, 84
esthetics: comedy's resistance to, 32–33; disconnected type of, 74–76; Joyce's development of, 89, 91–92, 97–98, 104, 111–12, 170n.23; Stephen's experience of, 73–79; Stephen's posturing in, 16–19, 58–59, 72; tumbling in, 46; unreal approach to, 40–42. *See also* art
Eucharist, 8, 21, 27
"Eumaeus" (Joyce), 106
exile: use of term, 80
eyes, 35, 44–45

fallen/idle: pairing of, 71
falling: use of term, 1, 4. *See also* tumbling

farcical: use of term, 124–26
feminist theory: on comedy, 20–21, 164–65n.33, 165n.36
Finnegans Wake (Joyce): comic in, 82, 154; grave and death in, 60; humor in, 14; Joyce's reading and, 99; list of names/places in, 18; *Portrait* compared to, 11, 119; rise and fall in, 4
fire: use of term, 132, 133
Flaubert, Gustave, 10, 106
Fleming (char.), 34
foster(age): use of term, 75–76, 79, 140, 146, 168n.20
France, Anatole, 98
Freud, Sigmund, 21, 32, 50–51, 167n.3
Friedman, Susan Stanford, 163n.17, 171–72n.11
Frye, Northrop, 163–64n.20, 165n.7, 167n.7
funnel/tundish: pairing of, 39, 135–36

Gabler, Hans Walter, 171n.10
Gaelic language: punishment for speaking, 46
gaily/gayly: gravely opposed to, 55–56, 57, 59, 71, 151
gender: conflation of, 5–6; confusion of, 9, 43–45, 156; inversion of, 79. *See also* sexuality; women
generosity: in *Hero*, 123–24
gentle/Gentile: pairing of, 62
Gifford, Don, 170n.14
gift of tongues (Pentecostal), 104
Gillespie, Michael: on comparing *Portrait* and *Hero*, 172n.19, 173n.24; on epigraph to *Portrait*, 171n.8; on irony in *Portrait*, 164n.23, 166n.9; on Joyce's development, 170n.17, 170n.23; on *Portrait*'s obscuring of scenes/sources, 172nn.12–13; on revision/response in *Portrait*, 162n.8
girl on the beach, 76–78, 79
Glover, David, 170n.21
goatish/gloating fiends, 64, 65, 79
Gogarty (Joyce's acquaintance), 113–14
Goggins (char.), 114
Gorman, Herbert, 171n.1

Gose, Elliott, 167n.9
gowns/skirts, 5–6, 14, 68
"Grace" (Joyce), 12–13, 104–6, 128
gravely: gaily opposed to, 55–56, 57, 59, 71, 151; lightly opposed to, 59, 69–70
Graves, Alfred P., 86
guerrilla activity: humor as, 165n.5

habits: use of term, 68
hagiography: severed heads in, 43
Hancock, Leslie, 172–73n.21
Hardy, Thomas, 98, 102
Harkness, Marguerite, 168n.23
Harmsworth, Alfred (Lord Northcliffe), 99, 100, 108, 170n.18
heads: as alternatives in portrait, 28–29, 31, 33, 42–47; in classrooms, 26–29, 45–46; doubling of alternative, 43–45; as intrusions for Stephen, 27–30; sticks and, 46, 48–49, 52, 166n.14; of turkey, 94, 95. *See also* surd
Heath, Stephen, 164n.23
heavenly: meaning of, 77–78, 168n.21
hell: use of term, 27–28, 61, 64
heresy: in classroom incident, 35–36
hero: temperament of, 144–45
Heron (char.), 35–36, 78–79
holily/wholly: pairing of, 60, 64
home/Christ/ale/master: wordplay and, 39–40, 133–34
home/stead: conflation of, 82, 169n.29
Homestead (periodical): Joyce's writings in, 103–4
homoeroticism, 44–45, 57, 166n.13
Horace, 135
House by the River, The (Warden), 99
humeral veil, 21–23, 70
humor: historical role of, 162n.12; irony's link to, 19–20; as irrepressible, 150; political oppression as point of, 166n.14; possibilities in, 152–53; removal/obscuring of, 121–26; as sidelight/alternate, 6–9, 12–13, 15–16, 18–19, 21–22; subversive effect of, 165n.5. *See also* comedy
Hungary: Iron Crown of, 43
Hynes, Joe (char.), 53–54

184 Index

hyperbole: effects of, 90–91; in inner/outer juxtaposition, 13; obscuring of, 145–46

Ibsen, Henrik: influence by, 10, 16, 112; interest in, 122; Stephen's/Joyce's paper on, 89, 124
Icarus, 73
identity: language as determiner of, 52–53
idle/fallen: pairing of, 71
imperialism: comedy's function and, 31–33; encoding of, 53–54; Morocco crisis and, 107–8; puns and, 50–51, 167n.3; turkey's link to, 93, 170n.12
inflict/afflict: pairing of, 61
intellectiveness: use of term, 145, 146
Ireland: comic writing in, 86–92; disdain for, 38–39; humor's historical role in, 162n.12; model for, 43; theocratic culture of, 6, 31–32, 165n.4
Irish Literary Society, 86–87
Irish Revival Literature, 170n.25
Irish Times (periodical): Joyce's writings in, 103
irony: in esthetic discussion, 16–17; humor's link to, 19–20; in instructional aim, 1–2; popularity of, 172n.20; in *Portrait*, 164n.23, 165n.7, 166n.9; prevalence of, 14–15, 164n.23; puns compared to, 51; in reader's response, 24–25; restrictions of, 13; Stephen's role in, 8; in valuing language, 131

Jesus: Joyce's humor and, 8, 81, 113–14
John the Baptist: head of, 43, 44
jokes. *See* comedy; humor; laugh/laughter
journalism: Joyce's reading of, 98–102, 107–10; Joyce's use of, 10, 106–7, 128–29, 172n.17
joy: in comic art, 15–16, 77
Joyce, James: art's meaning for, 53–54; as comic writer, 163–64n.20; confession of, 65; daemon of, 172n.14; dancing of, 158; on details, 168n.19; esthetic development of, 89, 91–92, 97–98, 104, 111–12, 170n.23; humor of, 2, 14, 98, 119, 150, 156, 161–62n.4, 173n.5; influences on, 98; model for, 97, 102, 103–5, 107–11, 112–13; reading of, 84–88, 89, 97–104, 107–10, 169n.1; use of correspondence by, 110–11; words hoarded by, 139, 142, 143–47
Joyce, Stanislaus, 98–100, 110–11, 172n.14

Kain, Richard M., 161–62n.4, 168n.18
Kane, Matthew, 106
Kenner, Hugh: on chiasmus, 167n.10; on "Circe," 173n.7; on critical terminology, 56; on irony, 13; on Joyce's characteristics, 2, 161–62n.4; on names, 162n.7; on vitiation of priests, 163n.15
Kershner, Brandon: on influences on *Portrait*, 51; on journalism, 170n.18; on Joyce's reading, 169n.1; on polyvocality, 84; on Stephen and carnival, 162n.10; on Stephen's disavowal, 165n.2
Kettle, Thomas, 161–62n.4, 173n.5
Kiberd, Declan, 163n.16
Kildare Street Club, 76
"King Kong" (film), 100
Kitty (char.), 157, 158
Krause, David, 162n.12, 165n.4, 172n.14
Kristeva, Julia, 21
Kuenstlerroman, 1, 144

lamp: as metaphor and real, 40–42
Lane, James Allen, 102
Lane, Margaret, 170n.19
lane/rue/adieu: conflation of, 9, 122
Langer, Suzanne, 163n.13
language: ambiguity in, 46; as art, 51–52, 133–38; confusion possible in, 44–45, 52–53; in critical discourse on comedy, 6; displacement of, 38–42; linked to body vs. intellect, 3–5; monk vs. rogue words and, 11–13; polyvocality of, 9–10, 84; value of, 130–31, 133–44, 146–47, 172n.19. *See also* common language; doubling; Gaelic language; wordplay
Lanham, Jon, 161n.3
laugh/laughter: absence/presence of, 126–27; hidden in serious, 17, 22–23; priests' furtive, 17, 20, 22, 36; use of term, 14–15; vocalization of, 37–38

"Lestrygonians" (Joyce), 144
Levenson, Michael, 169n.28
Levin, Harry, 161n.3, 171n.9
lightly: gravely opposed to, 59, 69–70
lists: as carnivalesque, 62–63; function of, 39–40
Litz, A. Walton, 171n.7
longing: comic and, 43–44
Lynch (char.): comic misrule and, 155, 156, 164n.27; esthetic discussion and, 16–19; name of, 78; pandying and, 157
Lyons, J. B., 161–62n.4

Macalister (char.), 28–30
"The Makings Up of Herbert Stagg" (Wallace), 108–9
Maple House, 76–77
marketplace: meanings of, 172–73n.21; revaluation by, 139–40, 142–43; speech of, 173n.22; value of words in, 41, 133–39
masks: memories paired with, 69–70; mirthless paired with, 70, 71
master/home/Christ/ale: wordplay and, 39–40, 133–34
masturbation, 18, 127
matches: use of term, 154
mathematics class: dating of, 85; rational/irrational in, 54–55; replayed in *Ulysses*, 155; surd in, 46–47; tumbling in, 45–46
McCann (char.), 113, 114, 115, 127
melody/mirthless: pairing of, 71
memories/masks: pairing of, 69–70; subjectiveness of, 148–49
Mercier, Vivian, 92
Meredith, George, 16, 87, 89
Metamorphoses, The (Ovid), 117–18. *See also* epigraph to *Portrait*
metaphors: for classmates, 112; comedy of common, 142–47; commonplace source of, 72, 76–77; reality's clash with, 40–42; in vulgar language, 131–32, 140
Mettle of the Pasture, The (Lane), 102
Middle Ages: comic in, 6
Milton, John, 138
mirthless/music: pairing of, 71

misrule: as alternate rhythm, 5–9; carnivalesque as, 162n.11; as cause of sins, 43; of chronology, 26; in classroom, 34–36, 45–47; comic Irishman as, 31; common speech in, 12; furtive laughter and, 17, 19; language as aim of, 140; location of, 52–53; reader's missed attention to, 25; rejection of, 10; surd's evocation of, 49; "vegetable world of," 10–11, 12, 71–73, 128
Mitchell, Breon, 161n.3
Morocco crisis, 107–8
Moynihan (char.): Shakespeare allusion of, 29; as stereotype, 87; as voice behind, 26–27, 28; vulgar language of, 4–5, 12, 30. *See also* comic Irishman
mulier cantat: meanings of, 74
Mulligan (char.): as comic counterpart, 114; as joker, 14; masturbation and, 18, 127; secondhand clothes of, 151; Stephen's memories of, 14, 149; as voice behind, 151–52
music/melody, 71, 74

names: alternate meanings for, 78; choice of Dedalus, 2, 162n.7; doubling of, 49–50; list of, 18; as onomastic caricature, 169n.24
narrative: abstraction in, 102, 111; ceremonial carving in, 92–94, 95–97; comic countermovement in, 30–31, 60, 68–69, 77, 80, 93, 150–51; common, humorous perspective in, 127–30; common language obscured in, 130–31; confusion in background of, 57; dual perspective of, 58–59; hegemonic forces in, 31–33, 50–51; interiorization of, 2, 7–8, 15, 33, 121, 124; narrator in, 113, 168n.17; rational/irrational in, 54–55; Stephen's distance from, 166n.9. *See also* counterparts of narrative; epigraph to *Portrait*; reader
"New Irish Humorists" (article), 86–88
Newman, John Henry Cardinal, 58, 132, 133–34
nightshade: use of term, 44–45
nomad, 138–39

186 Index

Northcliff, Lord (Harmsworth, Alfred), 99, 100, 108, 170n.18
novels: origins of, 117; resistance to hegemony of, 32–33; serializations of, 99, 108. *See also* narrative

olive/oval: pairing of, 78
"One Way of Carving a Turkey" (article): description of, 89–91; as possible source, 91–97
otherness: behind humeral veil, 70; epigraph's signaling of, 119–20; of Stephen, 33–34, 38–40, 42–43, 54, 78, 113–14; of *Ulysses* to *Portrait*, 149–51; of voices in classrooms, 26–29
oval/olive: pairing of, 78
Ovid, 117–18, 171n.2. *See also* epigraph to *Portrait*

pandying: in classroom incident, 35–38, 121, 153–54, 157–59
Paris Notebook (Joyce): on comedy, 15–16, 77, 91; context of, 89
parlor games, 155
Parnell, Charles Stewart, 96
parody, 92, 170n.25
paronymy, 44–45
Partridge, Eric, 170n.16
pastiche, 92, 108–9
peas/peace: pairing of, 80
penny dreadfuls, 85, 170n.18
Peter the Great (czar of Russia), 101
Peterson, Richard, 168n.17
physics theatre: carnivalesque in, 42–43; comic Irishman in, 88–89; ellipsoidal balls and, 4–5, 26–27, 156; misrule in, 67; solemnity and humor paralleled in, 11–12, 167–68n.13; Stephen's location in, 28–29; Stephen's memories of, 149; Stephen's vision in, 152–53. *See also* dean
pigs/children: pairing of, 62–63
Plato, 129
"Pluck" (penny dreadful), 85
Pola Notebook (Joyce), 89
politics: ceremonial carving and, 96; everyday juxtaposed to, 107–8; humor's direction and, 166n.14
polyptoton, 58–59
polyvocality, 9–10, 84
"pope's nose": ceremonial carving and, 96, 170n.16
popular literature: effect of, 47; influences of, 51; Joyce's reading of, 84–88, 89, 98, 169n.1; as source to react against, 91–97; Wallace's pastiche of, 108–9. *See also* common language
portrait: alternate perspective on, 6–7, 13, 37–38; complexity in, 2–3; confusion in, 57; focus of, 26; humeral veil for, 23; as image mediated by art, 43; meanings of, 1–2, 41; other heads as alternatives in, 28–29, 31, 33, 42–47
"Portrait" (Joyce), 111–12, 118
Portrait of the Artist as a Young Man, A (Joyce): as *Bildungsroman*, 1–2, 161n.3; carnivalization of, 173n.2; comic counterpart to, 104, 113–16; compound words in, 172–73n.21; ending of, 151, 153; focus of, 25–26, 136; *Hero* obscured in, 119–25, 126, 132–37, 149, 172nn.12–13; monoptic view of, 136; obscured/put behind by *Ulysses*, 149–51; overt humor in, 13–14; replayed in *Ulysses*, 4, 153–59; revaluation of, 139–40, 142–43; writing of, 134, 171nn.9–10. *See also* counterparts of narrative; epigraph to *Portrait*; narrative
postmodernism, 20–21, 163n.19
priests/teachers: concrete presentation of, 151; doubling of, 6–7; furtive laughter of, 17, 20, 22, 36; as jokers, 14; life of, 162n.12; Stephen as, 11–13, 21; "tumbling" of, 5–6, 26, 152–53, 155, 159; vitiation of, 163n.15. *See also* Cranly (char.)
profane: meaning of, 77–78, 168n.21
proparoxyton: use of term, 155
"Proteus" (Joyce), 11–12
puns: confusion of, 44–45; laughter and, 126–27; as repressed elements, 50–51, 167n.3; two heads and, 46–47

Radford, F. L., 168n.20
rays/raise: pairing of, 79
reader: classroom instruction for, 33–34; comedy as sidelight for, 50; common, humorous perspective for, 127–30; nearing/distancing of, 36, 57; response of, 24–25; Stephen as focus of, 8–9, 12; Stephen's otherness vs. real world for, 42, 54
religion: artistic vision's triumph over, 76–77; comedy's function and, 31–32, 127, 165n.4; confession in, 64–66; replaced with art, 66–71, 72–73; rising and falling in, 59–60; wordplay and, 56, 60–61. *See also* priests/teachers; sermons of the retreat
revelry, 6
revolution: in artistic gesture, 80–81
rhymes: comic source of, 61, 79
Richards, Grant, 87, 168n.19
riddles, 49–50, 155
Riquelme, John Paul, 167n.4, 167n.9, 169nn.25, 27
Rome: Joyce in, 99, 110–11
rue/adieu/lane: conflation of, 9, 122
Russell, George, 129
Russia: reportage on, 101–2, 113

Sanders of the River (Wallace), 100
Scholes, Robert, 161–62n.4, 165n.7, 168n.18, 169n.25
"Scylla and Charybdis" (Joyce), 152–53
self-communion, 70
Senn, Fritz, 171n.3, 171n.8
sensitiveness: use of term, 144–46
sermons of the retreat, 61–64, 167n.11
sexuality: confusion of, 43–45; directness of *Hero* and, 123–24; innuendoes of, 94–95, 157, 170n.14; oppression of, 32; wordplay and, 55–56, 57. *See also* gender
shadow: brought to fore, 150; comic as, 93; lightly opposed to, 69; number of appearances, 168n.16
shaft of thought: use of term, 29, 30
Shakespeare, William, 29, 43, 95
Sharpless, F. Parvin, 166n.9

Sheehy, Eugene, 161–62n.4, 173n.5
signified: representation of, 15, 164n.25
silence: in surd, 80–82
sins: causes of, 43; Stephen's, 55–56; water imagery for, 142–43
skirts/gowns, 5–6, 14, 68
"Solitary Reaper, The" (Wordsworth), 74
Sosnoski, James J., 164n.23, 166n.9
Staley, Thomas F., 164n.23, 166n.9
Stead, William Thomas, 114–15, 169n.29
steered: use of term, 80. *See also* Bull
Stephen Hero (Joyce): alleged burning of, 117, 171n.1; appeal of, 146–47; comic counterpart to, 104, 111, 112–13, 115–16; common language in, 128–32; confrontation in, 89; elephant in, 63; epiphany in, 168n.18; focus of, 136; generosity of, 123–24; journalistic material in, 10, 106–7, 128–29, 172n.17; laughter in, 126–27; length of, 118; names in, 40, 78; obscured by *Portrait*, 119–26, 132–37, 172nn.12–13; as origin of *Portrait*, 117, 118, 145; peasant in, 88; *Portrait* compared/linked to, 10–11, 12, 121–24, 171nn.2, 7, 172n.19; renunciation of, 139–40; writing of, 97–98, 118
stereotypes, 87–89, 166n.8
sticks: heads and, 46, 48–49, 52, 166n.14
stream: use of term, 141–44, 145
submit/admit: pairing of, 35–36, 121
surd: concept of, 46–47; contexts as, 83; irrational and absurd in, 54–55; laughter as, 126; meanings of, 48–49; riddle as, 155; silence of, 80–82; Stephen's confession and, 65; Stephen's interview and, 68; in Stephen's reaction to girl on the beach, 77. *See also* heads

"Telemachus" (Joyce), 151–52, 155, 173n.2
Temple (char.), 78–79, 114, 156
tendency: use of term, 141–44, 145
Tennyson, Alfred, 35, 112
texts: bridging of, 141; conflation of, 132–37; distancing from, 57; epigraph's function and, 117. *See also* narrative

Thomas Aquinas, 12, 17, 22, 30, 40
Thornton, Weldon: on irony in *Bildungsroman*, 15, 164n.23; on *Portrait* and cultural context, 162n.8; on *Portrait* as *Bildungsroman*, 161n.3; on Stephen's mind and displacement, 166n.12; on third-person presentation, 168n.17
Thrane, James R., 167n.11
Thurber, James, 109
Tit Bits (periodical): Joyce's reading of, 85, 99; Joyce's submissions to, 36, 86
touch/music: pairing of, 74–75
transgression: in classroom, 34–36
Trieste: Joyce in, 99
tumbling: as alternate rhythm, 4–9, 147; as antithesis of order, 45–47; as circularity, 3–4, 45; in comic confusion of gender, 43–45; of comic Irishman, 31; in critical discourse on comedy, 6; dancing as, 158; as deflationary process, 56; "falling" compared to, 4; as misrule, 5–6; necessary action of, 163n.13; possibilities in esthetic posturing, 58–59; pratfall as, 3, 80; reader's instruction in, 33; of seriousness, 25, 51, 140, 150; sins caused by, 43; in Stephen's essay, 36
tundish: discussion of, 38, 40, 41, 133; funnel paired with, 39, 135–36
Turgenieff, Ivan, 98
turkey: meanings of, 89–97, 157, 170nn.12, 14

Ulysses (Joyce): beginning of, 151, 153; carnival and, 162n.10, 173n.2; comedy's resistance to esthetics in, 32–33; humor in, 14, 39, 59, 75–76, 127, 141, 148–49, 163n.14, 163–64n.20, 165n.5; lists in, 18; names in, 78; parts of *Portrait* in, 153–59; plot of, 167n.7; *Portrait* compared/linked to, 11, 66, 114, 119, 148–49; *Portrait* obscured/put behind by, 4, 149–51; tumbling in, 4; writing of, 100

Valente, Joseph, 166n.13
verbal comedy: displaced effect of, 47
villanelle: critical discourse on, 169n.25; as higher art, 128; Stephen's habits and, 157; writing of, 32, 79
vulgar language. *See* common language

Wallace, Edgar: allusion to, 114–15; background of, 170n.19; common language and, 128, 131, 172n.17; Joyce's reading of, 98, 99–100, 101–2, 103–5; as model, 97, 102, 103–5, 107–11, 112–13; word pairings of, 115; writing of, 100–101, 103, 107–11, 170n.20
Wallace, Ronald, 163–64n.20, 164n.27, 166–67n.2
Warden, Florence, 99
water imagery, 40–41, 141–44, 149
Waters, Maureen, 163n.16, 166nn.8, 14
Weber, Eugen, 170n.12
wheypale: use of term, 29
wholly/holily: pairing of, 60, 64
Wilde, Oscar, 44, 79, 82
Wolsey, Thomas, 53–54
women: comedy by, 20–21, 164–65n.33, 165n.36; Joyce's removal of, 11, 163n.17; Stephen's focus on, 74–75
wordplay: alternative created in, 51–52; authority subverted in, 50–51; doubling as, 49–50, 52–53; in epigraph to *Portrait*, 121; essence of, 49; in interview with director, 67–71; in journalism, 101–2; pairings used in, 55–64, 61–62, 67–68, 115, 169n.27; possibilities in, 54–55; in sermons of the retreat, 61–63. *See also* irony; metaphors; puns
Wordsworth, William, 74, 146
word/wound: pairing of, 62

Yeats, William Butler, 32, 79, 86

Zoe (char.), 44, 154–57, 158

Roy K. Gottfried is professor of English at Vanderbilt University. His most recent book is *Joyce's Iritis and the Irritated Text: The Dis-lexic* Ulysses (UPF, 1995), winner of the South Atlantic Modern Language Association Book Award.